Theory and Practice of
SOCIAL CASE WORK

Theory and Practice of
SOCIAL CASE WORK

By GORDON HAMILTON

Second Edition, Revised

PUBLISHED FOR
THE NEW YORK SCHOOL OF SOCIAL WORK
COLUMBIA UNIVERSITY
By Columbia University Press
NEW YORK AND LONDON

Copyright 1940, 1951, Columbia University Press

Second Edition 1951
Ninth printing 1964

Manufactured in the United States of America

PREFACE

THE FIRST EDITION OF *Theory and Practice of Social Case Work*, published in 1940, was written during a rapidly changing decade which had seen the great depression, the extraordinary advances in welfare set in motion by the passage of the Social Security Act, and the tragic drift toward the Second World War. Because of such major trends, a radical revision of this book has been long overdue. Advances in psychiatry and in the social sciences have steadily clarified the concept of the psychosocial case, the interaction of environmental and emotional forces and conflicts, and the imperative need to bring scientific knowledge and values together. The social worker, traditionally concerned with the environment, is today committed not only to understand the structure and dynamics of personality but also to rediscover the use of environmental or social therapy. A period of deepening and enlightenment requires a closer integration of the social sciences and social work comparable to what has taken place between the physical sciences and medicine and, indeed, among all branches of science within the human professions in subject matter which calls for multi-discipline collaboration.

Until the thirties, casework had not felt the impact of ego psychology as it has developed from psychoanalysis, nor was psychotherapy distinguished from psychoanalytic procedure. Therefore, I have had to rewrite substantially the "therapeutic" material, since in the earlier edition I had assumed "psychotherapy" to be identical with psychoanalysis. I still believe, as I did then, that *principles* of psychoanalysis can be appropriately adapted for the use of many professions, but this does not mean that casework any more than psychology or education or other disciplines should take over a diluted sort of psychoanalysis as its own procedure. Social work, always attuned to the concept of the psychosocial event, constantly finds new perspective and therapeutic opportunity for its traditional role of helping persons in their living experience. Competence depends on relevant and exacting professional education and qualifications.

At the time of the first edition of this book, so-called "functional casework" had not become a definitive school of thought, nor were the implications of its diverging path easy to foresee. I should make clear that though I appreciate certain contributions from functional practice, especially in its earlier phases, my own point of view is based on the "diagnostic" approach. My frame of reference for the theories of personality and the psychodynamics of behavior described is essentially Freudian, a system which offers in itself an evolving set of principles and methods.

In Part I of this book I have attempted to show the basic processes which in various combinations define the area and characteristic method of casework. In Part II I have described the same processes through a systematic approach of study and diagnosis as the basis of treatment. I have included less case material than in the former edition, since case materials for teaching purposes are now readily available through the American Association of Schools of Social Work and a number of other sources. I have used, however, short extracts to clarify specific points of theory when indicated.

Again I owe thanks to several agencies for case data furnished either for the original or present edition: the Community Service Society; New York State Psychiatric Institute; the Jewish Board of Guardians; the New York Department of Welfare; the Neurological Institute of Columbia University; the Jewish Child Care Association of Brooklyn; also the Children's Aid Society and the Delaware County Committee Children's Aid Society, of Pennsylvania; the Department of Public Welfare of New Rochelle, N.Y.; the Barnard Free Skin and Cancer Hospital of St. Louis, Mo.

I wish to express appreciation again to those social workers and psychiatrists who have always so generously assisted me, and once again to thank my colleagues at the New York School of Social Work who have read and criticized the present revision. I am especially indebted to Anna Kempshall, Director of Family Service of the Community Service Society, for careful checking of the whole text against current practice, and to Carol White for her always thoughtful and adequate help in the preparation of the manuscript.

GORDON HAMILTON

New York, N.Y.
February, 1951

CONTENTS

PART I

PART II

CONTENTS

PART I

CHAPTER I

BASIC ASSUMPTIONS AND METHODS
OF SOCIAL CASEWORK

SOCIAL WORK rests ultimately on certain assumptions [1] which cannot be proved, but without which its methods and goals have no meaning. These axioms are, for example: human betterment is the goal of any society; so far as economic and cultural resources can be developed, the general standard of living should be progressively improved; education for physical and mental health and welfare should be widely promoted; the social bond between man and man should lead to the realization of the age-old dream of universal brotherhood. The ethic derived from these and similar axioms leads to two nuclear ideas which distinguish social work as one of the humanistic professions. The first is that the human event consists of person and situation, or subjective and objective reality, which constantly interact, and the second that the characteristic method of social work incorporates within its processes both scientific knowledge and social values in order to achieve its ends.

PSYCHOSOCIAL PROCESS

Man is a bio-social organism—the "case," the problem, and the treatment are always to be regarded by the social worker as a psychosocial process. A social case is not determined by the kind of client (a family, a child, an old person, an adolescent), nor can it be determined by the kind of problem (an economic disability or a behavior problem). A social case is a "living event," [2] within which

[1] Certain portions of this chapter have appeared in *Social Work as Human Relations*, under the title "Helping People—the Growth of a Profession."
[2] See Dollard, *Criteria for the Life History*, p. 26 *et seq.*

there are always economic, physical, mental, emotional, and social factors in varying proportions. A social case is composed of internal and external, or environmental, factors. One does not deal with people in a physical sense or with environment in a physical sense, but treats individuals in relation not only to their social experiences but also to their feelings about their experiences. So when one thinks of a social case one must always consider it in terms of both inner and outer interacting factors. Sometimes people fancy that a social case in a psychiatric clinic and a social case at a public assistance agency can have little in common, but this is not true. Fundamentally all social cases have "inner" and "outer" characteristics and consist of person and situation, of objective reality and the meaning of this reality to the one who experiences it. It is not possible to restrict the casework function to modification of "outer" conditions, since the problem is usually interpersonal, as well as social. Not only can one not successfully separate environmental and emotional factors, but the client's psychological insights are put to use in meeting "real" situations.

It is not easy to know another human being. People are complex, and when they come to a social work agency they may have lived a long time, and much has been woven into their lives which we can never fully understand. One knows that they are the products of heredity and environment and that constitutional elements and early surroundings will have affected their dispositions and partially determined their responses. Yet this knowledge does not in itself help one to "size them up." Two persons with the same low income may have, measured in a material way, the same deprivations, but actually one person will feel and act quite differently about the problem from the other. Two unmarried mothers may be facing about the same economic and cultural difficulties, yet they will react in totally unlike ways. It is hard enough to appraise the external social situation accurately without the additional responsibility for understanding something of the elusive inner life of the applicant. If social work is at a disadvantage in that all human relationships are intangible, invisible, complex, and because people feel strongly about them, it has the advantage that clients can talk and that one can learn to listen. Access to social resources makes it possible for the worker to offer concrete assistance, and knowledge of psychological subject matter enables him to offer assistance which is just as real, if less concrete, in helping the client to clarify the problem in such a way that he can do something about it if he wishes. Anxiety, distress, and incapacity are always personal and can best be understood through the individual approach. Any really helpful relationship must be an individualized one.

Both anthropology and psychiatry throw light on the factors involved in adequate personal adjustment. As Benedict expressed it: "Just as those are favored whose congenial responses are closest to that behavior which characterizes their society, so those are disoriented whose congenial responses fall in that arc of behavior which is not capitalized by their culture." [3] The person whose "congenial drives" are not provided for in his culture is in a bad way, and if what he desires is strongly disapproved by society he may be in a very bad way indeed. A person can, we are told, be well adjusted in a "closed" culture in which traditional and dogmatic influences perform the functions of a collective "super ego" or conscience. Ideologies to which people completely submit or which they completely incorporate into their lives seem to create a condition of tranquillity for the individual. In an open culture such as a democracy provides, particularly one in which many cultural forces interact, the adaptation of external pressures to the inner life may well conduce to a more delicate equilibrium of the total personality. In any event, experience pragmatically suggests, whether for child or adolescent, for the displaced person, the rural-urban immigrant, the second-generation citizen, the uprooted laborer, or the soldier, that dislocation without reference to cultural roots and customs, makes for tension, insecurity, and anxiety. No treatment goal can be envisaged which does not involve a value judgment which is itself culturally determined.

[3] Benedict, *Patterns of Culture*, p. 258.

SCIENCE AND VALUES IN METHOD

In applied social science, and perhaps this is true of all sciences, there is an increasing awareness of ends and moral purpose. In the pure sciences this awareness is not allowed to influence methods of measurement or otherwise obtaining facts, but in the humanistic sciences means and ends are indissolubly bound together from the beginning. When one says that human needs should be met, not ignored, frustrated, or violated; that the uniqueness and worth of the individual are fundamental values; that the interdependence of the individual with society makes it necessary to respect and live constructively with the members of widely divergent cultures and natures, then the values to be attained in the objective become themselves part of the discipline and of the method itself. Moreover, to help others effectively demands respect for human personality— a person's right to control his own life, enjoy personal and civil liberties, and pursue happiness and spiritual goals in his own way. The application of this principle means that social workers shall not impose upon the client their own goals or standards of behavior, their own solutions and morals, but shall concede the client's right to be himself and make his own decisions and plans. Concrete services and practical assistance are not contingent on conformity in behavior. Goods and services in modern social work, as in modern medicine, are given because the client has need of them. Self-direction, as well as self-dependence, is encouraged. The charter of human rights implies a democratic method of administering these rights, and the very nature of man allows him to be a participating, responsible member of his community and involved in social processes.

Historically, charity has always been concerned with religious, educational, and personality-building activities, as well as with the relief of destitution. Hospitals and orphanages, nursing services, assistance for the handicapped, organizations for the preservation or development of character, and "rescue" work of all kinds have often stemmed from consciously constructive impulses. That these impulses may be also guilt reactions to inner drives toward exploitation and aggression does not change their social value. The specific association of relief-giving with social work is of long duration. The trend cannot be fully understood without considering the cultural and economic conditions within which it was set and how the poor and dependent in American life, like certain alien groups, were not considered as worthy as the well-to-do and independent citizens.

Far-reaching changes in economic life and cultural relations such as the world is now experiencing call for constant redefinition and readaptation.[4] The purpose of "philanthropy," "love of men," has often been obscured by practices which have associated this attitude with the giver rather than the recipient, with the owning rather than the laboring classes. The essence of true "philanthropy" is reciprocity and should imply that every individual will have his assets realized and capitalized in a common purpose. The spreading of democracy first through political and then through economic and cultural institutions suggests a quality of human behavior allowing for self-determination, self-realization, and respect for rights, responsibilities, and cooperation as the foundation of society.

Throughout the centuries charity has always been focused upon services or care given by an individual to an individual. The true meaning of "charity," [5] as not seeking one's own, being not easily provoked, thinking no evil, being kind and long-suffering, suggests the indispensable elements in relating oneself constructively to other human beings, especially to those in distress, namely, the quality of "acceptance."

[4] Professor Waller, in "Social Problems and the Mores," makes an interesting distinction between what he calls "organizational" and "humanitarian" mores, saying of the latter (p. 925): "Probably the humanitarian impulse has always existed, but it has apparently attained group-wide expression at a relatively late period in our history, following the breakdown of primary group society. Social problems in the modern sense did not exist when every primary group cared for its own helpless and unfortunate. Social problems as we know them are a phenomenon of secondary group society, in which the primary group is no longer willing and able to take care of its members."
[5] 1 Corinthians, 13.

The worth of the human soul and the significance of the individual in society are not lightly held in American culture. Western civilization has been built upon ideas such as social justice, the scientific search for truth or knowledge, social security, duties and responsibilities, and—not least—the importance of human personality. Great cultures, such as the Hebrew and the Roman, have emphasized ideals and systems of social justice, as the Greek love of truth and freedom of thought and expression and the Christian love of one's neighbor and the value of the soul. While no one culture is responsible for all emphases, democratic society has assimilated so much that social work can hardly be understood except against this background. The fact that social justice, for instance, has been incompletely realized and developed more along lines of legal than of economic or intercultural justice does not alter its significance as a main objective of civilization. The element which brings it peculiarly within the democratic meaning, however, is its concern with individual needs, rights, and liberties. For belief in the inherent worth of the individual is the nucleus of several cardinal principles: equality of opportunity, the rights of minorities, the right of free expression. Democratic government means essentially self-government, and self-government is impossible unless one concedes that the individual is the best judge of his own interest and that free assemblage, collective bargaining, and other group activities for social ends are meaningless unless those who participate are free men. It is only if the individual is respected and allowed to develop through education, science, and free institutions that he is capable of creating the conditions under which he lives. That he does participate fully in his own socialization is the central assumption of casework.

It is not easy to estimate the concerns of social work—homes and families, work and play and education—because everyone has these experiences; but to have experiences is not necessarily to be aware of their implications, and certainly having them does not necessarily translate them into the warp and woof of social programs. The individual situation is the slide which must be put under the microscope.[6] In casework situations, one by one, can be found elements of a complete educational process. At its heart social action has a still small voice, speaking with the inflections of patient, accurate individual observations. Just as the individual is the touchstone of the family, so the family is the touchstone of the community, and so outward into national and international fellowship. Society would wage no wars if it really remembered the individual and his family group. It is said that the atom has in it such energy that the power would suffice for all the purposes of industry. In the same way the unit "personality" has the power to socialize the community, for quality of attainment rests ultimately on the development of individual personality. So casework makes no apology for its interest in the child at home or under foster care, in the troubled adolescent, the transplanted alien, and the disabled worker or housewife, but at the same time it makes no pretense that treating each case one by one is a substitute for changing the environmental systems which may fundamentally cause the unadjustment. The idea that casework is always trying to convey is that differences and unlikenesses must be considered in forming the pattern and in changing the pattern. Anyone who has worked with a state administration knows how impatient some officials are because each city and county not only wants to be a little different but actually *is* a little different from the others. It would be cheap and convenient if cities were all alike, just as it would be cheap and convenient if human beings were alike and did not want a hand in their own affairs.

Social reformers reproached the early caseworkers for taking too passive an attitude toward reconstruction of the social order through large projects or environmental shifts which might act as preventives of destitution. They conceived of the casework idea as narrowly related to relief-giving, not seeing its wider application. Some of the leaders of our own time are satisfied only with explanations which find all causes of distress in the economic struc-

[6] See Hamilton, "Contribution of Social Case Work to Modern Life," in *Family Life Today* (1928), pp. 205 *et seq.*

ture, whereas they think the caseworker finds the sole explanation in the deficiencies of the individual. This is as if one were to keep up a fruitless bickering as to which is the more important, heredity or environment, self-determination or social control. At times casework has overstressed internal causes of unadjustment, but one knows well enough that to understand a single set of relationships will take one not only far afield, but also close home again. One knows that growth depends first of all on securing the means of subsistence, then on opportunity, but finally on facing immediate reality, accepting responsibility, and working not only against limitations but also with and within them.

No one can presume to understand a problem of poverty without knowledge of human behavior, and no one can treat a problem of human behavior intelligently without reference to its economic and social framework. It is no accident that social work meets criticism and resistance, since fundamentally its objectives challenge men's choicest possessions and dearest prejudices. Social work, whether one calls it "welfare" or by the old term "philanthropy," is essentially radical in its objectives. For the moment love of our fellow men goes beyond lip service and into social and industrial democracy and a nondiscriminatory culture, hostility and resentment will be aroused. Political democracy and civil liberties must fight every inch of their way, and one can expect no easier road for social welfare. As long as welfare is thought of as the facile benevolence of friends and passers-by, as long as it is a tool of authoritarian government, whether industrial or political, it will not stir up much opposition, but in so far as it is considered as the expression of free men creating the conditions of their own well-being every advance will be attended by plenty of dust and heat.

In short, everyone wants welfare until it is made clear what it means to socialize the inner drives and the real wants, to accept ourselves and not only our neighbors but also those "out groups" which comprise other nationalities, races, and classes. The social worker has been accused of many things, and sometimes the criticisms have been just. Depending on who does the name-calling, he is palliative or red, angel or obstructionist; he serves a charity either "scrimped and iced," or extravagant and wanton. Yet the plain truth remains that he is committed to strive for a world in which social and economic security and social relationships are as complete and satisfying as possible. Social work is concerned with deprivations, dependencies, anxieties, aggressions, and hostilities in both their practical and their intimate personal expressions, and it is no wonder that progress is slow, hesitating, vacillating, and often blocked altogether. Yet there can be no doubt that if these objectives of welfare in its broadest sense—high income levels, full production, creative education, recreation, and public health—are not gradually achieved, civilization will fail with them.

It is impossible to understand the nature of either dependency or delinquency without reference to its cultural background, as well as to its economic and personal stresses. Men are born into organized social groups, but they have specific ways of behaving. The outer world imposes rules and regulations which the individual meets with a total but unique response of the whole organism. People differ not only psychologically but also with regard to the kinds of things which give them satisfaction. Gross physical and environmental deficiencies and strains, whether economic and cultural or arising from disease, war, or disaster, must be reduced, and a certain level of civilization, perhaps, reached before much can be attempted through interpersonal treatment.

SOCIAL PROBLEMS AND PROGRAMS

What kinds of problems and needs are within the field of social work, and through what methods does social work organize itself to deal with them? Since any profession must be a learned profession, what must students learn in order to be competent social workers? If one examines the reports throughout any ten-year period of the National Conference of Social Work or the biennial publications of the *Social Work Year Book*, one finds recurrent topics such as poverty, unemployment, transiency, "foreignness," illness, broken homes, family maladjustment, physical and mental handicaps, including those of old age, industrial injuries and low wages, limited recreation, inadequate housing, and problems of anti-social behavior. Looked at in terms of services mobilized to meet these needs, there are to be found family and child welfare, public assistance, social insurance, health and legal services, vocational rehabilitation, aid to travelers, resettlement, services for the crippled and the disabled, programs for the prevention and treatment of delinquency, child guidance, labor legislation and housing, recreation and educational programs for culturally disadvantaged groups.

Reduced to a simple statement, this enormous area can be compassed within two major fields and two major objectives of social work, namely, economic and physical well-being, or a "health-and-decency" standard of living, and opportunities for social growth through satisfying relationships and experiences. All professions would stake out an interest in these objectives, but there is little doubt that social work occupies a peculiarly inclusive position with regard to both, since the factors in economic and cultural security and individual behavior are interwoven. It is this integration which consistently has shaped social work and given it its distinguishable if not wholly distinctive pattern; it is this which gives it its complexities, its frustrations, its fascination, and its challenge.

Integration takes place only on the basis of differentiated function. One impinges on reality in many ways, but not the least through the single concrete human situation. In fact, there is no substitute whatever for knowing people one by one, because people do not live by averages, but by their own private visions of reality. There would be little social progress, indeed, if all people were case-minded or mass-minded. In welfare agencies, as "business" administrators have occasionally taught us to our cost, it has been possible to forget that the program was for the benefit of the client. It has sometimes seemed as if the program existed for the benefit of the accountant or the auditor or the statistician. So, too, the individual as a person can be almost overlooked in the routines of a big hospital. Whether one is thinking of Federal or state or local controls or the management of a single agency, the principle of "enabling" is sounder than the principle of "executive" administration. The strongest programs are built up from knowledge of individual clients and practitioners, not handed down. The truth is that we know, or can know, more about human beings than about almost anything else, yet many programs are put together with the individual reaction left out altogether.

Help is most effective if the recipient participates actively and responsibly in the helping process. Few persons are grateful for a "hand-out," and certainly not for continuous remittances which prolong dependency. The relationship of the benefactor to his client is proverbially uncomfortable and disillusioning. Some are not ready to use help wisely, just as some are not ready to learn. Readiness, however, can be stimulated and educated. What most people are grateful for in the long run, whether nations or groups or individuals, is a chance to help themselves—to work out their own solutions, at least to have a hand in shaping their destiny. The poor and the less fortunate have this desire just as strongly as the captains of industry. It is resources, capacity, and opportunity which fail them. Clients are usually satisfied in direct proportion to the degree to which this desire is recognized and means found to enlist them in efforts toward their own recovery. Poor job production, feelings of inadequacy, difficulty in getting along with one's associates, neglect of children, and delinquency can be explained in part by economic or political or cultural factors, but in part from the personality itself, and certainly few cures can be effective unless the personality is enlisted on its own behalf in the struggle. Caseworkers have learned pragmatically that self-help is essential in rehabilitation and recovery.

Complex as is its subject matter, social work is not a welter of activities. Potentially responsive to all phases of social living, it cannot shift with every wind of doctrine, though workers must always be aware of and sensitive to new trends and problems. They must specialize on significant and relevant problems in their own area in order to add to the content of knowledge. They must generalize and formulate principles, because a purely pragmatic and expedient methodology will not suffice. There must be well-considered hypotheses based on substantial data derived from both social values and science, or else social work policies and practices will serve merely for appeasement instead of problem-solving.

METHODS AND PROCESSES

There are mass needs and mass solutions, community needs and community solutions, group needs and group solutions, individual needs and individual solutions. In organizing itself to play a professional role in forwarding the objectives of a health-and-decency standard of living and of satisfying human relationships, social work has to date clarified three distinctive methods of approach, called, respectively, "social welfare planning" or "community organization," "social groupwork," and "social casework." The whole concerted movement toward the solution of mass problems in welfare, is sometimes called "social reform" and, more recently, "social action."

Social Action

Social action is by no means the exclusive prerogative of social work. Social action rests on the activities of all citizens using techniques of public education and propaganda, social legislation, and cooperative and collective enterprises.[7] When the social worker turns to the forces of community and government to achieve his objectives, rather than relying on individual initiative or voluntary group processes, this process is thought of as "social action." Social workers have long been engaged in the struggle to improve housing, reform the penal system, improve institutions, and socialize methods of welfare administration. Leaders have been vigorous

⁊ See Fitch, "Social Action," in *Social Work Year Book* (1939), p. 398.

campaigners for social security in the form of aid to dependent children, the aged, and the blind and for the extension of public health and constructive labor relations. Social workers see social action equally in terms of health, labor, industry, public assistance, recreation, social education, the prevention of delinquency, and intercultural assimilation.

There is always a polarity in social planning—to look at society from the basis of the whole and from the basis of the individual. Social institutions must be based on relevant interconnections, which means that the properties of the things themselves must be understood. It is equally fallacious to think one can solve the problems of the social order by the case method, or to think that one can solve individual problems with mass formulas. The case method addresses itself to individual adjustments and solutions, but the meaning of these cases taken one by one may prove to be of far-reaching significance.

Dr. Abram Kardiner has made an interesting analysis of the kind of "stresses which move to economic action." [8] He says they "have to do largely with the command, control, or exploitation of external sources of instinct gratification. . . . These are external needs which cannot be vicariously gratified" and "require control of the external environment in a rational way. . . . Each culture has its own values, necessities and defenses. . . . Other stresses lead us to more personal search and action." Social workers are beginning to differentiate more clearly between economic needs which necessitate control of the environment in a rational way and needs which in any economic system will require an individualized or so-called "case" approach. This does not mean that one can divide cases strictly into "employment" and "personality" cases, but that causes of unadjustment which are broadly economic will be seen as such, and appropriate long range action taken, while stresses which lead to "more personal search and

[8] Kardiner, A. "Influence of Culture on Behavior," *Social Work Today,* IV (February, 1937), 11–14.

action," whether or not the economic factor is involved, come within the casework objective.

There are unmanageable factors in the environment which the casework approach will not make manageable; broad-scale reorganization alone will bring them to terms. Human rights imply definition, classification, and uniform treatment; human needs require not only programs of security but also, within the broader classifications, individualization and differential treatment. The casework idea is now, however, fortunately no longer circumscribed by the practices of relief-giving, but may be utilized whenever a person's capacity to organize his affairs is impaired or he lacks satisfactions in his ordinary social relationships. Society is inseparable from the individuals who compose it; the more an individual develops capacities, the more truly he tends to find social expression for these capacities.

Now, as always, there are two fundamental approaches to social problems—through external structural reorganization and through the socializing of the individual and the group by educational processes. It is encouraging that casework and groupwork, developing the same concepts as to the interdependence of the individual and society, and the importance of self-motivated activity of the person and the group are drawing together to affect the dynamics of social action. Social work, like casework itself, needs more unification. It is not only clients who must be active in solving their own problems if they are to grow; social workers must develop a democratic method which releases activity in themselves and their fellows. If self-regard and self-esteem are normal personal incentives, so, too, is love of one's neighbor a normal incentive in group behavior. Too often clamorous raising of voices in public protest is assumed to be social action. Professional social action must rest solidly on knowledge of subject matter, on professional practices and disciplines which enable one to see the relation of these objectives to other objectives, and finally it should mean the release of individual energies less complicated with hostility and aggression and so more susceptible to cooperative social practices.

Community Organization

Until the last decade community organization had been thought of largely as concerned with private or voluntary agencies, developing as their techniques cooperative machinery, surveys, and studies; changing patterns so as better to fit resources to needs or to create new resources; approaching social education through interpretation, and so on. Today community organization is as much concerned with public as with voluntary functions and their collaboration. It must study the whole field of expanding human needs and forecast as well as interpret trends. Programs for economic assistance and leisure-time activities are far-reaching, the former are now almost entirely public; certain large-scale aspects of the latter, such as parks and playgrounds, are in the hands of public commissioners. Recreation, like housing, lies within the broad field of "welfare," although many professions must cooperate in furthering its objectives. Techniques in community organization are being constantly modified by these and other developments, although the essential basis of fact finding, of assigning priorities, and of eliciting full participation from the citizens who alike receive the benefits and pay the bills remains the same.

Certain functions, such as assistance and protection, rest squarely on tax-supported agencies supplemented by voluntary ones, while others may be approached through voluntary efforts, supplemented by public agencies. In some instances there will be joint enterprises. The consent and participation of the citizen in all types of enterprise is vital in welfare, as it is in the older aspects of government. It is in large part to secure his intelligent and informed participation through social agencies that community organization strives. It is important, however, to emphasize again the fact that the basis of understanding and support in social welfare planning must be steadily broadened if it is to be truly representative of the whole community. The cooperative efforts, not of the well-to-do alone but also of trade unions, religious and special-interest groups, client organizations, and the like, will be needed. Nevertheless, it would be proper also to assume, if social work is developing soundly and wisely, that a considerable proportion of the measurements, techniques, and social controls will evolve from those professional disciplines which are primarily directed to the study and treatment of human needs and of social relationships.

Social workers are interested in positive programs of welfare, as is modern medicine in positive programs of health. Each community is responsible for supporting, from time to time, skilled surveys of its needs, and as resources are created citizens should be educated to an intelligent use of these resources. Because social needs are interrelated, services should also be interrelated in a usable, effective pattern. While many cost studies have been made, the over-all cost cannot be once and for all determined, but practically all experts agree that hit-or-miss and inadequate programs cost the most in the long run. Mental institutions, hospitals, jails, diseases, and unemployability cost more than do strong, well-conceived programs of welfare. In its own way a slum is as deadly as the tubercle bacillus. Prejudice and racial intolerance are virulent infections to the whole of society. The individual has responsibility not only for himself but also towards the society in which he lives, and society has responsibility not only to allow opportunities for creative development and achievement but also to protect the lives and interests of all its members. As part of his activity the social worker helps the client to a more realistic sense of his responsibility to his community, tries to encourage him not only to make an effort on his own behalf but also to appreciate his role in the family and his role as a citizen.

Professional people who habitually practice the clinical and case-by-case method tend to resist attempts to segregate and classify problems as such. They know so well that each case is different that it is always an intellectual effort for them to look at the common attributes. Conversely, those who habitually are engaged in social-reform activities are often impatient of the slowing down that individual consideration inevitably entails. Nevertheless, intelligent community organization necessitates both classification and individuation, whether in health, labor, or welfare programs. Social work is slowly building programs derived largely from the "primary" techniques of group and casework, and the more far-sighted realize that the substitution of revolutionary tactics for everything else one has learned or can learn about human beings may not advance the culture so surely as programs in which comprehensive planning, social controls, scientific research, and the homely wisdom of studying particular situations will all find a place.

Social Groupwork [9]

Social groupwork is a psychosocial process which is concerned no less with developing leadership ability and cooperation than with building on the interests of the group for a social purpose. Experience in democratic participation in voluntary association is an essential technique not only in releasing the energies of a community but also those of political and labor units. In fact, the mass powers of great states will inevitably lead to bureaucracy unless local community opinion and participation can be mobilized through socialized group processes. It is the essence of social groupwork, unlike that of a lobby, that its efforts at self-realization and achievement include a contribution to the social life experience of all concerned.

The democratic way of life assumes that the individual as person and as citizen is of primary significance—his essential needs must be gratified, his rights protected, and his responsibilities shouldered through interaction with the culture and the political structure within which he exists. Each individual interacts with other individuals and groups through various cultural institutions as well as within physical and economic conditions, so that large-scale programs for reducing stresses in the economic, cultural, and psychological environments must proceed along with group and case efforts to help people adapt and maintain a satisfactory equilibrium within their immediate situations.

In another sense, groupwork methods are not only basic but

[9] See pp. 105–7.

also far-reaching, spreading their techniques through other fields. For instance, in the educational use of committees and conferences for community organization much can be learned through group-work disciplines. Creative community programs derive in part from creative group processes, and indeed effective social action, already discussed, will come chiefly through mobilizing the leadership of participating groups rather than that of single individuals. In the give and take of the socialized group, where the majority rules, but the minority is respected, and integration of ideas is the optimal result, progressive education becomes a reality. Social group-work and social casework, together with social research, are the basic processes in community organization technique, out of which spring welfare planning and action.

Social productivity, so essential to cultural survival, is increased through informed group processes. The individual contribution may often be effectively released and with enhanced satisfaction. Group interaction not only channelizes individual effort but also, through full personal commitment to a shared project, becomes in itself a dynamic experience. Groups cannot arrive at constructive solutions unless they acquire awareness of the movement and meaning of interpersonal and intergroup communication and are willing to modify the direction of their goal toward group interests, reinforcing one another's roles and evolving common paths of action.

The myth used to obtain that groupworkers were interested only in "normal" people, and caseworkers in "abnormal"—the basis for this being the fact that the child who was having difficulty with his social relationships would probably show these difficulties in the organized group and perhaps there being rejected would become the "client" or "patient," (the latter term being commonly used by social workers in medical settings,) in casework. The same child might be having difficulty with his family or in school, but the school is less free to reject the aberrant individual than is the voluntary group, and the family does not turn against its own except in extreme circumstances, the strength of the family being, as the witticism goes, that it is so uncongenial. Groupwork today has developed skill not only with the person for whom group experience is relatively easy, for whom education through group action can be readily experienced, but for the less typical person, who nevertheless can be helped to utilize group associations for his strengthening and reconditioning. Recently groupworkers have been expanding and differentiating their component processes along several paths, emphasizing administration, education, and treatment and putting into practice certain recent developments in group therapy.[10]

Respect for others includes respect for their differences. Social workers desire neither conformity with their opinions nor uniformity in cultural and individual patterns of behavior. Help is given without discrimination (legally so under Federal social security legislation). At its best, it positively accredits and builds on the richness of cultural variations, tries to break up meaningless labeling and derogatory stereotyping. Fear-hate cycles spring from frustrations of all kinds, of which intolerance is one of the cruelest and most damaging by-products. In a number of experiments to educate children to a great social and religious magnanimity, it has been convincingly shown that a purely ideological approach has little to offer in combatting children's attitudes of prejudice. If, however, warm and friendly associations across color and race and religious lines are provided, then concurrent educational efforts aimed at pointing up ideals of tolerance can have real effect. If children share a friendly living experience in a warm and permissive atmosphere and can be made aware of the implications of these satisfactions, tolerant attitudes can be integrated permanently into the personality. It was said of the late John Winant that his greatness lay in the fact that he really believed in the possibility of "the greater comradeship of man."

---

[10] It is always easier to define what is abnormal than what lies within the range of the normal. See pp. 111–13.

Social Casework [11]

In the various attempts to define the casework process the concept repeatedly elaborated is: the interconnection of personal adaptation of the individual and society's betterment. Of the many phrasings, those which still seem preferable were offered by Mary Richmond when she spoke of "processes which develop personality through adjustments consciously effected, individual by individual, between men and their social environment." [12] "Social casework may be defined as the art of doing different things for and with different people by cooperating with them to achieve at one and the same time their own and society's betterment." [13] Later definitions have clarified the means and the ends of the process by emphasizing that the problem is essentially the client's own and that the client is actively and responsibly engaged in its solution, but none states better the objective.

The main assumptions in all the accepted definitions are: the individual and society are interdependent; social forces influence behavior and attitudes, affording opportunity for self-development and contribution to the world in which we live; not only are all problems psychosocial—inner and outer—but most casework problems are interpersonal, that is, more than one person is likely to be involved in the treatment of the individual, and particularly in casework is the family unit involved; the client is a responsible participant at every step in the solution of his problems. At the center of the casework process is the conscious and controlled use of the worker-client relationship to achieve the ends of treatment.

The greatest gift is to enable another to realize his own capacities for change and growth. One cannot, however, release such energies in a client unless the helper himself has been taught systematically to understand the nature of motivation—how a person feels about

[11] The Reverend Swithun Bowers has performed a welcomed service in his several papers on "The Nature and Definition of Social Casework" by compiling chronologically all the important statements from 1915 to 1947. See the *Journal of Social Casework*, October, November, 1949.
[12] Richmond, *What Is Social Case Work?* p. 98.
[13] Richmond, *The Long View*, pp. 374 f.

his situation, about others, about the worker as "counselor" or "therapist." Only if the social worker in his professional education has been well grounded psychologically can he help the client to mobilize his feelings in the direction of change, growth, and adaptation to reality. In casework the client is stimulated to participate in the study of his situation, to share plans, to make an active effort to solve his problems, using his own resources and whatever community resources are available and appropriate.

There are several levels in this idea of readiness for change. For the relatively self-directing person caught in a tangle of external pressures or obvious difficulties the goal may be gained through the practical services and any necessary counseling to enable the person to change his own situation. As we have said, he is encouraged in so far as possible to do this himself and for himself. If the person is not well, weakened, or seriously handicapped, the worker must give him more support in his efforts, and even, perhaps, actively intervene in his environment to reduce social or personal pressures upon him. It seems to be a well-supported hypothesis that change in attitudes or mores can best be effected by creating new conditions within which new experiences and satisfactions may occur.

Individualization in social problems began largely with persons who needed relief.[14] The work of St. Vincent de Paul in the sixteenth and seventeenth centuries and of Ozanam in the nineteenth, through the art of friendly visiting, helped to individualize people at home; the German systems of the eighteenth and nineteenth centuries, directed, perhaps, more to the control of mendicancy than to the study of individuals, nevertheless yielded data on social conditions and on behavior. Edward Denison, Sir Charles Loch,

[14] For the historical setting of poor relief and allied programs, students should consult such indispensable texts as the Webbs' *English Local Government*, and Watson's *Charity Organization Movement in the United States* for an excellent chapter on foreign antecedents of charity. See also Warner, Queen, and Harper, *American Charities and Social Work*, Part I; Bruno, *The Theory of Social Work*, Part IV, and Millspaugh, *Public Welfare Organization*, chap. xii. For an interesting analysis of economic motivation from a casework point of view see Reynolds, "Rethinking Social Casework."

Octavia Hill, to name only a few of the English leaders, developed to a high point the theory and practice of personal service, personal responsibility, and careful study of each case. In our own times Mary Richmond set out the first rational and systematic approach to the analysis of individual social situations. Professor Garrett points out "that the attempt to modify the client's personality is not a recent and revolutionary undertaking of caseworkers but an evolutionary development from the beginning. . . . Then, as now, there was general recognition of the need to stimulate clients to want to change and to influence them to participate actively in the solution of their problems." [15]

Casework is characterized by the objective to administer practical services and offer counseling in such a way as to arouse and conserve the psychological energies of the client—actively to involve him in the use of the service toward the solution of his dilemma. Casework reflects a trend in complex modern society to offer help with the *personal aspects of ordinary living,* and it is still the only one of the "humanistic" professions wherein practitioners are educated for this function. Not only is every problem psychosocial, but casework treatment is inevitably psychosocial. The oldest function of casework, to supply practical services or to manipulate the environment, may suffice to put the client into balance, to help toward a successful adaptation. But long before the forces of the unconscious as factors in human behavior were understood, caseworkers recognized personality and character as essential in reconstructive efforts. Reorientation and reconstruction are achieved through a combination of psychological understanding and social services in an integrated participating experience with the client. Social casework as method does not often attempt total personality reconstruction any more than it attempts total environmental reorganization, but by direct counseling and therapeutic influences, as well as the release of environmental pressures, modification of attitudes and behavior may be possible. Casework

[15] Garrett, Annette. "Historical Survey of the Evolution of Casework," *Journal of Social Casework,* June, 1949.

is less often able to free its clients completely from disabilities than to help them live within their disabilities with the help of social compensations, but under favorable circumstances casework can mitigate or even prevent some of the crippling effects of deprivations or pathological exposures and traumatic events.

The interrelatedness of the personality with the environment has made for a professional discipline in which the focus is held to the individual who has a problem within a set of specific circumstances. This includes, however, consideration of causal and contributing factors. The client's reality and his feeling about his reality become the constellation of casework effort wherein familial and other interpersonal factors constantly impinge upon and modify diagnosis and the goals of treatment. Treatment is the sum of all activities and services directed towards helping an individual with his problem. It is concerned with relieving or solving the immediate problem brought to the caseworker's attention and, if made feasible by the client's recognition and participation, modifying basic difficulties and complications. Differentials are determined by the needs and wishes of the client, the resources of the community, the functions of the agency, and the skill of the worker. The professional purpose demands that treatment shall be in the mutual interest of the client and the community. As caseworker, one is obligated not only to help the person satisfy his social needs in an appropriate way, but to stimulate and release capacities for constructive social living; as social worker one is further obligated to continue efforts to create a better social environment for human beings. The obligation toward preventive action is implicit also in traumatic case situations as well as in programs of health, mental hygiene and welfare.

The concept of change is related to the client's capacity and environmental opportunities and resources. Every approach—direct and environmental—all combinations of services, counseling, and therapy overlap—may be employed in one case or quite differently weighted in another. Although the following are not precise coordinates—one implementing or overlapping the other—in the ensuing chapters we shall attempt to describe the casework method by discussing four characteristic processes: (*a*) the use of relationship; (*b*) the interviewing process; (*c*) the use of social resources; and (*d*) the requirements of agency practice.

A person is motivated to change because of the hope of satisfaction. He can be motivated to attempt to change his situation by an educational process which clarifies a course of action and offers the tools or resources with which to give satisfaction. All these may be achieved in the more rational aspects of counseling, but if a person is in any real sense to change his attitudes or his life direction, this can only be achieved by something more than a solely intellectual stimulus. Change in feeling can result from a major experience, such as a happy marriage, through great physical or mental suffering, through a significant relationship with one or more persons, or through religious experience. It is no accident that the doctor-patient relationship has received so much attention. So far as we know, it is only by means of a deeply felt experience in relationship that treatment can affect a person's attitudes towards himself and his fellows. We shall, therefore, begin our discussion of process with the dynamics of the casework relationship.

CHAPTER II

THE USE OF RELATIONSHIP

OUR MOST FUNDAMENTAL CONSIDERATIONS lie in the concept of human relationships—their importance, their dynamics, their use in treatment. Casework, groupwork, and community organization are alike grounded in the art and science of relationships. Every unit of behavior, moreover, is not only a complex of psychobiological facts, but is tinged with value considerations, since the behavior of one person interacts with the behavior of another. As Slavson puts it: "face to face relations activate intellectual and emotional processes, set attitudes and socialize the individual." [1] Relationships can only be experienced directly, although their meaning can be rationally and reflectively assimilated.

In certain occupations the worker who uses his hands for the performance of his tasks is thought of as a "manual" worker; for the use of head and hands at some sort of desk job, the American vernacular has contributed the phrase "white collar" worker. In all sorts of occupations, the relations of employers, employees, fellow workers, and the public have been found to be increasingly significant for successful operation. In any of the professions, especially those concerned directly with human beings, the total self must be fully and deeply engaged. Within the democratic frame of reference the professional relationship involves a mutual process of shared responsibilities, recognition of the other's rights, acceptance of difference, with the goal, not of isolation, but of socialized attitudes and behavior stimulating growth through interaction. Dr. Flanders Dunbar speaks of a "relational action in living bodies which, while producing changes in the bodies, at the same time

[1] Slavson, *Recreation and the Total Personality*, p. 81.

leaves the individuality of these not only identifiable and unimpaired, but even improved relative to their former states." [2] This is true of social, as well as bodily, relationships.

The professional relationship differs from most of conventional intercourse largely in the degree to which the aim must be the good of others (whether individual or group), in the amount of self-awareness to be attained by the worker, and in the techniques to be assimilated and consciously utilized. In social work most professional relationships are also conditioned by the fact of an agency setting rather than individual private practice. Agencies have programs, resources, and limitations—in short, functions—so that the relationship will be used by both worker and client with reference to what the agency is equipped to do and what other agencies in the community are equipped to do.[3] "The social worker must be a person of genuine warmth with a gift for intimacy. He must be willing to enter into the feeling experience of another, willing to listen to the other's view of his problem, and willing to go patiently along with him in his struggles for a solution." [4]

THE CASEWORK RELATIONSHIP [5]

The idea that the relationship of worker and client is important in helping people to help themselves—"not alms, but a friend"—is one of the oldest in casework. But it is not true that the naïve self is to be preferred in human relationships. The naïve self must be disciplined for work, for cultural requirements, for marriage, and for the religious life. It must also be disciplined for effective use

[2] Dunbar, *Emotions and Bodily Changes*, p. 8.
[3] In succeeding chapters we shall consider the use of "relationship" in the interviewing process, in the "living experience," and in the agency setting.
[4] See writer's "Helping People—the Growth of a Profession," in *Social Work as Human Relations*, 1949, p. 11.
[5] In *A Changing Psychology in Social Case Work* (1930) Virginia Robinson made a significant contribution on the use and control of the worker-client relationship in what was later to be called by the Pennsylvania School group "the helping process" in "functional" casework. Ferenczi and Reich in psychoanalysis had earlier formulated the theory of analyst-patient interaction and character patterns used as forms of resistance, and called attention to the treatment relationship as dynamic process.

in group, as well as individual, processes. Professional relationships are not just friendly associations. Contact is not for the sake of contact. Clients bring into the casework relationship feelings and attitudes and behavior which they have experienced with others. The family is culturally important because the person tends to carry into the world attitudes largely built up in familial settings, and the client tends to react to the casework or groupwork situation in ways derived from attitudes learned at home and conditioned also by other life situations. The professional self is controlled towards the end one is serving—namely, to understand and meet the psycho-social needs of clients. Techniques employed without this conscious professional purpose to better a given situation would be essentially unethical, but the democratic ideal requires that one's self may not be authoritatively imposed upon another's personality.

Object Relationship and Transference

One question commonly asked is whether all casework presup-poses a treatment relationship. When one says that treatment begins in the first moment of contact, "contact" is used in a special sense. In meeting and talking with a person a relationship is not necessarily established. It is only when rapport is created for a professional purpose that there may be said to be a "client." The extent to which the client will make use of the casework relation-ship depends upon the kind and quality of his emotional need and its place in the harmony of the personality. By no means do all casework situations call for equally strong worker-client relation-ships. Suppose an applicant is primarily in search of a social service. He is, let us say, a normally self-directing human being, his needs are practical, his cooperation excellent, he wants little except a secure income. Is a treatment relationship to be here presumed?

In so far as the caseworker is able to create a comfortable at-mosphere in which the client feels accepted and his need recog-nized as *his* need, in so far as his right to manage his own affairs is respected and his energies not dissipated in self-justification, a sense of failure, or a struggle of wills, he will experience a kind of "relationship." What conditions the client's use of the relationship are his emotional needs, the goal of treatment, and the function of the agency itself. The "pull" on the worker is both quantitative and qualitative; in all *direct* treatment, counseling and therapy, the worker-client relationship is inevitably accented. The relationship holds on a basis of positive feeling—sometimes with phases of negative or "mixed," that is, ambivalent, feelings— as long as the treatment continues. The relationship ranges from an objective relationship in which the worker is seen much as he is—liked or disliked, trusted or distrusted on the basis of his skill, courtesy, efficiency, and understanding—to one in which subjective feelings color the client's perception of the one who is offering treatment. The child and adolescent form their ideals through identifications. The adult can be sustained and to a degree, at least, stimulated to change by means of constructive relationships. The experience of having a friendly and interested worker listen attentively to one's troubles, not minimizing the difficulty, not criticizing or advising, tends to induce a warm response in the client, leading to a sense of being understood, which is the deepest bond in either personal or professional associations.

The person who is less well or less mature, with distorted perceptions of the real world (object relations), does not see the worker so clearly; all his reactions are colored by attitudes which are carried over from other, usually childhood, experiences to the present relationship. These are "transference" phenomena. Any worker operating in the family, children's, child guidance, fields or with sick patients must understand these complicated transferences or he will find himself involved in quite unmanageable situations. Such manifestations may be temporary—as when an acutely ill person worships his nurse only to find that when he has recovered she becomes again a perfectly ordinary creature acting as nurse. It is an aspect of the mature personality to see people objectively in the main, but fewer marriages would take place if it were not for the "dream girl" and the "hero" ideals which distort the everyday perceptions. Generally speaking, it is the childlike or the less

normal person whose perception of the worker takes on these color-
ings more or less habitually, particularly when circumstances force
him into a dependent or receiving role. The use of transference
forms of relationship for ego support or for strengthening the personality through limited insight directed towards better social
adaptation will be discussed in Chapter IX. In general, face-to-face
discussion of reality factors in the client's situation tends to reduce
transference phenomena. In all forms of psychotherapy transference is a major component in treatment, but in casework, reactivation of past feelings is less often the dominant focus than expressions of current and conscious emotions mobilized around specific
situations. Transference is only one aspect of relationship.

During the twenties, when caseworkers were assimilating the
truth that the subjective meaning of the experience to the person
was as important as the objective experience itself, they had em-
barked on a course of saying little except "how do you feel about
it?" or "it must be hard for you," or "we can discuss this further."
The idea back of this passivity was sound enough, but the technique
often led to difficult emotional material. Since the relationship,
where so little is given, can hold only if the client's emotional needs
are great, release of feeling must be not only appropriately encouraged but also appropriately recognized and worked with.

Relationship as the Basis for Interviewing [6]

While "relationship" is always involved in social casework, the
more intimate the history and the more disturbed the person, the
more is it essential that relationship be strong enough to permit
disclosure of the self. In giving history, a person's own story—his
impression of what has happened to him, the facts and events that
have significance for him—is of central importance. While history
is important for diagnosis and treatment, the ability of the client
(or the parent of a problem child or the relative of a mentally sick
person) to give relevant history is often a clue as to whether he can
assume further responsibility. When a careful, thorough history

[3] See Chapter III.

is needed, if the client understands the reason for giving it and can therefore participate in the process, and if the caseworker starts from the point where the client is, does not force the tempo, follows sensitively the feeling tones, then the relationship will not be adversely affected; on the contrary, the client will tend to appreciate what seems to him to be intelligent interest and concern. In explaining a child's behavior problem the parent is willing to give the obvious social facts readily enough, but when approaching her own handling of the child, her punishing attitudes, and so forth, she feels guilty and defenses are set up. Acceptance, permissiveness, and indeed active support must be given to enable the parent to feel secure enough to proceed.

People tend to think that their own emotional conflicts are very private, that this is an area of self-determination to which they must not admit another person. They may ask for help with "real" problems fairly easily, but less easily with emotional problems, unless they can project their difficulties upon some external factor like loss of a job or a problem child. Most of us have a constitutional dislike of being rescued. The parable of the ingratitude of the drowning man toward his rescuer has deep psychological truth. The caseworker's reticence in interviewing—miscalled "passivity," but actually the control by the worker of his own curiosity and impulse to save—may permit a healing self-knowledge in the client to be activated. We do know that the client's sense of being understood will not in itself remove his difficulties, but it will make it easier for him to turn from talking only about *things* to talking about feelings, even those inner and most protected feelings about himself and others, the recognition of which may help him to meet his difficulty.

Personal questions directed towards the interviewer may indicate interest in the worker—a growing sense of relationship, but perhaps more often they represent an area of emotional concern—a way of projecting one's own problem onto the worker. The client asks personal questions about the interviewer which indicate uncertainties about himself. They may be answered simply and quietly and so disposed of, but often it is best to turn the questions back so as to see what was really the client's idea when asking them. In therapeutically focused interviews this is almost always necessary. It does not really help or reassure a client to know about the interviewer, who is there to understand and help him. The worker must keep in mind that his purpose is professional and should gently recall the client into the appropriate relationship—"I think I can help you best if you will go on with what you were just saying," or something of that sort. Inexperienced workers who have let the interviewing ball go into the net often take refuge in personal chat. This deflects the professional purpose and confuses the client. This is not to say that at the beginning of an interview or when making a visit "small talk" may not take place in a friendly way, but one should proceed as rapidly as possible to the business of the interview. This is true of play interviews with children. We and they should know that they have come, not for amusement, but to be helped with their problems. On the other hand, the client often does not know that he has been helped through the relationship, although he may say, "It has done me good to talk to you." He is quite likely, however, to know only that he feels better and let it go at that, or he may attribute the improvement to some obvious, but usually irrelevant, factor.

Example of Worker-Client Relationship

It is not easy to show by a brief illustration in what ways a client uses relationship, since the variations are endless. The guiding principle is, however, that he tends to see and use the worker in terms of his own experience with other people, particularly (when transference predominates) with early familial figures. The following shows the use of a woman worker by a partially recovered 16-year-old schizophrenic girl.[7] She harbors great resentment towards her mother, a feeling that she always does the wrong thing, is never praised, and that unexpected consequences follow insignificant

[7] See reference to this case in *Journal of Psychiatric Social Work*, "Some Methods in Direct Casework Treatment of the Schizophrenic," Margaret M. Heyman, Summer, 1949. Vol. 19, No. I.

acts and incidents. In addition, the patient has a strong feeling that she has been pushed out of the life of her mother (who is a cold, aggressive, and rigid woman) by younger twin brothers. Excerpts from successive interviews taken in the ward follow.

Nurse on the floor introduced me to patient, who was pasting some felt on the bottom of a book-end. As nurse left, patient asked me to excuse the appearance of her cubicle, and said she "would be through in a second." I said I didn't want to interrupt and that the cubicle to me looked like a workshop. She finished the book-end very quickly and then smiled at me and took off her glasses. She seemed to be looking me over very carefully and then said she thought it would be all right if I sat on the bed, but she is not permitted to do that. I said I'd sit on the radiator. This brought another smile from patient, and she began to tell me how some of the nurses on the floor "irritate" her, and she hoped they would be transferred to another ward. I said that we all get irritated sometimes and I wondered what bothered her particularly. She said the way they act on the ward, but did not elaborate, and I asked no further questions about this.

All nurses to her are mother figures and, as we know, she has resentment against her mother. In this girl there is intellectual deterioration with depressive tinges, and as with little children, one must not startle or make aggressive advances. Like a child who has not had enough love and therefore has never established satisfying personal relationships, she lives essentially within herself. She will need much acceptance, will need to learn to trust if there is to be growth from self-preoccupation and dependency to some degree of independence.

I expressed interest in some of the things she had on her bureau, and commented about her use of color. At this comment from me patient's eyes seemed to light up, and she spoke with animation about her work. . . . She has only Sunday away from the hospital, and the libraries are closed on that day, so she can't go scouting for ideas in books. I said that if she knew what books she wanted perhaps she would like to have me get some for her. She showed some surprise at this, and then said her mother can't do things like that because she doesn't know what patient sees in a particular picture that she can utilize.

Gratified by the worker's interest, she immediately associated it by contrast with her mother's lack of interest.

Patient asked me how I liked the two dolls on her bureau, and I commented that they interested me, too. . . . She said she had originally made them for Christmas presents for her brothers, but "got attached to them," so that she couldn't bear to part from them. I smiled at this, and she joined me, saying, "It's hard to give up things you like," and I agreed that it sometimes is.

She could not bear to give her little brothers presents, and the worker accepts her feeling about this.

Patient then picked up a letter holder and told me she had to paint the bottom of it. She had taken it home to her mother, and the latter had noticed that it was not finished. . . . "When you make something for particular people who look everything over and find mistakes you have to be careful." As she said this there was a tone of hostility, and she asked me whether I had ever seen her mother. At this point she was standing over me with the letter holder in her hands and watching me very intently. . . . She said she knew I would be seeing her mother and did not mind my seeing her. Privately I wondered whether she really meant this, but I did not ask her. I did ask patient whether there was something special she wanted to tell me about my seeing her mother, and she said there wasn't.

She expected the worker to criticize her as did her mother, and again when no criticism was forthcoming there was a good response, and at the end of the interview the patient said, "It is no good to work all the time; it is good to talk sometimes."

At the next interview, when the worker took her out for refreshments, giving tangible proofs of liking, as with a small child, we again see her need for self-gratification—food, tips and so forth.

We stopped at the tearoom, and the table we got had not been cleared. There were several nickels on the table, and patient looked at me inquiringly. She made motions to pick up the change. I smiled and asked whether she had some question about the money. Patient said she always feels like picking up the tips before the waiter sees them. Why? Patient didn't know. She said she knows it is not right, and I agreed that the money was the waiter's.

The worker is noncritical, but helps her to consider reality. Over a chocolate soda the patient expressed again her fear of her mother, expressed resentment that she spanked her twin sons, identified with her brothers, saying with acute penetration that her mother should never have had any children, since she doesn't like them. They interfere with what she would like to do. She then complained, again with insight, that her mother was always urging her to make friends; if she would stop urging, she would be better off. Later she expressed resentment that a former worker had seen her mother more than herself.

Patient said that I was the first person she had felt she could talk to. I said I wanted her to feel she could talk with me; perhaps once she feels comfortable with me, she might be able to be comfortable with others and might make some friends. Patient told me how uneasy and apprehensive she is with people. I said I understood how she felt. I said also that she did not seem to feel that way with me, and perhaps eventually she might feel the same way with others. Patient said she hoped so; she would "love to have a bosom friend." She explained that it would have to be someone who shared in the same interests she had and one to whom she could "talk about everything."

With schizophrenics, gratifications may often more safely be offered through oral and other pleasures less contained within the relationship itself, since the patient may fear the warmth as aggression much as a little child does. The patient here used the metaphor ("bosom friend") of a baby, which she emotionally is, and the worker reassured her that she would see her every day in the hospital, but without emphasis.

Whether men or women are preferable for certain types of cases is a complicated problem in therapy which we cannot take up here, but we note that this girl has particular difficulty in having boy friends. In a subsequent interview, when preparation for the worker's leaving the case had to be made (it is particularly unfortunate to change workers frequently with this type of case), the following interchange took place:

She was given reassurance and encouragement and an opportunity was made to broach my leaving the hospital and the eventual transfer to another worker. Patient told me to "have a heart" when I casually suggested she might like a male worker. Her negative feelings were consciously expressed and amounted to, "How can you do this to me?" I recognized her feelings and told her I was glad she felt free enough with me to express herself. I also assured her that the new worker would be equally interested in her and her problems. Patient accepted this and made no further reference to my leaving. She used her interviews to discuss her art interests; her growing tolerance of her family, against whom complaints fell off quite noticeably. She enrolled in a YWCA Charm School and after about five weeks attendance asked me whether I thought she was acquiring "charm."

Obviously, what the patient meant was that she wished she could charm the worker into staying, but the worker handled this in general terms by bringing her back to a discussion of the reality of the school to which she was then going. It is not always wise to bring to the client's attention the things that we know are psychologically taking place. Later, however, the worker, not so wisely, and feeling guilty because she was letting down this patient by leaving, wanted to give her a present. The sense of loss, however, which this patient anticipated should have been recognized and frankly discussed. Often several interviews are needed in preparation for leaving such a patient.

Worker gave patient a charm bracelet, which she accepted with alacrity and admired, but for which she expressed no verbal thanks, and her facial expression conveyed to me that a bracelet was the least I could give her, since I was leaving her. She said good-bye unemotionally, but assured me she would continue contact with new worker. I gave patient reassurance and support by stressing fact that new worker would be very much interested in seeing her and helping her. At this, patient's face showed the first sign of feeling, and she commented , "You shouldn't have given me anything." I assured patient I wanted to give her something before I left and hoped she would like the bracelet, at which patient responded warmly, "Oh, but I do. That's why you shouldn't have given me anything." I suggested that my giving the bracelet was the most tangible way of showing her that she really mattered and that even though I had to leave the hospital and could not continue to see her she should feel that the new worker would really take my place. She looked at me and hastily turned her eyes away, saying, "I don't know. Good-bye," and walked away.

The girl intuitively understood the guilt reaction and actually remained hostile because this good friend was leaving her. She could not be bribed to accept the loss. As one might expect, the worker who picked up the case was greeted with considerable hostility, both expressed and disguised, because the relationship factor had not been adequately verbalized in preseparation interviews. Such factors, transparent in the mentally ill, occur universally.

ETHICAL CONSIDERATIONS

Every caseworker has a fourfold set of ethical obligations by which he is bound—to his client, to his agency, to the community, and to himself. Casework responsibility includes respect and acceptance of the client as a personality and a human being. This implies, for example, that the client is not a "problem," but a person *with* a problem. He may never be exploited, nor may his social situation be exploited for personal gain, and plans for and with the client must be carried out only on the basis of a considered professional judgment. Guidance should never be casual, impulsive, or hurried, but the emphasis should fall on release of the client's capacity for responsible decisions and actions. Appointments made with clients should be punctually and scrupulously kept, and privacy for interviews should be assured. Promises, always sparingly made, should be fulfilled; if in unforeseen and unavoidable contingencies they must be broken, the reason should be carefully explained. It is wiser, however, to make few promises and never to give false hope of one's ability to solve a problem or "cure" the person.

The Confidential Relationship [8]

One of the most important ethical considerations is the nature of the relationship within which the confidences of the client must be protected. The personal affairs of the client should never become the subjects of gossip or of public or private conversation. Tacit recognition of the fact that one can talk of intimate things in such interviews creates an ethical obligation for privacy. It is

[8] See also pp. 130–31.

part of the attributes of a profession that the nature of the confidential relationship assumes significance. In lay intercourse intimate things are told at the teller's own risk. Under authoritative external pressures or prosecution it is assumed that a person is not obliged to incriminate himself, but in law, medicine, and religion it is imperative for successful treatment that the person put himself unreservedly into the hands of his counselor or practitioner or priest. In a general way this is true of social work, and as professional competence has increasingly developed skill in the interviewing process, the client tends to yield himself fully, trusting in the worker's understanding and skill to help him. This requires that worker and agency safeguard the confidence of the client. A feature, not peculiar to, but accented in social work, however, is the fact of interacting relationships among various agencies on behalf of the client.[9] Here, too, the utmost care must be exercised to protect the confidential material. When the client reveals a situation detrimental to public health and welfare in a confidential interview, the caseworker is responsible for helping the client himself report to the proper authorities. In the double or multiple client situation, since several family members may be involved, each separate "patient" is helped to understand that what he says will not be communicated to the other partner or to a parent. Natural fears about this have to be handled if they arise. He should understand the basis on which confidential material is shared among the professional staff, and presumably will assent to this essential team responsibility.

Self-knowledge in the Relationship

It has always been observed that certain kinds of personality seem to be intuitively helpful; other personalities, quite as well-meaning, can prove dangerous or harmful in intimate human relationships. Students beginning casework may be astonished to find how often they themselves project into family casework treatment biases arising out of their own parental relationships and experi-

[9] For confidential relations between agencies see pp. 129–30.

ences. For the worker, just like a child in the household, may feel so guilty about his own parental feelings that he will oppose a family plan for separation or tend to approve only such filial attitudes, no matter how much resentment they conceal, as make a virtue of devotion or self-sacrifice. According to professional ethics he must learn to accept others as distinct personalities, with their own right of self-realization and self-determination.

In working through to attitudes that are neither moralistic nor coercive, the worker must first be able to understand himself and his own emotional drives and impulses before he can truly accept the "bad" feelings, aggression, or even love and gratitude in others. Caseworkers are trained to avoid "disapproval" of asocial conduct and to acquire understanding, which is neither tolerance nor intolerance. Social workers cannot and should not be impartial in the face of individual and social misery and evil. The place of value [10] judgments is always assumed, but they do not take the conventional form of praising or blaming the person who is to be helped. The attitude of detachment and acceptance is one of the products of the widespread scientific development of the nineteenth century and is not, as we sometimes imagine, wholly an innovation of psychiatry. Nevertheless, it is psychiatry, and more particularly some of the findings of psychoanalysis as to unconscious motivations involved in counter-transference which have helped workers to understand their own impulses to save or to punish, to indulge or to deprive. Insight and self-awareness are prerequisite in an ethical use of relationship; it is important to know one's self in order to be able to accept others; ability to live with one's self or one's feelings is important for being able to understand the feelings of others. Only if we understand to some extent our own motivation can we leave the client free to establish himself securely, first with the social worker and thus later with others. The caseworker will be of little use to clients unless he has a real interest in them—cares about them—but he can never be helpful if he exploits this interest in the form of curiosity or a desire to manage, or a need to

[10] See pp. 6–11.

have clients love him for what he does for them. If we must resist impulses to threaten or to punish, or to grant or to withhold favors, how much harder to see that each individual must make his own solution, not in the sense that he is master of his fate and captain of his soul in a reckless defiance of external reality, but because his goals and life objectives are unique for him.

There is ethical justification for the situation "characteristic of" the treatment relationship. Henri Bergson was not the first to point out, and he expressed the idea with great clarity, that it is very difficult and perhaps impossible to become aware of the nature of organic reality, or what the social worker would call the "reality situation," without entering into it, directly experiencing it, and, he would say, "interpreting it through sympathy." While the social worker who relies wholly on intuition to understand another person may become lost in mysticism, it is possible also to overestimate the intellectual approach to life as yielding real meaning. This truth the social caseworker learns the moment he tries to "treat" another human being. The highly intellectualized person may make a good research worker, but rarely a good clinician, because the intellectual quality itself inhibits him from a direct experiencing of relationship which is his surest touch with living reality.

In any of the professions aiming to help people knowledge of the self is essential for the conscious use of relationship. If one is to use the self, then one must be aware of how the self operates. Not only should the caseworker know something of his motivation for choosing this profession, but he must also surmount another hurdle by recognizing his own subjectivity, prejudices, and biases.

Learning to diagnose involves understanding not only the client's feelings but also one's own, that is, as distinct from the client's. At first a baby is unable to tell what is part of himself and what is part of actuality or objective reality. Gradually he learns that his toe belongs to him and other things belong outside himself. In the growing-up process many children dissociate themselves slowly from the world around them. In much the same way the beginning caseworker may confuse his own feelings with those of the client. He attributes to or projects upon the client fear, guilt, gratitude, or what not because he thinks this is the way everyone feels under the given circumstances, since he himself would feel so. There is a vast difference between being sensitive about oneself and being intuitional towards others. Gradually he learns to be sensitive to what the client feels or might feel. Thus he can identify with someone in trouble, but still keep his own balance; he must not be swept away by his feeling, or he will be pulled into an unconstructive over-identification or rejection. He may not permit himself to live within the client's experience—but he can understand his pain. Most people whom we think of as having "clinical" aptitude have a striking capacity for direct apperception in emotional and sensory areas, a quality of empathy, but all caseworkers have to come to terms with their own emotional experiences before they are free to understand emotional factors in a truly psychosocial perception.

Workers are not free from prejudice and intolerance and are not immune to the effects of irritating behavior, but to develop real tolerance for human behavior in all its manifestations requires fundamentally a warm, natural liking for people and beyond that a slowly developed quality of self-awareness as the worker learns to reduce and lay aside his own defenses against self-knowledge. He is able to do this partly because he experiences his teachers' and supervisors' attitudes of positive acceptance of him as a student and as a learner. In such an atmosphere he becomes secure and is therefore able more thoroughly to examine his own processes, his patterns of learning, and his patterns of professional behavior in ever-widening circles. It is not that he suppresses his feelings, but that more of his feelings—both negative and positive—are brought into consciousness and under control and therefore do not so much affect his response to another's emotion. He does not relinquish his sense of values—personal and social ethics—but comes to understand a wide range of emotions, attitudes, and behavior, without condemning the person. Sometimes the client expresses covertly or openly negative feelings which are disturbing to the young worker until he comes to realize that the expression of feeling is essential to treatment, and the problem is not only to recognize the client's reactions, but also to manage one's own.

The worker, as part of his acquisition of knowledge and skill, must to a considerable degree become willing to see himself in operation and observe how his acts affect others in his professional operations. In other words, if he is to use the self in his social skills in casework, groupwork, and community organization, he must understand the dynamics of self. He grows conscious of his role in all sorts of situations: in the interview, in group process, in surveys, in committees. During the field-training experience the student is helped to notice and to respond to feelings in clients, and by discussing his own mistakes, analyzing his reactions both to client and to supervisor, he gradually becomes aware of the meaning of interaction. Thus, he begins at one and the same time, as he lays aside his defenses against seeing his own patterns of behavior, to achieve a greater objectivity and control. The more a worker moves in the direction of therapeutically oriented casework, the greater are the demands upon him for self-knowledge and for the more complete use of the self.[11]

CLIENT-INVOLVEMENT IN CHANGE

Whenever we have to act for other people, as we do sometimes, we are called upon for wisdom, skill, and courage. Usually we do not have to be responsible for others; it is not often necessary to investigate without consent or to make arrangements behind people's backs or to coax and persuade them into decisions they could well make for themselves. It is to be hoped that society itself will achieve a wider and deeper liberty, based on more security, more cooperation, and less competition, so that a client's choices will be less determined by anxieties and frustrations. But in the casework process the choices as far as possible must remain his, not ours. It goes without saying that not all clients are equally

[11] Unfortunately it is not possible in this book to consider in any detail professional preparation for social work, for casework, or for administrative, therapeutic, or other specializations. See pp. 295–303.

capable of self-direction, and the obligation of society to protect and when necessary to control, remains. As society accepts responsibility for the security of its members, the cause can be advanced only as long as individuals feel responsible enough to engage in an active struggle for the kind of world they are willing to live in. Self-determination may be individual or group or collective; it is an encouraging sign that client groups sometimes constructively participate in welfare programs through appropriate channels. As collective bargaining is essential for labor and industry, the normal motive of self-interest can be developed through educational processes into an equally normal assumption of social responsibility for certain aspects of policy and procedure in welfare.

That a client has a right to be himself, to make his own decisions, to use his own abilities and resources, and to work out his own problems is an extension of the deeply rooted casework belief in self-help. Earlier concepts of self-help, like those of the role of the family, were, however, almost wholly economic. It was thought that the client should mobilize, in so far as he was able, his own resources, his work capacity, and the resources of his family and his community, and help was chiefly directed to eliciting this sort of activity from him. The social workers believe, not in "rugged" individualism, but in socialized individualism. Self-awareness, or finding oneself and being able to relate oneself to society are two ends of the same process. Behavior controlled by external authority leads to submission and the totalitarian ideal; behavior which follows its own uncontrolled impulses leads to anarchy; but if a person, in utilizing fully his opportunities for self-development, forms the habit of respecting "otherness," there is a sound foundation for reciprocally creative relationships—for the interdependent activities of a democratic society.

Medicine has for years been teaching diabetics to manage their own treatment, and medical interpretation is directed to teaching patients how to live within their disabilities, not merely to follow medical orders. Inexperienced workers frequently find it hard to believe that clients in an unjust economic order or in depriving individual circumstances can do anything to solve their own practical problems, but there has been an important development in the administration of public welfare with regard to the degree to which the applicant is encouraged to participate in establishing his own eligibility and to engage in efforts at rehabilitation. As in the intangible psychological areas, casework is less coercive and more reciprocating, at once more reticent and more understanding. Likewise, if clients have a serious disability due to illness, rehabilitation may seem to workers a completely frustrating experience, until they learn how to ally themselves with the personality strength of the client. Hardest of all is to understand that in order to "make good" psychologically a person must be allowed not only to make good by his own efforts but also to make good in his own way.

Early in the case we ask how severe are environmental pressures and strains and how troubled is the person, in order to see in which direction effort will be most immediately relevant and effective, yet we always give attention to the interaction. Gross pathology should always be reduced first, if feasible. Since the personality functions socially and culturally, treatment seeks to release capacities for self-direction and social adaptation within the person and to discover resources and reduce pressures in the environment. While increased understanding and acceptance by the client of himself in his relationships and social role is usually a by-product and sometimes the goal of direct treatment, changes in a situation may also effect changes in feelings and attitudes so that the client can relate himself more successfully to his associates and in general perform more adequately. In other words, in the psychosocial formulation treatment may begin at one end or at the other or at both ends, provided the aim is clear and both the aim and the means are based on proper diagnosis.

Besides understanding to what extent there is a practical problem, with the possibility of a practical solution or gratification, and to what extent the client may have projected his other problems onto the external and obvious need, the worker has to estimate the degree of self-help which may be expected. Not everyone is equally capable of self-help, and the amount of help one must give people is directly inverse to what they can do for themselves. The very young, the very old, the sick, and the feeble-minded need more care, protection, suggestion, and active interference than the more self-directing Even so, the caseworker does not assume that the client is helpless in the face of his difficulties or that there is no part of him which can be roused, but he tries to stimulate him to think and act for himself—to make his own decisions. The idea of self-help in casework was first construed largely as economic; later, psychologically—in terms of readiness to use help actively and to change one's circumstances or one's attitudes. But the concept is fundamental, calling forth the caseworker's skill to motivate the client to use both personal and social resources in working through his difficulties and achieving his own solutions.

THE USE OF AUTHORITY

Although authority is occasionally exercised in the interest of the client through suggestion, advice, and so forth, in any casework setting such authority, arising largely from the prestige of the worker's status and his expert training, is not used as coercion or threat. In certain settings, however, such as the courts,[12] the compulsory educational regulations, the child protection services, and similar agencies, authority exists. It is a mistake, however, to assume that eligibility is confined to security programs and authority to public health or the courts. Nevertheless, certain public agencies have a large degree of authority vested in them.

Authority cannot be used "clinically" without full understanding of the growth and development of the personality—the incorporation of restraints used in normal training—the rebellion, aggression, or neurotic character deviations which stem from inadequate parental handling or other traumatic events in childhood. The psychologically well-equipped worker is not afraid to use authority on a positive basis after it has been diagnosed as appropriate for the individual and the function of the agency. Much protective work is

[12] See pp. 288–93.

simply casework with deeply disturbed or neurotic parents. Case-workers have had to learn about authority just as they had to learn about the principles of "rights" and "needs." To a large degree the clinical use of the "release of feeling" is under-stood, but one is just beginning to understand the clinical use of "restraint of impulses." For example, in working with pri-mary behavior disorders, psychopaths, character disorders, certain phases of psychosis, and all those who act out their impulses, one must help to develop internal and external restraints, and until the client can do so the social worker may have to exercise restraint or authority. Children need to be restrained, just as they need to be loved—restraints are internalized because of loving, nurturing rela-tionships.

Whereas some people have internalized their response to au-thority so that they are in the main guided by their own inner sanctions, others have not. The latter turn quite naturally to a court to settle their problems, even quite minor conduct problems. They may have need for an authoritative political party or religion or ideology or judge. It is to be assumed that this need derives in part from unresolved parental experiences and from other social and cultural conditioning. In mild disturbances in family life, the objective of treatment would be to help the person to face reality and to balance it with his own inner authority or conscience. "I am a man under authority," said the Centurion in the Bible. Both caseworker and client act within reality situations of which au-thority is part of the framework.

A great deal is now known about building up the ego by means of approval, the heightening of self-esteem, success, acceptance by a group, and the development of skills which tend to strengthen the personality. The person who has a stronger ego and a reasonable super ego has a better sense of reality, but delinquent children have distorted ideas of reality and of punitive relationships, thinking that everyone is ready to hurt them. When, through actual experi-ence with a skilled worker they find that such a relationship offers a different reality, they may begin to change their attitude.

MULTIPLE WORKER RELATIONSHIPS [13]

The problem of sharing a relationship with more than one worker has several considerations. Any social case may present concurrently or in quick succession several problems, for instance, an economic problem may be coupled with a health problem in the same family. Or more than one *patient* may be involved—husband and wife, parent and child, ill person and relative. A team approach in a cooperative case is easiest when there is more than one focus for treatment in quite distinct areas, such as an occupational adjustment for an asthmatic boy and an old-age allowance for his grandfather. Here medical social, and public assistance, workers can readily work together, since there are not only distinctive problems but also separate clients.

It is, however, less easy to assign clean-cut functional roles in cases of marital or parent-child conflict. The disputants in a law suit will engage separate lawyers; in social work there will probably be a great deal of cooperative effort between two or more workers. In family counseling one worker may interview both spouses in marital-conflict situations, or if treatment is to be intensive, two workers may be used. In child guidance the two-worker (especially psychiatrist and worker) set-up for parent and child is common, except in the case of very young children, where treatment of the parents, particularly the mother, may be sufficient—the child receiving only incidental or occasional observation. Each case must be considered according to its own dynamics. Nevertheless, in general one might say that social workers are especially equipped to handle family interaction, and it is often practicable to have one worker so long as the focus is on the interpersonal relationship. Whenever the "client" moves out of the social resource and counseling context and he becomes a "patient," he is likely to require a worker for himself. Whenever there is antagonism between marital partners or between child and parent, whenever emotional separation is the chief aim of treatment, whenever a worker finds himself

[13] See also pp. 141–43 and 299–302.

identifying with or being more interested in one partner than in the other (and this is a natural circumstance)—more with the adult than the child, or the reverse—it is better to have two or more workers closely collaborating.[14] It is essential that the several workers have joint diagnostic and treatment conferences frequently when dealing with marital or parent-child problems. In child placing the gap between treatment of the parent and that of the child is often too wide; this has been partly owing to the tradition according to which two agencies carried the same case, and partly to a mistaken notion that "family work" and "children's work" could be kept apart. That a case is "child centered" should not mean that the parents are left out, but rather that they must be actively involved in treatment so long as they are in the picture. In any phase of treatment, harmonizing the several possible goals for the family group is essential.

Another aspect of the multiple worker approach arises from the way intake is managed in most agencies. Because of the agency setting and the distribution and allocation of case loads among the staff, intake or admitting is done by a worker who may not and probably will not carry the case. This necessitates control of the interview in favor of getting necessary facts for the determination of "presumptive eligibility" and preliminary diagnosis, engendering a climate of good will toward the agency rather than toward the individual worker—when the client may be prepared for a second worker. No one likes being shunted from one worker to another, but resistance to such changes can be partially neutralized if the intake worker does not get too deeply involved, if emotionally loaded material is avoided, and if the agency's procedures are carefully interpreted. When it is necessary to transfer the client to another worker, the new worker may be introduced. Agencies should be flexible enough to let certain cases with special emotional problems be carried by the initial worker, just as agencies should be flexible enough to let workers with certain interests and aptitudes

[14] For further discussion of the team approach in psychiatric and medical settings see Chapter X.

specialize to some extent. The practice, however, of permitting intake workers to carry cases for many interviews is not usually desirable. It tends to make the intake function so involved that it virtually becomes an agency in itself, and this complicates the relationship in cases which are continued.

Staff turnover is an aspect of social work practice to be reckoned with, and it is particularly unfortunate when sustained treatment must be carried on. However, if the basic therapeutic attitude is present in each relationship, workers can be changed without too much damage to the client. Careful preparation for the new worker and recognition of the client's natural feelings of resentment and disappointment, often disguised in general criticism or in a wary flattering of the new worker, may reduce the traumatic effects of such change. But it goes without saying that unnecessary shifting from one worker to another should be avoided as far as possible. Relationship is not a mystical union, and transfer can be achieved by preparation and permitting all the inevitable feelings to be aired with the original worker and his successor.

The mature and realistic client who is chiefly concerned with getting a practical service does not invest too much emotion in the relationship. Because he will be aware that his problem has been intelligently grasped and his self-respect preserved, a positive feeling toward the agency will be aroused. But he will not object to going ahead with someone else who also seems to have a good idea of what it is all about (an advantage derived from well-recorded intake interviews). The anxious and disturbed person tends to invest more of himself from the outset, and the intake worker has to watch lest the relationship become too meaningful. In general, this may be controlled by keeping the client's attention upon the reality aspects of the problem and his feeling about his situation rather than his relationship with the worker. Explaining and discussing the agency's methods also tend to dilute the initial relationship by involving the client with the institution as a whole rather than with any individual. This is one of the basic interviewing techniques which will be discussed in the next chapter.

CHAPTER III

THE INTERVIEWING PROCESS

SKILL IN INTERVIEWING and in the professional relationship are so
intimately related to skill in the approach to the living experience
and the social resources of the community discussed in later chapters that any separation here must be regarded as an arbitrary
device for the sake of simplification.[1]

THE CLIENT'S OWN STORY

Because a human being can think and talk as well as feel and
experience, what he can tell us of his situation becomes the chief
medium for exploration, discussion, explanation, and establishing
a positive relationship. Communication is essential in all forms
of interpersonal relations, whether among individuals, families,
races, or nations. In many aspects of social work, as well as in casework, the interview technique is a basic skill to be acquired. The
particular techniques employed depend upon the nature of the
professional problem and the purpose to be achieved, whether to
obtain information, furnish an appropriate service, clarify a decision in counseling, sustain or support the client emotionally, or
motivate a change in attitude and behavior. The worker learns
gradually how to offer a social service not merely as a "commodity"
but also how to help the client use it actively and responsibly, and,
finally, the worker learns how to use himself fully and with self-
awareness in a face-to-face relationship, with or without the appeal
of a practical benefit to reinforce the interviewing objective.

[1] Various purposeful adaptations of the interview in application, social study,
and treatment processes will be discussed in Part II, but here, in a preliminary
way, I shall outline some recognized principles.

Interviewing skill [2] rests on a fundamental professional attitude called "acceptance." This means acceptance of the other person as he is—in whatever situation, no matter how unpleasant or uncongenial to the interviewer, with whatever behavior, aggressiveness, hostility, dependency, or lack of frankness he may manifest. This attitude can come only from respect for people and a genuine desire to help anyone who is in need or trouble. It is translated through courtesy, patience, willingness to listen, and not being critical or disapproving of whatever the client may complain of, request, or reveal about himself. The first requisite in any interview is to make the person feel welcome and comfortable, and for this the interviewer himself must be relaxed and friendly. Initial resistance [3] to telling one's troubles may result from personal or cultural inhibitions, or more likely from both. A person may be ashamed to admit what seems to him to be failure to manage his own affairs, and his particular problem may also be culturally stigmatized. Poverty, unemployment, unmarried motherhood, certain diseases, including mental disease and neuroses, inability to control one's children, and delinquency are in one degree or another frowned upon by the community. Even being one of a minority group may have aroused fears of and defenses against the dominant groups. There are, in addition, all the vague fears of the unknown to make applicants hesitant and cautious about giving information as to their circumstances, fearing the listener's reaction thereto.

Social workers are taught how to recognize and disarm such initial resistance. Courteous reception, immediate attention to a request, explanation of any inevitable delay, verbal recognition of the person's right to apply, use of the appointment system (always, however, with provision for attention to emergencies), information, screening, and steering to determine whether the client seems to be in the right place for his initial need, genuine kindness and consideration for all clients, from the switchboard operator to the porter, give clients a first glimpse of that "acceptance" which is so

[2] See Garrett, A. "Interviewing, Its Principles and Methods," Family Welfare Association of America.
[3] For discussion of handling resistance in treatment see pp. 210–11.

fundamental a part of the whole experience. Resistance [4] mobilized later as a reaction to treatment is a more complicated phenomenon. Detachment and objectivity are, however, as important as identification and acceptance, lest the client feel that the interviewer is "too good," "too nice," and so be unable to express criticism or verbalize antagonism. Recognizing and working with the defenses erected by the personality is an area calling for great technical skill which is, however, indispensable in professional interviewing. This will be discussed later in various connections.[5]

Accrediting and Acceptance

Respect for a client is shown through the discovery and building up of his strengths, as well as understanding his needs and feelings of inadequacy. For any effective use of a service, still more for any change in attitudes and behavior, the client must be encouraged to put something of himself into the treatment process, to communicate what is necessary by way of social facts, social history, and his feelings, and to make an effort on his own behalf, which must be recognized and accredited verbally whenever necessary in the interview. From the first moment when the application is interpreted as a "right"—as under social security provisions—or as wise and self-respecting—as when seeking help for a personal problem—the interviewer supports honest efforts to participate, to cooperate, and to work actively toward a solution. When dealing with difficult and painful details a good deal of backing and reinforcement may have to be given, but without pressure or curiosity. Always, however, the worker should avoid raising false hopes or giving false encouragement. Capacity to participate varies from person to person and from time to time in the same person, so that dependency needs must be accepted, as well as potential and actual strengths recognized.

Young workers are apt to reassure too much and about the wrong things. They tell the client to "buck up" or "cheer up," that he "will get well soon," or that "it isn't as bad as it looks," or the like.

[4] See pp. 266–67.   [5] See pp. 169–77.

Real assurance occurs from conveying that we are interested in the problem and intend to try to help him, getting the fears released rather than making him repress them because of our cheerfulness; and planning out concrete and immediate steps to take together. Nothing relieves anxiety so much as appropriate activity. The worker not only tries to stimulate the client's capacity and will to do for himself, but whenever necessary he offers some of his own strength and active assistance.

Casework has always emphasized principles of self-direction and self-help. As a reaction against overmanaging, overactivity in history-taking, asking too many questions, interpreting too much, there was a phase of "passivity," in which the client was allowed to struggle into his story with little if any help. Interviews were punctuated by long pauses which the worker would not break, and while often this procedure did have the effect of putting a certain pressure on the client to divulge what was on his mind and of showing the worker areas of resistance or "blocking," frequently it did not give the client enough support. Naturally the client expects and needs response. Another disadvantage of an over-passive technique (like that of premature interpretation) is that it tends to make the client go below the surface at a time when he may not be ready to do so. Silence may be an effective, even aggressive means to get the client to unlock his heart, and it tends to involve the worker in an emotionally charged relationship. Worker as well as client may be made to feel insecure by prolonged silence, unless the contact between the two is strong and old. Anyone who has sat next to a silent dinner partner has known a feeling of compulsion and pressure. Caseworkers often find themselves tempted to break in on the slow or inarticulate client because of their own tensions, rather than because the client should be assisted to his own self-expression. Quick guesses and clever deductions, like leading questions, are often barriers to understanding. Unless workers start with a natural love for people, a concern about them, and a sincere desire to help them, they probably never will be good interviewers, but their whole professional discipline teaches them to abstain, to listen, to avoid meddling, and they must have first learned to listen fully and to respond tranquilly before they can be usefully active in terms of what the client needs to tell, not of what the caseworker wants him to tell. Just as it can be said that nobody is fit to use authority until he has stopped *wanting* to do so, active questioning can be used helpfully only after one no longer has the compulsion to rush in. Once free enough to listen, the caseworker can stimulate the client in all sorts of ways in order to get his story. A client may not be ready to discuss certain materials, but permissiveness to do so must always be in the worker's mind. The importance of letting the client tell his story does not mean that the interviewer should not assist him with appropriate questions as to what we shall need to know in order to be of assistance. The incidents of relevant history and specific facts are explored in terms of the presenting problem and request.[6]

Beginning with the Request

One must always keep in the foreground the client's request for assistance. This is the first professional bond between worker and client. The applicant is initially reassured by our acceptance; he is further reassured by our willingness to try to help him. One must, therefore, find out early what was his idea in coming for help. Did he come of his own volition? Who referred him, and for what? One tries to help him verbalize his reason for coming, not only because this will lead to understanding his own sense of difficulty, but also because his request for help, in his opinion, is the immediate point of contact. The interviewer, therefore, tries to get him to discuss it. Clients are often vague because they feel ashamed and too insecure. Young workers, equally insecure, may evade discussing the request simply and realistically either because they think the reasons for it are obvious—one can easily be mistaken about this—or because they are afraid it will be impossible to grant the request, or because their own personal insecurities and dependency make them fear the demands being made

[6] See pp. 159–61.

upon them. However, progress can only be made if the client's purpose is early made clear, and our resources and functions equally so. It is usually better to find out *what* the client is looking for than to ask *how* he expects to be helped. He does not know our methods in advance, and it is in many instances our unknown reaches of power about which he may be fearful. What will we try to do to him if he asks for help? We make it easier for him by explaining in a general way the role of our agency or department—what services we can offer, both practical services and counseling—and we can see what lead he picks up. Thus, joining his ostensible request with our service, he may feel more secure and feel that his coming has not been taken amiss. In describing our role we explain, whenever indicated, any special limitations of our function and what other resources are available in the community.

In the first interview the worker makes a preliminary formulation of the situation, of the diagnosis, of treatment aim, and next steps in procedure. This operates to involve the client responsibly and consciously in working towards a solution of his problem. If the client at first requests a practical service and as one proceeds to discuss the implications it becomes clear that the problem has been "internalized" and that meeting the immediate objective need is no real solution, then formulation of other therapeutic possibilities with the client should be undertaken. One should not, under the guise of a practical service, treat the client for a "personal" problem without his full knowledge, consent, and active wish to be involved in this way. Proceeding with the initial request for service and discussing its implications realistically often leads to a request for less tangible psychological help, but this will not occur unless the worker understands the emotional elements of the case. Any shift in treatment goal should be discussed.

We have spoken above of recognizing and meeting initial resistance through courtesy and acceptance. Resistance may be mobilized further the moment the client glimpses what is involved in getting his problem solved. He may not wish to meet the conditions of eligibility for service or treatment; still less may he be disposed to change his behavior towards spouse or child. Often parents who have displaced their own failure on a child's behavior, will withdraw as soon as they take in how they themselves will be involved in the treatment, saying that the child is behaving better or giving some other excuse. In certain instances a single interview or a few interviews may be sufficient; no resistance is involved, and termination of the treatment is mutually agreed upon. Often, however, early termination by the client is a sign of unwillingness to finish the treatment, and verbal recognition of his resistance may help the client again to attempt to move ahead. Sometimes resistance dies down and flares up again. Commenting that it is difficult, yet perfectly right, to ask for help, or indicating that reluctance to take certain painful steps is perfectly natural often reduces the initial resistance. Workers should be slow, however, to pounce on a broken early appointment as indicating resistance; they should not say too glibly, "It must be hard for you to come." The subway really might have delayed them; or the child might have been taken suddenly sick, and such a comment may be threatening to an already anxious person. As they discuss the client's request they try to let him see what it is they have to offer; they bring out his expectations, express interest in his plans, perhaps introducing some doubt if his proposals seem too optimistic, but not refusing to consider various possibilities. They are justified in expressing an active interest, yet cannot overplay the role of helper if the client really does not want them to help. Starting wholly on the client's terms is rarely wise, but with slight concessions the worker may move in, and together the two may proceed. What finally convinces the client, if he is at all well disposed toward treatment, is recognition that his needs are understood and that the worker grasps what is really involved both in the psychological and the social means of help.

Specific Facts and Responsive Questions

The professional purpose requires enough facts to determine eligibility for service and sufficient acquaintance with the situation to begin to understand the client. The interviewer should not be afraid to ask questions in order to clarify the nature of the problem. Although usually it is well to let the client talk without too much interruption, especially at first, essential facts must be obtained. Few clients resent questions relevant to the immediate situations they have presented. In fact, if the interviewer's attitude is one of acceptance and helpfulness the average client regards questions as evidence of an intelligent interest in him. Questions which can be answered by "yes" or "no" should be avoided, but specific questions in social and psychological areas are necessary. As the interviews progress, it will be important to add further details about such things as employment, health history, income, and other identifying data, as well as the specifics of behavior and feeling.

The essence of the interviewer's skill here is to ask questions which are "responsive" to what the client is already saying, not routine queries as from a questionnaire or outline. He will have general areas [7] in mind, but he will approach the problem from the client's angle and in his own terms and language. "I cannot manage because the cost of everything is so high and rents are out of this world," says the client. "Let me see, what rent are you paying now?" asks the worker quietly. "My child behaves terribly all the time." "What does he do? When did you first notice it? What seems to set him off especially?" and so forth.

There is a great difference between taking case histories in a routine way and in a "responsive," way: for instance, in talking about her domestic situation a woman referred to herself and her husband as being quite happy and having made a good many plans when they were married. Worker A, following a "logical" track, might ask about the marriage date and acquaintance with her husband before that, and the client might say they had known each other almost seven years before their marriage in 1940; that they had met when working in a restaurant, and so forth. Worker B., however, following the emotional tone, might say, "What sort of plans?" and thereby bring out her frustration because she had

[7] See Dollard, *Criteria for the Life History.*

not been able to have a baby. Or a man is saying irritably that his wife is constantly attempting to pick fights and to hurt or annoy him. "Why do you think she does that?" asks the interviewer, and gets vital sidelights on attitudes, behavior, or feelings.

Any caseworker will admit that it is difficult to learn to catch the overtones and to respond to them. The natural tendency is to cut across with ideas of one's own or some intellectual discussion, since in social conversation most people have the habit of thinking about what they are going to say next rather than really listening. Nevertheless, the art of taking histories is dependent upon the ability to relate questions to the main themes in the client's story. One learns to work from the current situation to its background— from top to bottom, as it were—but the quantity, tempo, and quality of material will vary with each case. The giving and taking of social history is a reciprocal process made more possible and effective by the use of relationship, or, more accurately, skill in taking social histories is one factor which tends to establish the relationship. Although at any stage helping the client to reveal specific facts and feelings has the double purpose of giving the worker understanding and helping the client to see his own role in the situation, in the more sensitive areas of feeling the client becomes responsible for being willing to disclose himself, and the timing is almost wholly his. Both kinds of history taking, as information and as "abreaction," that is, reliving an emotional experience, may be seen in a single interview, but the former is more common in initial phases of contact. The client tends to generalize; the worker tries to help him to be specific, both as to the situation and how he is meeting or has met the problem before. First because in this way the worker can understand the problem more quickly and, secondly, because in telling his story the client himself sees more clearly what has been going on and, perhaps, how he now wishes to proceed. It is always an advantage to ask about the immediate onset of the problem. When did it start? What precipitated it? What has he already done about it? Repeated interviews may be necessary to get the relevant facts about the social milieu, the family set-up and relationships and the client's reactions to them, and the structure of the personality as patterned by the life experience. Early exploration elicits objective facts and the more obvious reactions and feelings; later exploration seeks also specific information, but now about the more intimate facts of life experiences and feelings, which come to light only by way of the treatment [8] relationship and as a relived "therapeutic" experience rather than primarily, as at first, for information and diagnostic purposes. Inexperienced workers often shy away from getting the necessary facts because they fear they cannot deal with what will be revealed, but the facts, whether pleasant or unpleasant, must be known. It may be that much of what is divulged will not be treatable, but to know all that is relevant enables one better to determine what should and what should not be treated. Inexperienced interviewers also tend to change the subject—introduce new topics, go off at a tangent—because they do not really listen to what the client is saying or because of anxiety over what the client is expressing, often rationalized to themselves as reluctance "to probe." The client always knows intuitively whether the worker is ready and willing to listen. As the interviewer proceeds, he will draw the client out about the facts presented—not only what happened, but how he feels about what happened and how he reacted to the circumstances. Meanwhile the interviewer is noticing the client's behavior—tension, withdrawal, signs of anxiety. Observation, along with attentive listening, gives us some idea also of the client's level of functioning, his readiness to use help, and the like. This is one approach to appraisal of ego strengths.

In noticing such behavior as silences, trains of thought, and so forth, workers have sometimes leaned too heavily on the idea of free association to gauge feeling. The conditions of the ordinary casework interview do not offer a favorable opportunity for the use of the free association method, either in the psychoanalytical or the laboratory sense. To listen to the "heart beats," the emotional undertones, one has to develop not only infinite patience

[8] See pp. 252–58.

in listening to the natural flow of the narrative but also, like the doctor, a sort of "percussion" technique. One does not use an instrument or tap with a finger, but one does "tap" gently nevertheless in the form of responses which help the client to be more specific as to both events and feelings. In discussing a person's feeling toward another member of his family—wife, child, or relative—it is important to stay with the feeling of the client—not be drawn into an identification with or a defense of the relative being described. One must always "keep one eye on the ball"—that is, talk to the person immediately concerned, not switch to another subject or, which is even more difficult to remember, veer away from noticing the client's emotions about another person as one follows his complaints and he discusses the other partner's circumstances and behavior.

Noticing Points of Stress and Conflict

The interviewer at all times should notice the emotional tone—pauses and blockings in giving information, evidences of pain or anxiety. He must be always sensitive to these points of stress, although he may or may not make any rejoinder. In teaching inexperienced interviewers to notice and respond to indications of feeling it used to be customary to suggest comments such as, "You worry about that?" or "It must be hard for you," the intent being thus to sensitize the learner to respond in some natural way to points of stress. The client knows well enough whether an interviewer is aware of his feeling or not. In many instances the effect is produced merely by repeating the word used by the client, either in recognition of the pain or as a gentle stimulus to proceed with his recital. As a general interviewing principle—stimulus questions and interpretative comments are best made in the clients own words.

In the case of a young girl burdened with three dependents family tension had been increased by the establishment of a joint household with a married sister. Crowded quarters, lack of privacy, and financial strain produced frictions and a sense of social frustration in that she felt her chances of meeting men and marrying were being diminished. Her accumulated hostility was of a rebellious nature—a protest towards an inhibiting outer world.

Laura, coming for her third interview, appears tense and uncomfortable. She speaks of bad weather. Worker says, "It must have been hard for you to come here today." Laura says she dreads returning home at night because of the constant quarreling that goes on all the time. [Notice that this interpretation does not "take" as it were. It is "hard" not to come here but to go home at night. The defenses are operating.] She feels her anxiety is affecting her work, as she is unable to concentrate because of all this worrying. She just cannot make her income stretch over all the family's needs. Worker says she quite understands how Laura must resent all the responsibility she is forced to take. . . . (This comment is accepted and she goes on.)

Laura says that since she was thirteen she has worked on Saturdays during school vacations in the summer. She had had to work because her father never had an adequate income. The $100 monthly that she earns would be quite sufficient for her if she did not have the responsibility for these other people. Worker says she must feel angry and frustrated, working so long and having so little real life of her own.

In recording the interview the worker makes occasional comments, such as, "Laura shows reluctance to face the business at hand by evading practical discussion of the budget," her "tendency to set conditions," her "characteristic response being resistance quickly translated into resentment." These observations as to characteristic response and patterns of behavior may later be communicated to Laura whenever she is ready.

It is not possible to say when a client should be encouraged to go on by a comment such as "Please go on" or "What happened next?" or other gentle stimulus, and when one should respond by picking up and focusing on what is being said. Interviewing is safely active as long as the worker is following closely the facts and feeling tones in what the client is telling, not talking about topics of interest to himself, no matter how informative or instructive they may seem. The good interviewer never "lectures," and is slow to interpret isolated incidents until he is on sure ground.

The interviewer learns to keep the conversation moving ahead, just as the tennis player has to concentrate on getting the ball back over the net. The client makes a drive—an emotional expenditure—often hoping to finish off the conversation, now going too fast for him, by "a smash." "So you see our marriage didn't work out as we had figured"—finality, a "that's all there is to it" tone "Didn't work out?" says the interviewer, or "How did you figure it?" Only the skilled interviewer knows how to time his questions and responses, whether to move ahead or to slacken off for the present. But in general skilled interviewing is responsive to points of stress—helping the client to *bring out* rather than to keep back relevant facts and specific feelings. This is essentially what gives an interview "movement," as it is called.

The caseworker can usually respond safely to expressed feelings and those which lie near the surface, whenever the worker-client relationship is secure. In the case of Lucy, aged seven, as the relationship strengthened it was possible to point out a bit of the disturbance and aggression engendered by a frustrating hospital experience.

Abruptly Lucy challenged me with, "Have you a candy store?" I said, "No." "Have you an automobile?" she continued. I said, "No, why?" "If you had an automobile would you give me a ride?" I would like to. She persisted, "Any place I want to go?" Where did she want to go? Lucy seemed unprepared to answer. Evidently her need for nearness to me and for something positive from me was more important than the outcome of her fantasy as resolved in an automobile ride. . . . She reverted at once to her primary purpose, which was apparently to test me. "Do you go to other little girls?" she asked. I said, "Sometimes, but not now. Now I come to see only you." She said rather coldly, "Suppose I move out?" I suggested that I could find out where she lived and come if she wanted me to. Lucy said, still in a detached, casual way (as if afraid to give too much), "My mother could tell you when she goes to the hospital." I agreed with this. . . .

She spoke then about not liking to go to bed. "Do you have dreams when you sleep?" She answered "No," but added, "Sometimes." Lucy immediately went off into a long string of incoherent words and sounds. She produced these noisily and with considerable aggression and agitation. I asked, "Are you angry?" She replied, with a gay smile, "No, I just want to talk for fun. I want to be a midget." More incoherent sounds followed. To my question, "Why a midget?" she said, "Just for fun," then, "I make teasing. You can't stop me." I felt we were touching a source of some of Lucy's antisocial behavior. I said, "That's how you get even with people, isn't it?" Lucy responded readily, "Yes, they start up with me." I said, "Then you get angry?" Lucy replied with strong feeling, "Sure, I sock them in the eye; I throw them on the floor; they get black and blue. They can't start up with me. I get a hammer and an ice pick and I split their heads open. I'm tough." She looked to me for approbation. I said, "You want to be tough, don't you? In case they start up?" "Yes," Lucy replied intensely, "they can be in the hospital with their eyes." I said, "You're angry you had to be in the hospital with your eyes?" She again went off into incoherent sounds that seemed to help relieve her tension.

The interviewer never minimizes the seriousness of whatever the client complains of, never laughs it off or suggests that it shouldn't matter so much or tries to encourage him with false reassurance— nor does the interviewer ever minimize the real difficulties which may lie in the path of treatment or recovery. Facing together what can be dealt with is no less important than facing together what cannot be dealt with now, or perhaps cannot be dealt with at all within the agency's province or because of external factors which cannot be shifted. Release of impulsive feeling may be contra- indicated in mental illness and other forms of psychopathology. Rather the worker may, in collaboration with the psychiatrist, help the person repress his feelings and adapt to reality situations. The application of general principles of interviewing calls for specialized training as one moves more in the direction of therapeutic aims. An interviewer, skilled in treatment, learns to notice and respond to emotionally charged verbal and behavior, as in a child's play, communications, and release more feeling in constructive ways. Obviously there are occasions when release of feeling should not be further stimulated.

INTERPRETATION AND EXPLANATION

Interpretation takes several forms in the interviewing process. The most familiar types are: explanation, clarification, pointing out patterns of behavior, and interpretation of motivation, the last being sparingly used within the range of social casework method.[9]

Explanation may be clarification of policy and procedure or stating the nature of statutory requirements and eligibility, as in public assistance, a medical regime, or some similar program. The skilled worker seldom attempts this through formal exposition, but in discussion, responsively, as in most interviewing, getting the client to formulate his own questions, watching the emotional components, noticing whether there is an anxiety reaction which blocks or an anxiety pattern assimilation of the information given (a form of defense). The client is not merely informed as to those procedures to which he should relate, but is helped to understand their purpose, especially if to carry them out will be confusing or painful. Policy should not be given as fiat or edict, but within the democratic concept even structure and policy are open to discussion and criticism by client, citizens, workers, and are therefore subject to revision. This does not mean that the worker can unmake policy and procedure at the client's whim, but always there is the underlying assumption of the person's right to know, to understand, to comment, and to question. Explanation of other resources available in the community are given whenever the need indicates a referral. In this respect the chief precaution is that the worker himself shall be noncompetitive and nonpossessive of the client. Professionally oriented, he knows institutions and agencies and is committed ethically to a cooperative undertaking for the welfare of each client whenever and however his best interests can be served. He, therefore, interprets other agencies' functions and limitations as generously and as accurately as his own. He does not let feelings of rivalry or superiority or inferiority trick him into unreal promises which dazzle, or guarded recommendations which effectively warn the client away from applying elsewhere. On the contrary, he must be direct, sincere, and realistic; he does not discuss details of the other agencies' procedures, which is *their* business; he does not advise the client how to manipulate or "wangle"

[9] See pp. 249–53.

a service or a benefit; he does not tell the client how the other agency will treat him; he neither oversells nor depreciates. His chief preoccupation, in fact, is to see that the client is not too bound to the agency to which he makes the original request, is indeed free to leave, for it is usually the worker's unconscious clinging to the client, or hostile attitudes, which makes it hard to help the client use another agency.

Furthermore, he will let the client who has sufficient strength manage his new contacts for himself. On the other hand, he will not hesitate to help the immature, dependent, or ill client to make a difficult contact—telephone for an appointment, write a letter, even accompany him if necessary. The fashion has swung from too much escorting and arranging for clients who do not need such support to a severe "noninterventionist" policy, which may be little suited to the less mature clients and the complexity of interagency practices. In fact, the client is often supposed to bridge in his own person many poorly organized and inefficient community operations. The intake practices of some agencies are formidable. Until these are changed and the community resources are better integrated, indeed, whenever the client needs backing, the worker is prepared to be warm, flexible, and supportive in his handling of referrals, evaluating his client's ability to function in a complex agency world and collaborating with workers in other agencies as members of the fraternity of professional service.

Clarification [10] is the level of much interpretation—which is usually thought of as rational discussion about education and physical, economic, or other problems. Interpretation of a medical problem to the patient and his family is primarily the function of the doctor or the psychiatrist, but the social worker will be constantly called upon for additional reenforcing interpretations of the medical regime and the meaning of the disability for work or family life. The essential requirement is that the worker be thoroughly conversant with the medical or the psychiatric implications and able to take the time, which the doctor often cannot do, to

[10] See Hollis, *Women in Marital Conflict*, pp. 150–52.

carry on a discussion which will enable the patient to bring out his fears, dependence, and resentments. The urgent seeking for information in disability cases, as, indeed, in most problems, is driven and sharpened by anxiety, which, recognized under its various disguises, must be allowed to come out. Interpretation of the relationship is so emotionally charged that a therapeutic context is always to be assumed.[11] Comment on behavior, as indicated earlier, is reserved until the client's patterns are well understood.

In general, whenever the client expresses a conflict or a dilemma the interviewer picks it up and restates it, using the client's own words. This has the effect of further clarifying the problem and may lead to a shared formulation of a plan of work. The client may insist upon a solution through authoritative advice, whereas in effective counseling he must be helped to embark on a series of interviews designed to help him explore the factors which have placed him in the dilemma. By encouraging clients to bring out their ideas and cultural superstitions about the social problem or the medical program, by giving factual information, not minimizing fears, always being sensible of the patients' subjective version of the experience, the caseworker can use interpretation to effect adjustment and strengthen the determination to go through with even very difficult treatment.

The caseworker who spends sufficient time in coming to understand what is really troubling the patient about his operation or disability or social situation is in a strategic position to help in interpretation and adjustment with the patient group, employer, and so forth. Although the following interviews show the sort of interpretation which is admittedly part of a physician's task, in most hospitals the responsibility of working through the patient's fears is shared fully with the medical social worker.

This patient is referred to a caseworker in a clinic for assistance in arranging treatment for carcinoma of the cervix.[12] At first Mrs. B.'s attitude is nonchalant, and she gives the impression of being entirely free from anxiety. Worker begins interview with a brief explanation that

[11] See pp. 252–53.
[12] Condensed from the first edition of this book.

there is additional routine information the hospital would like to have about her in order to be able to keep in touch with her through the subsequent years. She answers questions almost flippantly until the worker inquires how long she has been feeling badly and how she happened to come to this particular hospital. Almost immediately her manner changes, and she becomes quite emotional as she relates the experiences which led to her arrival in the clinic this afternoon. Last July she began to have a vaginal discharge for the first time in her life. This was distressing to her, because she always dreaded having a body odor of any kind. She stresses the importance of cleanliness to her throughout life. After the discharge began, she started to take douches in an effort to cure herself. She says she has always kept her body clean, and she can't imagine how she could have cancer. "It's always seemed like such a filthy disease. I'm sure I'm a clean person . . ."

As in other forms of illness, the patient may translate the disease in terms of his own phantasies, both personally and culturally determined. This is especially true in carcinoma because of the organs most often threatened. It is clear that Mrs. Barger had displaced deep conflicts upon her condition. The caseworker's role is not to interpret the unconscious background of these phantasies to the patient, but to bring out the conscious fears and help reconcile the subjective ideas with the scientific "reality" with which Mrs. Barger is being met in the hospital setting.

Finally, her family doctor told her frankly that she had cancer and needed immediate treatment. "I never had such a shock in my life. It never occurred to me that I might have cancer. I never thought of getting such a thing wrong with me." She came to the hospital as fast as she could get here and then learned that the clinic would not meet until afternoon. "I was just as cold as ice all over and shaking from head to foot."

Worker gives a brief explanation that the doctor has recommended X-ray treatment for her in order to arrest the discharge and "clean up" any infection and inflammation which may be surrounding the tumor in her cervix which is giving the trouble. There is a good chance that these treatments may give her immediate relief from the discharge which is so objectionable to her. After the X-ray treatment is completed the doctors will reexamine her and determine whether she should have an operation or be given radium. The patient listens attentively to this explanation and then comments: "Well, I'm glad you can do something for me, anyway."

The medical approach—with its microscopic examinations, X-ray, and so forth—frequently causes tension to mount. Acceptance of the "funny" ideas which patients are ashamed to admit and at the same time explanation of medical procedures often, as in this case, relax the tension and help bridge the gap between the phantasy and the reality. The caseworker is careful to give only justifiable reassurance, as, for instance, that the X-ray will relieve the discharge, thus pointing to a concrete bit of help within the all-enveloping fears. In hospitals the traditional atmosphere of blanket reassurance often alarms the individual, who feels himself threatened in a special way. The social caseworker, by patient listening and individualized interpretation, puts himself in a strategic position to meet the diffused fears and resentments which helplessness and uncertainty engender.

She is glad they told her that she had cancer, although she has talked with a lot of patients who don't know what is the matter with them. She thinks it is much better to know exactly what is wrong. However, there are two things she would like to know in order to rest easier. She would like to know definitely what the doctors are planning to do next to her, and she would like to know exactly when her cancer began. She says, "I feel if I have already had it a year it might prove that I would live longer because it would show that I'm big and strong and could stand it better than most people." She heard someone in the clinic say that for a very long time before they knew they had a cancer they suffered from neuritis. The woman who told her had cancer of the breast and neuritis in the shoulder, but she thinks that her case might be similar because before she knew she had cancer she had "neuritis pains" in her knees and legs. "Do you think that could have been my cancer coming on?" Worker explains that it is not possible to tell just when her trouble began. Patient sighs heavily and comments: "That's the trouble about cancer. When you find out you've got it, it's too late to do anything about it." Worker explains that the doctors do feel that she can be helped by treatment, even though she does have cancer. Patient replies promptly: "Well, I'm thankful to hear you say something can be done. Having this disease makes me feel inferior." Then she talks about the two douches she takes daily and describes her frantic efforts to scrub and sterilize the bathtub afterwards. She is really frightened about other people using the same tub, although she has been told that cancer is not catching. At the time of her first examination she was too frightened to answer the doctor's questions correctly and did not tell him that cancer does run in her family. Her own grandmother and an aunt died from it. Patient says she would rather have an operation than any other kind of treatment—"I want them to cut it all out of me." Worker encourages patient to talk more about her feeling of having something "bad" inside of her; she would like "to have it all cut right out of me." Very abruptly she puts her hand on worker's knee and says, "Honest truth, do you think I'm getting along all right ?" Worker replies that she seems to be looking well and inquires, "How do you feel you are getting along?" She sticks out her tongue and says she has a terrible taste in her mouth, which makes "her wonder." She has had severe attacks of nausea. Worker comments that these are both by-products of X-ray treatment.

Mrs. B. has been terribly frightened by a broadcast from Mexico which advised against X-ray treatment. The caseworker discusses this and other misleading impressions which the patient had received from reading, and comments reassuringly on her continuing with the hospital in spite of her misgivings. She says that the patient's own ideas about cancer are important because they are making her nervous and anxious, and explains again that both the X-ray and radium treatments are designed to retard the growth and activity of the cancer. "Tell me the truth, how many times can I have radium?" Worker explains that will depend upon the number of hours the radium is left in her cervix, since it is the total amount of radiation which is important and not the number of treatments. Patient says: "Do you think they'll use it all up on me the first time? I'm scared to death that this thing will come back on me and you folks won't be able to do anything to stop it." The worker replies that it is only natural that patient should be frightened after reading the terrible descriptions in the pamphlet. The worker also comments that the thing which she is actually afraid of is death itself, and not any specific form of treatment. The patient agrees emphatically with this. "Everything I've ever had in my life has gone hard with me, and I'm sure this would too." Her mind is filled constantly with ideas of what is going to happen to her. "I feel my abdomen all the time and it doesn't feel different, but I know there's something in there, because I feel it when I stoop over or try to move around. It's just like a big hard lump. And when these doctors go probing on the inside of me I get pains that make me think I am in labor." Worker comments that there is a lot of pain connected with cancer and that many of the symptoms of which patient complains are present in all cancer patients. However, Mrs. B. seems to have discomfort and anxiety caused by certain ideas or pictures she carries about in her mind. Some of these ideas are accurate—cancer is a lump, and it does grow and get larger, and it does cause pain, but there are other ideas she has which need to be untangled and straightened out. The worker is always willing to talk with her about anything she wishes, even the ideas which seem queerest. Since patient has asked her to do so, worker will always be absolutely frank in sharing any information with her which she may have about her actual condition or plans for treatment. Patient interrupts to say that she feels worker is the only one who knows just how scared she is and she did trust her until the matter of the operation came up. Worker agrees that she is justified in being angry if she feels she has been deceived. She sighs and says: "I told the doctor just how I felt about the operation, but he said I was too far along for that. Then the lady who gave me my appointment said they weren't going to operate on me because my stomach was too fat. I hardly know whom to believe." Worker comments that both statements were correct and offers a simple explanation as to the difficulty which fatty tissue would present in any operative procedure. . . .

The caseworker saw Mrs. B. on three successive days after her radium treatment, listening to her expressions of anxiety and apprehension and explaining the common features of the discomfort which she was experiencing. In the fourth interview Mrs. B. discusses her conceptions of the radium capsules quite simply and without especial effect. Then patient asks whether she is going to continue to feel better. Before worker answers, she says: "You know you said yourself that when all this is over I'm going to feel fine." Worker agrees that this is what we all hope for, but that there may be discouraging days before that time comes. Patient sighs and say that she feels the worst is over and she is certainly grateful to the hospital.

We see Mrs. Barger reaching a point where she can in part reassure herself, although the worker paves the way for disappointment, an essential precaution if the patient's confidence is to be held. Mrs. Barger, like other anxious people, has to go through a phase of articulating many fears and phobias around such ideas as cleanliness, "something bad inside of her," or projection of her fears upon other people—she "must get well for the sake of the children"—before she can admit openly her great fear of death which the worker meets without evasion.

It is interesting to observe how often a person will move through a phase of ostensible information-seeking to face the basic problem if, and only if, the caseworker is sensitive to the anxiety which motivates the request for information. All of us have, expressed or unexpressed, a feeling of the terms on which we are willing to be helped. The caseworker who senses this only as a challenge on the part of the client to control the situation is less helpful than the one who, understanding the usefulness of resistance in the economy of the personality, interprets actual procedures in such a way that it is easier for the client to come to grips with them. Some clients have patterns of domination just as they have patterns of ambivalence—a person both wants to be treated and does not want to be treated, wants you to know about him, but does not want you to know so much that you will thwart or criticize him. But attempts to control are as often defenses against anxiety as they are expressions of aggression.

Because a person tends to behave in ways customary for him, patterns can be discerned by the trained eye and ear; but one must also remember that persons acutely ill or upset may temporarily behave unlike themselves. Children may show very changeable behavior from one day to another, and the well-known shifts of adolescence must be allowed for. An acute fear or aggressive reaction should be distinguished from an anxiety pattern. It is best to listen to whatever the client brings out and get to the core of the situation, except in very special situations concerning near-psychotic patients or patients near a panic state. Every individual who has anxiety has developed defenses against it. Of course, occasionally an individual is overwhelmed and without defenses, but in the majority of cases clients can handle the anxiety which the interview brings out.

Pointing out or Pointing up Patterns of Behavior

In counseling, especially in interviews therapeutically focused, the clients' pattern of behavior gradually emerges; for instance, one tends to be extravagant and reckless about spending money, another is compulsively neat and exacting in the household; another may be managing, or fearful, or inhibited. When the worker catches the pattern of behavior, he calls the client's attention to it if it is important for the solution of the problem that the client recognize the way he tends to behave. The worker usually makes the observation as to the behavior in the form of a mild question, and only when the client's presentation shows that he already glimpses what he is doing. Timing is of great importance.

In any ordinary life situation the mature person may have enough understanding of himself and the nature of the problem to use the social resources or to come to a decision as to a course of action on the basis of explanation and analysis of the issues. The person grasps the elements in the problem and moves on sensibly or comfortably to meet it. But if the person is anxious or disturbed, if the person's behavior and feelings block any solution, "he gets in his own way," as in the popular phrase; or if his aggressive or delinquent actions bring him into conflict with society, then for solution the person must come to see that his patterns of behavior are part of the problem itself. The reality he must now face includes his own behavior and possibly its meaning, and if one is not behaving well, this is hard. Caseworkers must sometimes bring to the attention of the client ideas and feelings, whether acceptable or not, of which he was previously unaware. These ideas and feelings are in the antechamber of the mind or, as Freud calls it, the "preconscious." Such thoughts can become conscious in appropriate circumstances. The caseworker deals most with accessible memories and feelings about which the client may have defenses; within the scope of the ordinary casework interview, however, he does not have ready access to impulses lying deep in the unconscious, for which analytic procedure would be usually indicated. Derivatives of the unconscious, however, are constantly worked with.

Rarely can the client bear to see himself in his actual role unless the worker-client relationship is "stepped up"; unless there is strong positive feeling of trust in the worker's willingness to understand and ability to help. Inexperienced workers wish to point out the behavior immediately and expect the client to agree that it is undesirable and so give it up; but the matter is rarely so simple. We seem able to change ourselves (except in the most superficial ways), only in a deeply felt emotional experience. The greater the change expected, the stronger must be the client's emotional involvement. At the deepest level such changes seem to come only "out of great tribulation" and in transference relationships.[13] What a wise parent knows intuitively or learns quickly is that the child becomes "good," gives up or represses his naughty behavior, when he identifies with a loving parent, through an understanding relationship. The client can allow himself to see his patterns of behavior only when he believes in the worker's acceptance and noncriticism. The therapeutic attitude, of which we repeatedly speak, alone makes it possible for him to face and accept the self.

For instance, in a case of marital counseling Mrs. P. has repeatedly represented herself as a good and patient parent to her step-son, Fred, age 10. She has projected all the blame for the boy's trying behavior on his previous up-bringing and on her husband. Eliciting her story, the worker notices that the situation is quite otherwise; that the step-mother's behavior towards Fred is actually harsh and depriving. As the relationship deepens between the worker and Mrs. P. she reveals more and more of her real behavior and feeling—unconsciously lowering her defenses. Finally, in the fourth or fifth interview, the moment comes. The step-mother is spontaneously describing an incident when something had gone wrong again between herself and the boy. She is complaining about Fred as usual, but the incident shows her harsh behavior, and the worker senses that this has now become an "admission" which offers

13 See pp. 26, 256.

an opportunity for bringing it to her attention. Reporting the interview the worker writes:

It seems that Fred is allowed to use only the back door of the apartment, taking off his shoes and leaving them on the porch before he enters. Mrs. P. thought that her husband agreed with her that "this was a practical procedure that kept the house cleaner. Other children in the neighborhood do the same thing." I found upon inquiry, however, that Peter (her own son), had not been made to do so when he was a little boy. She laid this difference to the fact that she was then not working, could make sure that he wiped his feet at the front door, and she had more time for cleaning up. (Towards Peter she is always indulgent. It is Fred for whom she cannot clean up.)

The difficulty the other day had centered in the fact that Fred had come home at a time when no one was there, had not been able to get in the back door, then had gone away. (She does not allow him to have a key lest he bring in some of his friends when she is not at home.) By the time he returned she was already at home and was busy so did not answer his knock on the back door immediately. He then went to the front steps and sat down and waited quietly, so she was not aware that he was there until Mr. P. came home and found him cold and crying. Her husband was very critical of her about this. (She is really critical of herself, but can only admit it in this indirect way.) His criticism hurt her, and she thinks she got excited and said things that perhaps she should not have said. I said to her gently, "You said things?" "Yes," she had burst out that "Fred just sat there and cried to get her into trouble with his father." "Did you really think this?" "Well, it is like Fred; he is sneaky; he wants to hurt me; he wants to turn his father against me!" She cried a little, and I asked her if she could think of anything she did which would make Fred feel this way about her? Well, she supposes she does this sort of thing to Fred because she hates what he has done to her marriage; he must know she hates him, and he hates her the same way.

An admission of this sort tends to make the parent guilty, and she will require considerable emotional support from the worker. Perhaps this should not have been elicited so soon, but in this particular case Fred was a refugee, only recently brought over to join his father, and there were many ways in which he was behaving in a difficult manner in meeting a situation of considerable tension and urgency—a fact which the worker had sympathetically responded to in all previous interviews. At any rate, once this step-mother, at heart a quite warm person, was able to see that her own behavior had been a factor in the child's difficulty, the treatment could be formulated on another level, giving her more opportunity to participate in seeking help for herself as well as for Fred. The first phase of the case had indicated that the child, Fred, was a problem (specific social and cultural history and facts of behavior were furnished by both parents). Next, the worker, who saw the step-mother's contribution to the problem, disguised as it was by displacement, denial, projection, and other defenses—she had presented herself as a good mother—helped Mrs. P. to notice her own behavior and to express some awareness of her real feelings.

To a young couple chronically in debt one might say: "What usually happens when you borrow?" To a veteran who cannot get his compensation because he quarrels with each doctor and leaves the clinic before any examination is completed, "Do you think that your 'getting mad,' as you say, 'so easily' may really stand in the way of your getting the money adjustment you want?" "Do you get mad easily at other frustrating experiences?" This kind of calling attention to patterns can best be done when the relationship is strong enough to bear it; when the client will not feel it as the worker's criticism, but as a verbalization of his own admission, therefore already in consciousness or near consciousness, and when he is genuinely seeking and using help in the solution of his problem. Interpretation may be too early, may be shrugged off, may be wrong, but no great harm is done if the worker is non-critical and warm and if motivation is not touched upon at a deep level. When timely and relevant, a new orientation thus gained may lead to some change in attitude and behavior in respect at least to the situation immediately brought for counseling. One should not overestimate one's ability either to help or to harm the client, as at best one's powers are limited. Reality always imposes certain limitations upon the worker's and the client's phantasies of omnipotence.

Interpretation at the Level of Motivation [14]

Interpretation as to motivation, such as early psychosexual conflict (infantile neurosis), is not attempted in limited types of therapy. Primarily this technique lies in the area of psychoanalysis. The *level* of motivation is usually unconscious and cannot and should not be reached under ordinary conditions of interviewing.

Most caseworkers would agree that it is possible to interpret attitudes and feelings which the client brings forward of which he is already aware or half aware—always realizing that actions and feelings determined by unconscious motivation have to be understood, but often let alone. The wise caseworker is cautious about appearing to know too much or too soon, interpreting too deeply or too early, if the client does not himself want to face or wish us to understand the meaning of what he is telling. Any interpretation may make him feel as if he were getting caught. While in many instances one can count on the client's dismissing the explanation if it does not suit him, premature reality testing is ineffective, especially when the client is projecting his difficulties upon other people and things. However, if a relevant and responsive attempt is made to point out the source of his difficulties, no great harm will be done even though defenses operate as resistance.

Most people have defenses against learning unpalatable truths about themselves, and the well-trained interviewer perceives a good many elements in the problem which he may or may not think it wise to share with the client. This is partly a matter of timing and partly a matter of the goal in each given case. In determining eligibility the worker is obligated to interpret the nature of the right and the function of the agency, and if the client's behavior is interfering with the exercise of his right and responsibility to his family, the worker may be obliged to share this, too, rather directly. But if in a request for a nursery school placement the worker recognizes a basic rejection of the child by the parent, probably this

[14] See also pp. 264–66.

fact would not be shared so immediately with the parent, who may be unconscious of her own motivation in making the application.

For instance, in the case of Mrs. P., just cited, the reasons the step-mother behaves as she does towards Fred may stem from her own experience in childhood with an indulgent father, an ill and partially rejecting mother, and younger brothers, towards whom she held a great deal of resentment. These elements of early (oedipal) motivation which are caught up in the current marriage and focused on Fred were not interpreted, although in certain interviews Mrs. P. discussed childhood situations quite freely. Interpretation in the interview rarely attempts to show the reason for anything which is not already conscious. It is not easy to learn the reasons and usually a client does not want to know. Interpretation in the briefer and more limited forms of psychotherapy deal with what and how, rather than why. "You are afraid I won't understand you," verbalizing an unexpressed thought. A child says, "Do all small boys have fathers?" "I think you are wondering, Teddy, where your father is, aren't you?" As the client is helped to talk about emotionally significant material, he will make such associations for himself, and his recognition of them is one of the safest forms of interpretation, for he will best know whether they are true or not.

Inexperienced workers should be cautioned that appropriate forms of interpretation are explanations of practical external current problems and conscious feelings and behavior. Interviewing designed for insight into the unconscious determinants of behavior should be reserved for those with special and, indeed, rigorous training. Fortunately, moderate changes may be effected by situational adjustments, counseling on a conscious level, clarification of real issues, without the goal of "insight," which may be gained only in a special sort of emotional experience. The reintegration of the personality through insight is the goal of psychoanalysis which affects the total mind-body structure. Radical changes take place only as a result of radical treatment. Obviously, interviewing with stimulated rather than free association does not lend itself to such fundamental reorganization; it can only furnish the basis for effectively pointing out current patterns of behavior both in a heightened use of and the control of the transference possibilities in the relationship.

TREATABILITY AND TERMINATION [15]

The termination of treatment is always related to the original request and its shared reformulation with the client. If a new treatment goal is formulated later, one may proceed, but one does not "hold cases open" to see if something will happen. No one can imaginatively relate himself to experience until he is an active participant, but in "therapy," as in casework, he is asked at first to relate himself to certain procedures or "rules"—policy, time, appointments, fees, and so forth—which are realistically discussed. In counseling or interviewing treatment, it is important not to drift along with vague gratifications and indistinct goals. As at the beginning, the approaching termination of treatment must be sensitively recognized and appropriately timed and discussed in terms of favorable shifts in feeling and environment.

From the outset one must realize that the modification of character, so commonly the concern of social work, may be even more difficult than the relinquishment of neurotic symptoms. From the outset the worker must estimate the kind and extent of help it is reasonable to offer or expect. The client knows to some extent what he wants, but he cannot know what to expect either from the mobilization of the self in the treatment experience or from the agency. Dissatisfaction may arise either from real limits and frustrations or from unreasonable expectations and demands. Again, from the outset the worker must be clear and firm as to reality factors affecting the use of practical resources or other known limitations, without, however, imposing artificial restrictions. Joint planning in itself suggests a course of action with implied termination. Just as in establishing eligibility for public assistance one

[15] See pp. 236, 267.

should provide for review, so in treatment one allows for reviews and reformulations which sharpen the sense of direction and possible ending, the awareness of and the use of time.

A period of exploration may be usefully determined with the client, or an approximate, or in some instances definite, date for review or termination discussed, but the allocation in advance of a set number of interviews renewable almost in contractual terms or the assumption of a rigid time system does not seem relevant to the complex interaction of psychosocial factors involved in characteristic casework processes. Casework which is not diagnostically based or in which the treatment aim has not been clearly formulated has tended to be either diffuse or mechanistically controlled, but one of the greatest strengths in diagnostically based casework lies in the plasticity which working with the total psychosocial configuration permits.[16]

Nevertheless, one should not make promises for one's own agency, and still less for a cooperating agency, which it is impossible to fulfill. The inexperienced worker may confuse his own wish to help with the actual realities of the situation itself—the client and his own similar wish for magical solutions. The desire for treatment, except in situations of great emergency or urgency, is almost always complicated by the phenomenon of resistance [17] already discussed. In the range of casework services the client may wish help for his concrete problem, but not for himself, or for both—in therapeutic efforts these goals are inseparable. In casework, access to the problem may be had at either end, but if the problem is formulated as situational, termination is then defined by these same terms. However, in casework, since self-involvement is encouraged, the client's persistence or his desire to discontinue enters into the matter of termination. Usually his helplessness at the beginning and his effort to put all the burden onto the worker are kept steadily focused within the treatment situation. The worker's effort to give all or do all for the client can lead only to in-

---

[16] See FSAA, A Comparison of Diagnostic & Functional Case Work Concepts.
[17] See pp. 177–78.

creasing demands, frustration, and anger on the part of the client, since retreat from this position is inevitable, and the worker's intentions and capabilities will become equally suspect.

As drifting along with undefined goals is unproductive, so termination discussed prematurely, or with aggression or challenge, arouses anxiety and hostility which are detrimental to the client. The immature or weakened ego may need long periods of practical and emotional support, but this goal, too, calls for purposeful review of the agency's resources on a planned basis at appropriate intervals. The painful aspects of terminating a helpful relationship are diminished by the client's own growing sense of strength, by a comforting feeling of improvement because of the channelizing of his activities into ego building and enlarged social activities and interests with the realization of the worker's continuing good will and the fact that he can return to the agency if necessary. At one time it was believed that reapplication meant that there had been failure on the part of the client or the worker or both, but this idea came from the false assumption that there could be magical and complete results from treatment.

Fortunately changes in the client situation may take place outside as well as inside the relationship, either because of the growth of the client's personality or for causes unrelated to agency activities. New factors or the recurrence of old problems may again require intervention. No stigma should attach to reapplication in social work any more than for medical treatment. It is well to remember, however, that periods of regression and clinging to the agency or worker are common when the client contemplates the withdrawal of emotional support. This may be verbalized, accepted, and worked through as a normal phase of termination. The chief technical problem is to determine the goal and method of treatment as based on psychosocial diagnosis and evaluation. The practitioner is attuned to what actually is occurring both in the objective situation and as shown in the client's readiness and functioning. He does not proceed toward arbitrary and artificial conclusions, nor should theoretical assumptions blind him to the fact that what is supposed to happen may not take place. Measurement of success [18] and failure is still in its infancy. Systematic observation, careful recording, discussion of progress and results obtained, and participation in experimental research projects should, in the long run, make for informed qualitative, instead of opportunistic, judgments as to treatability and termination.

[18] See Hunt and others in bibliography.

CHAPTER IV

THE USE OF SOCIAL RESOURCES AND THE LIVING EXPERIENCE

THE DISTINGUISHING CHARACTERISTIC of social work is its attempt to integrate the psychological approach in the interview with the realities of the living experience, since they interact.[1] Man is a social being, living within a variety of cultural patterns. Changes occur in what is normal for the individual as development within the cultural group takes place. Similarly, when there is movement from one pattern to another, the concept of what is normal changes. Social workers need to understand established cultural patterns as well as what is involved in change within a cultural group or in the move from one group to another. An understanding of the effect upon the individual and the use he makes of the patterns of the in and the out groups in relationship is essential. The meaning of apparent deviation can be evaluated only through this understanding. An outgrowth is the attitude of acceptance and even of enjoyment of differences, as well as likenesses, between people.

The casework situation is that of a person in conflict with environmental factors or with a deficiency which must be compensated for by community resources; or the typical situation may be one in which the conflict has been to some degree internalized, so that the client is in conflict with himself as well as with society. It is well known that the effect of a harsh social environment, too restrictive a cultural milieu, and curtailment of educational and social opportunities hamper or weaken the integrative ability either to adapt to external circumstances or to cope

[1] See also for social agencies Chapter V and environmental treatment pp. 243–49.

with inner conflicts. Gross social pathology, denial of civil rights, traumatic and unfair employment or social practices, discriminative segregation, or other isolation affect the personality much as the restriction of mobility, disease, or physical handicaps may adversely affect the growth of the child. Maturity, adequacy of response, freedom from excessive anxiety or aggressive hostility can take place only if there is a favorable balance between man and his social environment. If the difficulty lies between the person and a depriving or traumatic reality we may regard it as a primary reactive conflict in which the balance may be restored by making available the resources of the community to sustain and correct the deficiency or by arranging a more favorable living experience. Overprotection and a too-indulgent security (although in our society, no doubt, less of a present danger than is deprivation) may also weaken the personality through lack of vigorous challenge to growth, constructive activity, and self-reliance. Any drift to conformity, failures in imaginative enterprise, and dependency are at least partially met through wholesome primary identifications with parents, group acceptance, and opportunities, and the assumption of individual and social responsibilities through educational means rooted in sound mental-hygiene principles. Intra-psychic conflict,[2] as such, is not the preoccupation of casework treatment, but rather the balance between person and environment where, by attention to the less conflicted parts of the personality the client can be helped to better social functioning and adaptation. The essential nature of basic conflict must, however, be understood in any truly therapeutic endeavor even though such conflict is not touched directly in limited forms of therapy.

KNOWLEDGE AND SKILL IN THE USE OF SOCIAL RESOURCES

The social worker must have a thorough grounding of knowledge as to the socio-economic factors in the community which have an influence upon individuals: population make-up and trends,

[2] See pp. 264–66.

industrial and health conditions; history of the community, political or governmental structure, educational provisions and standards, religious influences, ethical standards, and so forth. He must know the social organization of the community, the significance of the family, what group activities the individual may be a participant in or affected by. Because of such knowledge he will come to understand social needs—what they are, how they change, ways in which they are being met, through both organized and unorganized efforts. Furthermore, he will comprehend resources for meeting social needs—statutory and voluntary, sectarian and nonsectarian, individual and group—and the social agency's relationship to the community, to welfare planning, to community organization; he will see the agency as part of a constellation of community effort.[3]

Knowledge of the various social agencies includes understanding the personal, group, and social needs which the agencies are set up to meet; their diverse origins and auspices, their varying structures, functions, and concepts of service, and the degree and quality of their interrelationships. Such understanding leads to a broad perspective. Agencies are seen as part of a composite picture in which the diversified aspects have a common relationship to the meeting of human needs. Narrowness in viewpoint of the kind which considers one agency or one area of service the hub of the professional universe is discouraged by this perspective. Only on such a basis can the worker learn how to help his client use resources effectively to better his situation. In giving practical services the emphasis falls on helping the client to use, either in one's own agency or through another agency, the community resources necessary to meet his need. Exploration of the need, clarification of the problem or situation, mobilizing of the client's own efforts to change his situation through the use of the resources are the dominant considerations. Information, interpretation of policies, procedures, community resources, and so forth are, however, given through the psychosocial processes of casework interviewing, and experience is structured for growth and development.

[3] See pp. 129–31.

To meet the requests which clients make for help with the problems of everyday living, social work has taken over earlier traditional "philanthropic" endeavors, many familiar services, and developed others, such as financial assistance, relief in kind, institutions and shelters, foster and boarding care, homemakers, day nurseries, camps, and certain kinds of rehabilitation work for the handicapped, and so forth. Cooperation with educational and religious organizations has been a long-standing, accepted obligation. In addition, referral to medical, nursing, dental, and similar resources, as well as to employment and legal facilities, has increasingly been refined as a characteristic form of service, based on established practices of inter-agency collaboration. Community resources are fully utilized. Health needs are seen in their relationship to the client's request and to other problems, and treatment is geared to foster the total well-being of the individual and family. The needs of the applicant are explored to the point of determining where he may best be served, and if it is clear that he is eligible for and would profit by the service of another agency he is helped to make the necessary connection.[4] This form of service not only protects the interests of the client and the community but also makes selection at intake effective for each agency's distinctive service. As in other problems, the educational and treatment aims are flexibly approached, and freedom of choice and initiative are so far as possible left to the client. For the best results, the client must involve himself by recognizing his needs and trying to improve his situation. The caseworker, however, promotes these efforts toward physical and emotional health and intervenes in acute situations by arranging the proper care.

Since every case may be said to be psychosocial—practical services are given with an understanding of the person and his emotional reactions; counseling and therapy are often accompanied by practical assistance. Just as caseworkers had to learn not to give money for vague emotional purposes, so, too, in each case they deal with specific requests and related problems, not with gen-

[4] See pp. 179–80.

eralized and diffused misery. To do some little thing which seems to be relevant to the client's purposes for himself is better than to try to do everything.

One might say that the two services around which the casework idea was most developed were relief-giving (assistance) and child placing. In these two fields the social worker was traditionally the "expert," for in the use of money to maintain the home the caseworker must evaluate the wage-earning, supporting, child-caring, and home-management functions, and whenever there are children, inevitably he must evaluate the child in the home and the effects of parental and sibling experiences. The caseworker, using institutions and foster parents in child placing, encounters not only the child himself but also the effects of the child's parental experience in his adaptation to foster care. Around both approaches accessory services such as day nurseries, homemakers, home economists, and so forth have been developed. Family maintenance and substitute home care will later be discussed as living experiences rather than as social resources.[5] We shall continue first to describe the common practical tools, such as financial assistance or money as income.

The Use of Money

There are two major concepts or values to be differentiated here, one stemming from the recognition of community responsibility for social welfare and the rights of the citizen, and the other from "clinical" recognition of economic, as well as other needs, on a diagnostic basis. In the former instance, financial assistance, as income, to meet certain lacks or deficiencies is an end in itself; in the latter, assistance is usually a component in or an adjuvant to a therapeutic goal.

Since in Western civilizations stigma still attaches to the status of financial dependency, social work attempts to counteract the negative cultural attitudes throughout every step in the rehabilitative process promoting a "health and decency" standard of living by adequate grants; and sustaining the right of free and independent

[5] See pp. 95–102.

status even though economically dependent. Other values and techniques include: "unrestricted" money payments (by which is meant that the eligible citizen's expenditures are not supervised); the recognition of dependency attitudes and defenses and support of the ego philosophically and technically; participation in a frank process of determining eligibility, including explanation of one's rights in a democracy and of reciprocal responsibilities; preservation of confidentiality; acceptance of individual differences and the measurement of cost of living and special requirements through the budget as a measure of need. What basic needs may be satisfied at public expense is culturally determined, but at least the recipient of public assistance should be assured of proper nutrition, housing, education, medical care, civil rights, and economic opportunities. Advice as to financial management is offered as a counseling service, but is not made a condition of eligibility.

The maintenance of family life threatened by disintegration only because of loss of income is properly the responsibility of a tax-supported agency through social security provisions. A progressive program should include a broad scheme of social insurance and compensation, with casework services made available to insured persons who desire it; public assistance, either in the home, in boarding homes, or in properly classified institutions for various age groups for delinquents, and the mentally or physically ill and disabled. Besides adequate housing, food, and clothing, these institutions and agencies should provide all the usual resources of individual and group treatment, recreation, and other programs made effective through qualified and adequate staffs.

Within the insurance, veteran affairs, and similar large-scale facilities, a social work department, in our judgment, should be set up much as social services are now available in medical and educational institutions. Such a department might be conducted as a center for referrals to public and voluntary agencies in the community. It is essential that such a function be staffed by adequate professional personnel equipped to make diagnostic and evaluative judgments and to offer economic and family counseling relevant to the insurance payments, as well as to put the client in touch with appropriate agencies carrying responsibility for social treatment. It is well known that many domestic problems are brought to light in connection with the administration of financial matters, but the worker trained for the operation of a social security provision does not thereby become, though he is often tempted to do so, a family counselor. Social workers skilled in family and children's problems should be employed both to handle short contact requests for advice and to steer the applicant to the appropriate community resource.

Whatever may be the pros and cons of "categorical" appropriations, there is general agreement that the public assistance structure should be administratively integrated and that in all forms of assistance workers must understand sound methods of budgeting, family income management, and principles of human behavior, so as to be able to individualize the person in the economic, as in other social, situations. They must have a good grasp of property adjustments, indebtedness, the utilization of liquidated assets, the psychological, as well as the financial, potentialities of liable relatives, occupational referral, vocational training, housing problems, and the like. Not all recipients of public assistance desire or need social services other than income,[6] but a large number do, and, as we have shown, particularization of the economic situation by budget, by understanding the applicant, by eliciting strengths and by putting the client in touch with community agencies is not only appropriate but also essential for rehabilitation. As the insurance program is broadened, the necessity of operating public welfare as a family and children's agency, offering all the established social services on a high level, becomes not only obvious but urgent. The preventive features of such a positive welfare program are apparent. Economic security while basic to a productive society is only a half way measure without individual and family responsibility and stability. Sometimes clearing up the immediate emergency by financial assistance will improve the psychological

[6] See pp. 243-46.

situation also; sometimes it will not, and then another formulation with the client of his problem and what he is willing to work on may be necessary. Inexperienced caseworkers, knowing that reality issues may be pressing and resources meager sometimes shy away from the discussion of money, but this evasion is futile. It is better to explore the situation, no matter how painful this may be for the worker—not only to see if anything can be done but also to share, if little can be done, the frustration, the inadequacy or the limitations of services frankly with the client. This takes both courage and common sense, but the worker is neither omniscient nor omnipotent, and if there is sympathetic understanding between them the client can better tolerate denial than if put off with excuses or unrealistic attempts to divert his preoccupation with what he conceives to be of great urgency. Conversely, when the need or conflict is obviously psychological, yet displaced on the economic situation, the worker should also examine the situation so as to precipitate the underlying need and possibly to stimulate a request for psychological help. Knowledge of defenses, timing, discussion of possible courses of action, emotional support, and so forth are no less important when the need is financial than in any other area. In fact, the problem of money in Western culture is so emotionally charged that the ego may be as much threatened by economic loss as by the effect of severe illness or other handicap.[7]

Eligibility as a Casework Process

Earlier, caseworkers interested themselves chiefly in those cases in which character or personality problems were displaced upon or interwoven with "the relief situation," creating a "clinical" problem calling for a treatment skill. But as casework has spread within governmental agencies, new techniques evolving from the concept of rights developed, and thus new content was added to established practice. The function of maintenance requires that a money grant be given if the client fulfills statutory conditions of eligibility, the determination of which is a casework process.

[7] See pp. 294–97.

The administrative aspects as laid down in policy and procedure must be translated into the basic technique of discussing the request in such a way as to bring client and agency service together or, if appropriate, lead to a constructive referral elsewhere. The common stock of casework has come to include not only understanding economic social need, but the *person* who has the need. Both psychiatry and economics have taught indispensable principles of self-awareness and democratic values in "relief" administration, as in other forms of casework.

Whether in public or voluntary agency settings [8] it is necessary to be firm as well as clear as to the amount and kind of help a client can reasonably expect. On the one hand we do not deny the client material aid if the economic situation warrants assistance, and on the other, we try to isolate "real" needs from exaggerated dissatisfactions or self-punishing inhibitions. The caseworker in public assistance who is unable to distinguish the client whose limitless demands for relief and attention are forms of neurotic behavior from the client who asks for shoes and a stove and a bed because he lacks these vital necessities, will find his case loads relatively unmanageable. Not only does the use of the itemized budget make it possible to measure needs but also in discussions with the client the worker may help to sort out objective reality from emotional demands.

When providing monetary assistance, a home economist may be an invaluable consultant in determining realistic budget standards and allowances and giving counsel on problems of management, homemaking, meal planning, and marketing. As in other services or counseling, the caseworker starts with the request [9] and with the client explores its reality. When practical requests are made, it is usually important to meet them or arrange to have them met elsewhere as promptly as possible, not only because food and shelter and ordinary subsistence needs are primary but also because a prompt response with regard to such details symbolizes to the tense and anxious person the concern and interest of the worker. Close

[8] See pp. 123–25.　　　　[9] See pp. 159–61.

attention is given to understanding what is involved in unemployment and emotional responses to loss of self-maintenance. Although there is a general tendency towards a flat grant under specified conditions, one hopes that the use of the budget, already proved so valuable in counseling, will remain a tool of the skilled interviewer for household management and other appropriate problems.

As a "Tool in Treatment"

Technically there have been many developments in the use of money as a "tool in treatment." [10] It has long been recognized that because of stigma the applicant may ask for some other service when he really wants relief, or he may displace all sorts of inner conflicts, fears, and hostilities upon the economic situation. The first essential is a diagnostic approach to determine to what extent the conflict is really economic and how much intra-psychic and inter-familial tensions are involved. In most voluntary agencies financial assistance is given, not with the goal of maintenance (except for certain groups that are ineligible because of residence or other restrictions for public welfare), but with the specific purpose of helping the client change or improve his situation, to retain or to regain independence, to create opportunities which will develop his capacities, to improve physical and emotional health, to protect family life in a period of crisis, to create a special living experience for a child or adolescent, and so forth. Money grants used in treatment should favorably affect the progress of the case, constructively support ego strengths, or else the treatment aim should be reconsidered.

Planning to review at regular intervals the need for a money grant and preparing well in advance for its discontinuance, reduction, or renewal permit the client to participate in the process. A client who demands a sum of money without being able or willing to state his problem may be blocked by anxiety, have little

[10] The phrase was first used by Grace Marcus in *Some Aspects of Relief in Family Casework*, 1929.

sense of reality, or actually be in no need of help. He may make a financial emergency out of a long-standing condition in order to escape from working out a more general personal economic difficulty. The actual economic situation, as well as the person's feelings about money, must be understood and worked with as a unit if a constructive outcome is to be achieved. Our culture places a premium on the ability to maintain oneself and one's family, and it is money which enables the individual to do this. The client who asks an agency for money believing that he is admitting a personal inadequacy may react with shame, with anger, or with fear of what this experience will bring. Because ordinarily getting money from others involves giving something in return, the client may feel that he is sacrificing his independence. All the feelings surrounding money which the client brings to the agency serve as clues which, if the worker is able to observe them accurately and objectively can be valuable guides.

Lack of money may create tensions within the family, disrupting the normal interrelationships. When the father is no longer the provider, both husband and wife may be tormented by fears lest the family will not be kept together and by doubts as to whether they really want to go on together. Within the family group money is closely tied up with love, aggression, and ego factors. Unwillingness to discuss financial matters, to share responsibility for money management, to give or share money when able may indicate immature, narcissistic, or actively hostile attitudes. To the young adolescent beginning to earn money earnings represent concrete evidence of growing independence and emergence from childhood. Caseworkers in public, as in voluntary, agencies must be adequately trained in order to recognize the more usual symptoms of personality disorder, not because they will be called upon to treat emotional illness as such, but so that they will not let themselves be drawn naïvely into impossible therapeutic activities. To the skilled worker behavior in regard to money is often a fascinating study in defenses; the release of feeling around specific financial situations and the pointing out of roles, repetitive attitudes and patterns is as significant a form of therapeutic casework as in any other form of family and child guidance.

In appraising what he knows about money, the caseworker should begin by reviewing his own attitudes, which will depend partly on his economic background and personality. How he spends money and the value he places on its importance will be involved in his feelings about relief. If the caseworker has negative feelings about financial assistance, these may interfere with his relationship with the client. Because of early frustrations, a person may not be capable of giving or receiving, may be afraid that too-heavy demands will be made upon him, and may feel that the regression to dependency is too great a threat. Money symbolizes love and denial, adequacy and inadequacy, power and compliance. One may feel that money, as is love, is one's right, and in proportion to one's sense of affective deprivation in other relationships a person may demand money and all its benefits. In any phase of childhood growth, where there has not been a satisfactory adjustment, the idea of money may become later tinged with the conflicts of that earlier period, and to understand the adult's reaction to money it is necessary to understand the developmental picture.

In dishonest behavior in money matters, as in delinquency, the worker must be realistic, scrupulously fair, and incorruptible. The temptation of the client to withhold or distort information about his resources is most reinforced by that worker who, out of his own ambivalence, unconsciously or consciously connives at this sort of evasion. It is best to be frank, though not reproachful, whenever the client attempts to make the worker his accomplice in disingenuous behavior about unreported resources. No matter what the actual level of assistance or the hidden earnings, if any, the worker should draw up a fair and honest budget, compute the balance or deficiency, and so help both the client and the administration to face the economic facts. If the assistance grant falls below the cost of subsistence, representation of the real picture should be made to the community in appropriate ways.

In order to handle money as a tool in treatment, the worker must be diagnostically competent in regard to the motivation of behavior. He must be able to distinguish the impulsive character's spending from typical behavior of the compulsive neurotic, who tends to use money as a power instrument with which to punish or control. Nor can fees be successfully administered without, on the one hand, a realistic scale based on ability to pay and, on the other, recognition of how a client may use the fee situation to serve his dependency needs and aggressive or hostile drives.

THE FAMILY AS LIVING EXPERIENCE

The primary constellation in American culture is the family unit, the interaction of whose members affects negatively or positively the life of each individual, particularly in the formative years.[11] Using "group process" in family life does several things: it locates and clarifies the problem through discussion; it permits expression of opinions; it dissipates anxiety for each child, because the situation is shared with the other, as well as with the worker; and this participation releases ability to move toward action. Work with families inevitably includes children, adults, adolescents, young married couples, and the aged; none of these can be treated as isolated problems, because of the nature of social relationships themselves.

Social casework is directly concerned with the family as living experience and, related to this, to the provision of substitute family care in foster homes, cottage institutions, temporary shelters, and camps, through homemaking and housekeeping services, day nurseries, and so forth. Furthermore, social work is concerned with the social component of school, recreational, and occupational life, with delinquency and disability, which play an adjunctive role in the educational, medical, court, and legal systems, and increasingly in the field of labor and industry.

Casework has always been concerned with the family as the pri-

[11] The approach to the family unit should draw both on groupwork and casework processes, since there are considerations of family balance and behavior as a group as well as from the point of view of each individual member.

mary social unit within which concepts are formed which have a profound bearing on social adjustment. It would be difficult to define socially acceptable or unacceptable behavior without fully understanding parental roles as conditioned by cultural factors. According to earliest casework concepts the family was the "unit of work" in that the caseworkers gave services to the whole family in terms of wage-earning, supporting, and home-making activities. The individual, too, is a "unit of work," and so is the group; but the role of the family is immensely important in understanding both the individual and the larger group. Today the family does not as commonly maintain itself as an economic and physical unit as it did in the preceding century. Subsequent study has brought out the affectional and relationship aspects, the concept of family interaction and balance, both normal and neurotic, as of greater significance. That social workers do not feel compelled to keep all kinds of pathological families together by assistance and counseling does not mean that there is any less recognition of the importance of the family as the prototype of society or of the fact that it is the natural place for the nurture and development of children. It is still the best place to learn to love, to be loved, to accept oneself and others, and to work out problems of aggression, rivalry, dependency, and submission. It is still the best place in which to acquire an understanding of some of those deep and relatively inaccessible impulses out of which society is largely shaped. The family may no longer be the place where economics begin, but it is certainly the place where feelings begin.

In the normal growing-up process parents learn to relinquish gradually their protection of children, and children learn to differentiate themselves from their parents. In more pathological family relationships the parents may overprotect or neglect, cling to, overshadow, or project their own difficulties onto the child, or, conversely, they may fail to relate themselves to the child, as shown by various forms of rejection. In either case, the growing-up and healthy differentiating process is inhibited. In amenable instances the caseworker who is able to diagnose the parent-child relationship can offer treatment either toward the growing away or toward the integrating process within the family unit. If, however, the movement observed definitely indicates the advisability of family separation, either because of structural defects in the family or because of emotional deviation rather than differentiation, placing techniques will be desirable. The caseworker knows, however, that the physical removal of a child from a home does not remove the impress of the emotional traumata felt in the home, although in mild disturbances constructive opportunities and stimuli may prove entirely favorable to development in the new environment.[12]

What caseworkers have come better to understand are the psychological as well as the economic factors which condition the movement toward integration or separation in family life. This movement may be either relatively normal or pathological. In the normal course of development the child, first through identification and then through increasing the psychological "distance" between the self and the persons around him, moves healthily out of the "undifferentiated unity," to use a current phrase, of parent-child relationships. In so far as he is able to love and so to recognize others as personalities (object love), he is more capable of relating himself to his fellows on a social level.[13] Aside from homes broken by death or enforced separation, one of the commonest problems in casework arises through deviations in the integration-separation movement.

One may see, even in such otherwise constructive programs as public assistance, that in certain cases a money grant throws a sort of ring around the family group which makes constructive differentiation harder to achieve. One is familiar with conflicts among second-generation children of immigrants—when the absoluteness of parental authority creates such problems. Parents who turn to family or children's or guidance clinics are often found to dominate and overprotect their children consciously or, more often, unconsciously. In such instances the caseworker may play an extremely

[12] See pp. 281–87.
[13] The norms for psychosocial development are, of course, more complicated than in the trend noted above. See Irene M. Josselyn, "Psychosocial Development of Children," and other psychiatric references in bibliography.

significant part, just as the group leader does, in shifting the balance to more democratic procedures in the family setting. The worker with families, either own or foster parents, has to develop a light touch, not a heavy hand. For it is easy to come between parent and child and so threaten the parental role. If one forms too direct or too intensive a bond with the child, it may well separate him from the most important persons in his natural group. Neutrality of the caseworker in the family and his acceptance of all members—spouse, parent, child, siblings—is a basic social technique.

In noting the parental fixations which condition so much marital discontent, one must remember that complete emancipation is not always a realistic goal. Response to parental claims and exposure to a reasonable amount of marital aggression is normal and does not necessarily harm children, but on the other hand caseworkers understand that between many of these apparently irreconcilable couples there is a mutual dependency, on a neurotic basis, which makes it impossible for them to keep apart long. Caseworkers make careful diagnoses as to which types of family strain are due to external traumatic situations, which may be reduced through interviewing, relief, and all the ordinary casework services, which types justify moving apart to a real separation, and which are of the interlaced, neurotic dependency type. For the children caught in these consuming parental struggles, neurotically weighted, the outlook is not promising. Diagnostically one must distinguish cases of gross parental pathology from amenable problems of economic and cultural reality, which can be attacked, modified, or corrected. Although the larger economic and health hazards can affect family life psychologically, it is observable that given parental security children can weather most of life's threats. One cannot expect the neurotic child, however, to adjust to the environment since the problem is already internalized, although in mild cases some improvement may occur. That is, a favorable environment may allow the neurosis to subside. Direct treatment of the neurotic child while in placement is desirable, as well as environmental therapy. Only the well-adjusted child can react favorably to placement without direct treatment. Guidance to parents is as essential before, during, and after placement as when the disturbed child remains at home.

Family Guidance and Placement [14]

A chronically disturbed child is likely to be indicative of not only a disturbed parental relationship but also a disturbed family. Traditionally, as we have shown earlier, the "family field" held a large incidence of those unhappy families which did not break up but continued to take out or act out their neurotic problems and character disorders through and on each other. Many "good" mothers receiving social security assistance, who superficially appear concerned to bring up their children properly, are rigid and compulsive, or narcissistic, controlling, demanding, and so forth. Much chronic indebtedness, leading to insufficient income, gambling, and alcoholism, stems from the root of character neuroses. It is now better understood how one may act out his conflicts through intrafamilial disorders rather than through psycho-biological processes (symptoms and diseases). For the most part parents do not seek psychiatric advice for themselves as "*patients*," but for the solution of the child's problem, usually seen by them as bad behavior due to physical causes or other circumstances, when actually the child's behavior is a "symptomatic" attempt to adapt to the family conflict in some fashion.

Either parent or both parents may express their neurotic conflicts by contributing to the making of a child's behavior problem by partial or complete rejection, which may lead to child placement, because of acts of overt delinquency, neglect, and abuse. Such parents may invoke the protective offices of society in behalf of the child. In any one of these expressions of deep-lying disturbance the dynamics must be understood in order to treat the social aspect of difficulty. In general one cannot hope to cure a child either physically or emotionally against the unconscious opposition of the parents.[15]

Working with the parents at home ("guidance") or during a placement experience is essentially the same—calling for a fusion

[14] See pp. 273–87 for child placing as "field."   [15] See pp. 282, 297.

of psychological and social skills. One should not expect of parents an easy adjustment to frustrating reality. The whole trend in casework is greater frankness and directness in sharing the process of treatment and its aims with both parent and child. Mothers and fathers already often know the overt facts better than we do, but to face responsibility for a problem child is hard for the guilty parents. Only mature persons can be rational about reality, and this sort of reality is peculiarly disturbing. One cannot apply reality testing, therefore, in a blanket fashion to family disorders. This is being learned in sex education, and most agencies have learned that there are no ready-made solutions for all the complicated forms of parent-child relationships, or for how and when interpretation may be attempted of family dynamics.

Caseworkers have had experience with parents who seek, apparently wholeheartedly, to place a handicapped, feeble-minded, or crippled child "because it will be good for him" or "for the other children" at home, only to find that when commitment proceedings get under way the mother breaks appointments, cannot find time to take the child to the clinic, mislays papers, all the while insisting that the worker should alone carry through the proceedings. If the worker, failing to recognize the defenses, takes over the responsibility of commitment, he should not be surprised if the parent, in the not-too-distant future, will remove the child from the institution, blaming the worker or the institution, or both, with fine impartiality. When the child is a pawn between two incompatible parents, placing the child may merely shift the battlefield to the foster home.

Most parents—at least to some extent—want the best for their children. One does not coerce them into a course of action, but is not afraid to give an expert opinion if sought. This is true of the married as well as the unmarried parent. Parents are not always capable of making a sound decision, and they have a right to ask the worker to put his experience at their disposal. One should not be afraid to give immature parents counsel if they seek it. There is no disrespect for parental responsibility in so doing. In dealing with ambivalent parents advice is of little value, but one may be able to sustain them in a constructive decision and in carrying through a difficult course of action. It is often better for masochistic parents to be allowed to blame someone other than themselves if things go wrong. Parents who remain in the picture with a long-term placed-out child for whom they are unable to make a home are usually immature or exceedingly ambivalent. They will need understanding and acceptance of their feelings in order to bear not only the separation but also the experience of competing with the foster parents. Workers must really like parents—some do not, if they have not worked through their own parental relationships; some psychiatrists do not like parents either. The more the treatment succeeds, whether in child guidance or in child placement, the harder the experience may be for the parent. One may expect interference, obstruction, and withdrawal. Ungrudging acceptance and respect for the parental role even when relatively ineffective will do much to pave the way for guidance.

There are certain pertinent considerations in the approach to parents and children, both in guidance and in separation. From intake on, parents are encouraged to participate in planning for and continuously to involve themselves in the child's treatment. One technique in eliciting participation is to interpret, prepare, and help the parent to take the necessary procedural steps—make appointments, arrange for examinations, furnish consent and the essential document. The worker should try to find out their idea in coming for help or asking for placement. Why have they come *now*, and with what expectation for the child and for themselves?

Only genuine empathy with the parent will permit him to assume a role in helping the child. Moreover, if parental attitudes are not too destructive the parent is encouraged to remain in the picture so far as is feasible—attending the day nursery and visiting the foster home or institution or camp. To keep parents acting responsibly when the child is placed with foster parents is even more difficult than helping them function wisely in the child-guidance situation. The parent must now observe and adjust to the possible success of the foster parent, which is even harder to accept than improvement of the child with a psychiatrist or a worker, who are "experts" and not just another and better set of parents. The more the dynamics of the parental emotional involvement are understood as basic in the total treatment and the stronger the support given the parent, the more likely it is that anxiety and guilt feelings can be reduced and the parent enabled to maintain a constructive role in the treatment. How much awareness the parent achieves, either in the guidance or the placement experience, is like any other degree of insight, variable. Warm and steady support to the parent, combined with direct or environmental treatment, or both, for the child are often the most practicable goals. It has been repeatedly observed that direct psychotherapy for the child may be relatively ineffective unless something can be done to modify his familial and other social reality, since these are often causally related. If in sustaining the familial focus, with the child as "patient," the parent should come to see the need of therapy for himself, and he thus may be said to turn from the status of "parent" to that of "patient," another worker may be sought who is equipped for psychotherapeutic casework, or, in severe instances, the adult may be referred to a psychiatrist or psychoanalyst. For psychopathic parents, the treatment goal may be to help them relinquish the child altogether to permanent placement or adoption.

OTHER SOCIAL ADJUSTMENTS

Social institutions are the framework of the average person's living experience—the family, the school, the labor market, and the religious and recreational groups. Within these customs and regulations the person acts out his impulses rationally or irrationally, constructively or with anxiety and aggression. Within this framework he is constantly striving, testing reality, and seeking satisfactions and ways of adapting his behavior.

Adoption

Adoption, with the attendant traditional secrecy stemming from the stigma attached to an out-of-wedlock child, has long been an isolated field. Now, with increasing legislative protection and cultural tolerance toward mother and child, the adoption process is aligned with tested family and foster-family practice. Although there are too many technical and cultural complexities in the current scene for full treatment here, a few trends may be briefly noted. Since the security and happiness of a young life is at stake, careful home finding and evaluation of prospective parents is of central importance. On the other hand, skill in the evaluation of parental strength and balance and greater confidence in education for adoptive, as well as natural, parenthood is developing more effective processes. The chief defects of the adoption field have been the false secrecy, leading to a black market in babies and an anxious caution on the part of under-equipped agencies, which can only be corrected by adequate staffing and skilled and therefore, earlier diagnosis of the child and evaluation of the adoptive parent. As cultural discrimination is reduced, the importance of racial and national "matching" of child to family will diminish, and improved levels of general standards of living will allow for wider choices of both foster and adoptive parents. Middle aged parents for young children are usually regarded as unsuitable, and precautions against placing the child with impulse-ridden characters, severe neurotics, or other disturbed persons are essential. Given reasonable evidence of warmth, tolerance, mature capacity to love others, not overrigid, compulsive personalities or those with narcissistic demands, the ordinary applicant may prove a "good risk." One no longer expects perfect parents in the natural home or the foster family. Perfectionist parents are never good risks, since they will want too high standards for their own or adopted children.

The practice of telling children that they are adopted, have been chosen out of love, and the reduction of cultural stigma make the whole procedure nowadays more commonplace and permits the adopting parents to seek guidance if problems arise, without undue feeling of guilt. Telling a child that he was "illegitimate" is a delicate technical problem, which often is handled in foster care and sometimes after adoption. As in any other painful area, the child must be in a secure relationship, and his phantasies and other defenses must be carefully worked with. It is important to know what it is that a child really wants to know about his own family and respond to that. He is rarely interested in the abstract question of illegitimacy. If we puncture a child's phantasy prematurely or in the wrong way, without building in something constructive in its place, he will merely use other defenses to protect himself from the unbearable. Careful research into the use of study homes and trial placements, especially for babies and young children, is needed throughout the foster-care program. There are many controversial factors which must be examined. Experiments in the use of prospective adoptive homes as controlled and limited foster placements are worth watching. Obviously only the most outstandingly good homes, and after surrender, would be used on such a trial basis, and the testing of the child may well be done during the trial period. While it is harder to remove a child from such a home, the risks of occasional failure must be weighed against the hazards for the baby of undue delay, institutional trauma, and other preadoptive vicissitudes.

The trend has gradually shifted from protecting the adoptive parent against the ordinary hazards of rearing a child and a sometimes perfectionist standard held out for adoptive parents, to the common sense aim of finding as many reasonably good homes as possible for ordinary children, even those with some defects.[16] The

---

[16] The trend in Canada, as in the United States, seems to be toward greater flexibility and imagination in placement across race and nationality boundaries formerly thought to be barriers, and to find successful adoptive homes for children of mixed parentage, and also for physically and even mentally handicapped children, although here additional precautions must be taken. "The adoptive parents chosen understand our aim in placement of these children, willingly accept, as do natural parents, what risks may be involved in rearing a child, and willingly agree to the extended probation period." Ruby McKay, Superintendent of Child Welfare; in the Annual Report of the Social Welfare Branch of the Department of Health and Welfare, British Columbia, Canada, 1949.

number of children in long term *placement* who have never had a permanent *home* is still alarming. This makes social workers turn with fresh determination to find those who have a natural gift for parenthood and those who can learn to become successful adoptive parents. Such homes offer possibilities not only for one child but for several. One must also remember that good, whether natural or foster, parents may include constructive brother and sister relationships, and increase the effect of the atmosphere of the good home.

GROUP . PROCESS AS LIVING EXPERIENCE [17]

Understanding the individual and understanding his social development inevitably are complementary processes. Because social-welfare planning rests quite as much on the cooperative functioning of groups as of individuals and because group experience is a way of meeting needs and developing healthy interests and the contributions of individuals, social group work has a well-defined place as a basic method in social work. Groupworkers have been discovering the importance of the case method, and caseworkers of the group method. Casework and groupwork, like education, have evolved from authoritative and "top-down" disciplines to fresh orientation based on how the individual really learns, grows, and becomes socialized. Early group work offered clubs and classes, swimming pools, and shop work, Boy Scout troops and summer camps, just as early casework dispensed relief, convalescent and health care, and home economics as "commodities." The idea of the reciprocal nature of all social work relationships—of give and take between teacher and pupil, caseworker and client, club and leader—has stimulated new techniques and new ways for caseworkers and groupworkers to think about interaction. Respect for personality, whether in the one-to-one relationship, or the one-to-several, or to the group as a whole, means to give up manipulation and indoctrination in favor of letting emotions and ideas be expressed. The caseworker releases tensions largely by means of the one-to-one relationship and family interaction; the groupworker

[17] See pp. 19–21.

releases tensions and drives through larger group interaction, but there is much common ground. Both are concerned with the individual's development from self-centeredness, dependency, and aggression to social attitudes and interests. Not everyone need be gregarious—many creative artists have little social tolerance and should be permitted to have their own solitariness—but the ordinary range of happy and useful living depends on comfortable and constructive ways of relating ourselves to our fellows. Children and young people need a reasonable amount of inhibition, but not too much—if the impulses completely master the individual there is antisocial behavior, and if the impulses are too much denied or repressed there is also unsocial or neurotic behavior. Everyone needs affection, acceptance, and recognition in his family, in school, on the playground, in his daily work. Only so can he readily give affection, tolerance, and recognition to others. Social workers understand how groups other than the family can assist in the socializing process, although the family remains the primary influence.

In a worker-client relationship the technique of acceptance is relatively uncomplicated; with a double patient—husband-wife, parent-child—"acceptance" has to be nicely balanced and controlled so as to minimize a sense of discrimination, partisanship, and the like. The problem is especially delicate in relation to large groups. In all variations there are the same several basic concepts: acceptance of the client's feeling, with understanding and tolerance, encouragement of participation, cooperative activity, and recognition that activity must express itself in a setting of social reality, whether family, group, or world at large. Most groupwork has been developed in what are commonly thought of as "leisure-time activities," such as have been undertaken by settlements, churches, Scouts, and youth organizations. The caseworker utilizes as a form of treatment all the ordinary community resources, from "Y's" in the city to 4H clubs in the rural districts, on behalf of his clients. The objective may be simply meeting a lack or a need, or it may be educational or therapeutic, to assist the client's growth or development. The spread of Federal "white collar" projects during the Second World War—worker and parent education, little theaters, art centers, orchestras—have suggested new opportunities. In a large proportion of cases community resources for group participation, whether occupational, educational, or recreational, are made available merely by introducing clients to them.

Fresh-air camps have been developing, as have other forms of groupwork, from wholesale recreational "commodities" to educational and, when indicated, to therapeutic opportunities, and the interaction between casework and groupwork is becoming increasingly effective. The groupwork process is concerned with developing both the capacities of individuals for social participation and the ability of the group to attain its common purposes. Experience in democratic participation in group relationships is essential not only for releasing and channeling the energies of the community but also for realizing the potentialities of individuals for social growth. Political and economic democracy is impossible of achievement in the modern state unless its citizens are capable of responsible participation in the social groups on which the pattern of communal life is based.

The following cases show children for whom careful preparation and concurrent and subsequent family treatment have had good results.

Elsie Evans, aged thirteen, was unable to make social contacts. The parents were considering separation, and the child was over-serious and withdrawn. At camp she rejected the leaders' interest at first, and then identified with them against the group. She was critical, dominating, and intellectually superior. When she failed to gain a following, she withdrew. She became interested in the boys at camp and a little more acceptable to the group. On her return she was able to assist her mother for the first time with household tasks. There was coincident treatment by a psychiatrist, who commented on the evidence of socialization.

· · · · ·

Olga Harris, aged fourteen, was demanding and attention-getting. Her father had deserted, her mother was inconsistent, and Olga herself was somewhat rejected. The atmosphere in the home was of nagging, quarreling, and hysterics. In camp when Olga refused to cooperate she was ignored by the leader and came around. As she found the group liked her better when she was pleasant, she began to behave. In the casework contacts the mother was able to follow the interests built up in camp, and this was a bond to draw Olga and herself together, which the child needed very much. On the whole the interests developed at camp seemed to have a very good effect on her home problems, and these gains were fully utilized in subsequent treatment.

. . . . .

Peter, a physically well-developed and bright boy, IQ of 130, was showing childish behavior, enuresis, and withdrawal. After some preliminary casework contacts, he was sent to camp. Peter was fond of his father, an invalid, but feared that when he grew up he might be like him. There was continuous friction between Peter and his mother, on whom he was very dependent. He resented her demands that he accept a responsible role in the family and reacted with defiance and on the level of a much younger child. The smaller children in the home made Peter wish that he were not so smart and that he were a baby. He fought and quarreled with them. Peter had not been able to develop friends among other children. He fought with them and would attack bigger boys if they angered him. Teachers found Peter inattentive, and his "naughty" behavior disturbed them. There had been a carry-over from the home situation into the relationships outside. In the schoolroom he was unable to meet the demands made of him. Because he had not been able to relate himself to other children of his own age, he was in a situation of conflict in his play relationships and other relationships with children.

For two days Peter showed the most difficult behavior of perhaps any child in camp. He got into countless fights with his bunkmates, had temper tantrums, struck the counselor, and threw dirt in his face. He refused to cooperate in any way or to participate responsibly in the activities of the group. During clean-up he was put outside the bunk and kept there because he was disturbing to the group. At night he persisted in annoying his bunkmates and keeping them awake. During these days the counselor had been extremely patient and passive, and the boy went to great lengths to test the counselor and to see if this were real.

The camp fire provided the medium for Peter to make bids for attention before a large audience and to attack and further test his counselor. Peter made ridiculing comments while the counselor told a story, and interrupted him to have the Indians in the story swoop down on the counselor. Once he became silent, the leader invited him to participate in the story-telling, and Peter proceeded to "stick all the spears into the leader and roast him." Following camp fire the leader walked back with Peter. The leader praised Peter for his story-telling ability and told him how much he had enjoyed it and invited him to write it up for the newspaper (non-retaliation). The music counselor found Peter very pleasant, quiet, efficient, and really helpful with the other boys. He had no inclination to fight there. His attendance was good. It was also noticed that Peter had rather unusual mechanical ability, and this provided an area where he could readily get satisfaction. In this group he also got a lot of attention and approval from the leader. This activity also did not require Peter to relate himself closely to others. Here he could work on crafts at his own level of ability and rate of speed. Peter did not make friends with other campers, but this seemed understandable in the light of his own development. There was progress in that he took more responsibility for getting dressed; he did not dawdle at the table. It was evident throughout the experience that he was constantly begging for attention and fighting to get it if necessary. One of the most important developments was the boy's growing insight into his own problem. During one of the discussions with a counselor he commented on his own infantile behavior and related this to his father's being an invalid.

On the one hand, Peter was hard pressed by the intensity of the group situation; on the other hand, he discovered an adult who was not "hollering on him" or making unusual demands of him. The counselor gave this deprived and hostile boy special attention, placing value on the boy's achievements and making possible a relationship with adults not so tense as was the home experience or even the casework interview, since at camp the boy shared the experience with other children. Individual treatment or group and individual treatment concurrently can continue to build on his improved condition.

A soft answer can turn away wrath, and in the vicious circle of frustration-aggression steady and friendly acceptance is a major tool for case and group processes alike. Therefore it is to be expected that the selection and use of camps and other such opportunities by caseworkers will be put more upon a diagnostic basis and that there will be a sharing of treatment objectives with the groupwork agency from the start. Group experience can develop capacities for participation, for acceptance of others, for leadership, and for personality development, and is now being extended in therapeutic forms.

In healthy growth, drives should not be repressed, but managed and utilized in acceptable ways. One way to learn how to manage drives and unsocial impulses is provided by the therapeutic group. The problem child has often a strong inferiority sense and a weak ego. A natural group may on a purely competitive basis make him feel more inferior. In a controlled group the leader, like the caseworker, can offer steady support and acceptance, which enables the child better to meet his fellows. While the natural gang often serves a useful purpose as the outlet of the aggressive impulses, not all children are sturdy enough to utilize this successfully, and in the therapeutic groupwork process the leader can supply a nonauthoritative, quasi-parental relationship which is reassuring and steadying. The somewhat "diluted" parental role may be easier for the aggressively reacting boy or girl to accept. What we have come to see is that an understanding group process, beyond that of the primary family experience, is important in many forms of casework treatment. Conversely, one can scarcely understand a child's use of the group without understanding the primary family experience. Group relationships, like family relationships, are essentially *natu-ral*, but in this discussion we are regarding the group primarily from the angle of a professional operation.

Groupwork,[18] closely allied with the aims and methods of progressive education, is directed especially to the development of socialized personalities. Group experience can develop cooperation, self-reliance, and integration, in so far as its programs are not rigid or imposed from without. Groupwork is increasingly developing processes which encourage initiative and participation and provide stimuli to growth and change. Groups must be thoughtfully selected, just as in casework aims, with consideration of age levels. What one expects of a nursery school in socializing the youngster is quite different from what the Boy Scout troop or the adolescent club will attempt. A boy or a girl during pre-puberty identifies with the Scout leader or teacher as parental surrogate, and almost casually takes over

18 See pp. 19–21.

aspects of his role, in a way that the adolescent, breaking away from parental authority, would not do.

When parents are inaccessible to individual guidance, they may be able to accept a group experience, which seems less threatening to parental prestige than would treatment of the child in the office by the worker. When parents are accessible, they may, by observing group interactions, especially with younger children, notice unexpectedly self-reliant behavior of their over-protected child, which may encourage the parent to release the child from dependency. They may also notice, both because of the attitude of the group worker and through direct observation, the noncensorious tolerance of "bad" behavior, and so relax a little of their own rigidity and repressive tactics. As a version of home experiences extended through these activities, the group can prove educational to the parent as well as helpful to the child.

The use of the group therapeutically has also been found significantly helpful with handicapped and feeble-minded children, spastics, and others.

William Dix, aged twelve, was failing at school. He had had a birth injury, with long childhood illnesses. He had always been overprotected by his mother. He had never had a satisfactory relationship with his father or other men adults, with whom he always developed a rivalry situation. Sent to camp, he chose first cooking and solitary sports. While he was away in camp and things were easier at home, William's needs and interests were interpreted regularly to the parents. William went on with the "Y" after his camp experience and began to make better social contacts. Coincident with his ability to relate himself to the boys and the leader, there was improvement at school and some release of dependency on his mother.

Common parental attitudes of overprotection or rejection may be aggravated by such handicaps, and again the group can afford a more neutral medium than the family for relieving some of the pressures. The competitive situation is reduced, mutual aid finds a natural setting, inferiorities are minimized. At its most successful level the child should be able to move on with his new securities in relationship to less protected situations, and the parent may be able to use at home the gains made in the group. The essence of the therapeutic use of the group is to discontinue segregation as soon as the child develops capacity to relate himself to others in a nonsheltered environment. In cases of severe handicap, however, just as with disabling illness, the child or the adult may have to learn to live with varying degrees of permanent dependency in sheltered surroundings.

Group therapy [19] is a specialized form of group experience, much as psychotherapy is a specialization for casework. It is being used to effect change and growth for people who are having difficulty with their social relationships. At one time the aggressive or the shy withdrawn child could make little use of the neighborhood house because he did not fit in anywhere. That was his problem; so that if he got himself there he could not relate himself successfully to the other children. Such children quickly excluded themselves or were excluded. What workers now understand is that such a child has already been frustrated or hurt in his primary group experience, the family. What they also understand is that in many instances he can be helped to a better adjustment through the group process, as well as through family modifications and direct treatment interviews.

Aggression may be released within the group experience, and there is little attempt to arbitrate quarrels, the theory being that noncritical acceptance of the behavior combined with the interaction of fellow members, will help the child work through re-

[19] One of the earliest exponents of "activity group therapy"—in fact the invention of the phrase, as well as the special character of the project is attributed to him—is S. R. Slavson at the Jewish Board of Guardians in New York. The chief characteristic of group therapy, as Slavson describes it, is its similarity to the family. Its aim is to create and stimulate relationships that would approximate as far as possible those of an ideal family. He states the main principles of "group therapy" as follows: "Every child needs the security of unconditioned love from his parents and other adults who play a significant role in his life." "The ego and sense of self-worth which are frequently crushed in problem children must be built up." "Every child needs some genuine interest to occupy his leisure time." "In group therapy we provide activities in the constructional, plastic, graphic, and other arts and occupations to rebuild distorted personality." Other variants of theory may be found in the literature.

pressed hostilities. The amount and kind of aggression which can be permitted in group experience varies with age levels, form of expression, severity of the problem, and so forth. In general, freedom leads to disorderliness, which, in turn, under skilled guidance, leads to inner controls and integrated creative activities. In both casework and groupwork the child will test the worker to find out whether the worker can really accept his bad behavior and bad feelings without retaliation. In the casework situation the worker may, if the aggression is too violent, have to limit the destructive behavior or, in child placing, move the child; in the groupwork situation some of the controls will be supplied by the group itself, although controls beyond that will have to be directed. Sibling rivalry may be worked through realistically in the same group, although in many cases where there is sibling domination separate groups are used for each child. Here the competitive situation, in the absence of praise or blame, is modified by the presence of others under the unobtrusive and "accepting" guidance of the group leader.

Group therapy is reaching a significant place for both young patients and adults. As a method it includes both "activity" and "interview" forms of treatment. Group therapy is as closely related to casework as to groupwork or, more correctly stated, it is based on the same clinical principles but the multi-person situation is utilized as the means of treatment. Primarily resting on the consciously controlled tool of leader-member's relationship as the chief dynamic, it affords opportunities for release, sublimation, the use of the self through creative experiences, with ego-strengthening goals. Situations may be also structured for moderate or graduated frustration, reality testing, and so forth. Self-awareness is promoted both through the reciprocal interaction of the members and, wherever indicated, by the leader's interpretation of the behavior displayed. Particularly with children of five or six years of age, verbalization of the meaning of the acted-out behavior is often readily assimilated. The principles of group selection, such as a diagnosis of socially adaptive age levels and maturity considerations, must be grasped by understanding how ego ideals are developed. Knowledge of psychodynamics, object identification, acting out, neurotic inhibition, variations of transference, countertransference, the nature of defenses, and similar concepts all bring some group processes within the general area of therapy, but as a specialization calling for the same rigorous training as is required by any form of psychotherapy. Psychiatric consultation should be readily accessible.

CHAPTER V

AGENCY AND INTER-AGENCY PRACTICES

THE TRENDS in modern society toward the administrative practice of law, of group and institutional practice of medicine, the history of social work as essentially agency rather than individual practice have drawn attention to the different fields or settings for practice.[1]

FIELD AND SETTING

According to one writer, social work practiced in a social agency may be regarded as operating in a "primary" setting, whereas a social work department or service in a hospital, court, or school is operating in a "secondary" setting. Moreover, there are "primary" settings, such as a children's institution, in which the living experience is supported by casework, groupwork, and other services.

Generic and Specific

One of the basic concepts to be mastered is that of the generic aspects of various agency and institutional settings. Tested and sifted knowledge is a slow and painful result, neither lightly achieved nor easily assimilated. Basic assumptions and common principles act as unifying and integrating forces in the practice of generic casework.[2] Specific practices, tested, compared, and abstracted, lead to new levels of formulation for general use. Unchecked by specialization, generalization becomes facile and arid. Interaction and

[1] Perlman, H. "Generic Aspects of Specific Casework Settings," *Social Service Review*, XXIII (September, 1949), 293–301.
[2] See *Social Case Work Generic and Specific; a Report of the Milford Conference.* 1929. For further discussion of "fields" see Chapter X.

integration of the generic and specific spell movement in any profession. It is usually a sign of arrested development when any group relies overmuch on its own setting for prestige values. "Generic" does not mean "elementary," but rather the basic knowledge of social factors and dynamic psychology for effective operation in any setting, calling for the same essential skills. Settings [3] are not in themselves marks of specialization, nor is the walling off of practice in a secondary setting conducive to the discoveries of true specializations within the whole range of professional practice.

Although the "settings" of casework are usually thought of as the family and children's fields, psychiatric and medical social work; probation, parole, and social work in schools (formerly called visiting teaching), the fields are also thought of as being divided under public and private, sectarian and nonsectarian auspices. But the essentials of family, children's, medical, and psychiatric casework are the same whether practiced in tax-supported or in voluntary agencies. Because of the legal basis and the framework of regulations and because of the size of caseload, casework under public auspices is usually less flexible and experimental than that under voluntary auspices, but this is not inevitable. Almost all rural welfare work is under public auspices, so that the difference between work done under public and that done under private auspices lies in the administrative elements, not inherently in the professional content and quality. Basically, too, Jewish, Catholic, and Protestant social work is alike, and the casework has certainly differed professionally in no demonstrably significant way.[4] Jewish social work, perhaps because of its relation to immigrant and refugee groups, has always stressed concepts and practices of mutual aid. One might say that Catholic charities have always stressed problems of conduct and of character and therefore have been especially interested in programs of child care, probation, and the like, but whatever philosophical emphasis or religious motivation, technically the practice of

[3] For "fields" and settings see Chapter X.
[4] See articles in *Social Work Year Book* under "Jewish Social Work," "Catholic Social Work," and "Protestant Social Work" for discussion and bibliographies.

casework in sectarian agencies is similar to that in nonsectarian agencies.

As structure and function are developed, interdependent or cooperative enterprises in the community arise. Division of labor becomes possible only when there is a clear sense of the total needs and the related parts of the necessary service, with each separate agency accepting responsibility for distinctive lines of practice. During these stages of development, as is natural, confusions arise whenever important functions are shifted or new structures created. One such shift occurred in the rapid expansion of public welfare; another in the convergence of family work and children's work; another in the status of the protective function; another arose in the expansion and contraction of war-created agencies. The mental hygiene approach has become the common element in all modern casework. Workers in medical and psychiatric settings are finding common ground in the growing understanding of psychosomatic medicine and the psycho-social elements in all disease. Child and family guidance cannot be offered exclusively under medical auspices, but has long been recognized as a function of the social agencies dealing with the problems of parents, children, and youth.[5] Neurotic characters do not commonly see themselves as ill, nor disturbed behavior as being a symptom. The presenting problem may determine the client's choice of agency or institution, but the underlying conflicts will not be found to be peculiarly the province of any one professional group.

THE SIGNIFICANCE OF FUNCTION [6]

No one can set down a design for permanent structures in a shifting cultural scene. Functions must be altered with new problems, new needs, new facilities, and new technical and scientific knowledge. In early days in America the emphasis given to taking the child away from home was in part conditioned by the lack of adequate

[5] See p. 125.
[6] For the technical and philosophical use of function from another approach see pp. 127–28.

economic provision for children at home. The great slogan from the White House Conference of 1909, "no child should be removed from the home because of poverty alone," could not be translated into reality until the provisions of the Social Security Act made care for children on a large scale possible. Child welfare services are closely related to the maintenance of children at home, as well as to caring for children away from home.

If the cultural idea which now regards the family as socially valuable were radically changed, at once the pattern of much of social welfare would be shifted; if concepts of the welfare state should come to replace instead of to implement concepts of self-maintenance, or collectivism replace democracy, new techniques would have to be found for the development of the individual. Therefore, any attempt to clarify the meaning of contemporary structures and functions must be grasped in its theoretical aspects, rather than as a static explanation of an agency found in a given community today. For one characteristic of social movements, aside from their fluidity, is the variety of drifts and tendencies even within quite small geographic areas. Often there is more variation between agencies supposed to be in the same "field" than between those in different fields. What we mean by function is appropriate, cooperative, and integrated division of labor, based on an understanding of the welfare structure as a whole. It is important not to underemphasize or to overemphasize function: if function is vague and diffuse, both worker and client will be confused in their objectives; if function is inflexible, arbitrary, or captious, sporadic efforts to compensate for its rigidities will start up in the community. Administrative costs mount if parallel or categorical structures persist, either within a single agency or among agencies in the community with similar functions. From time to time, in a growing profession, reorganization and integration of structures is indicated, with resulting redefinition of functions and new procedures for collaborative effort.

Agencies, like biological organisms, often start with undifferentiated functions. Primitive structures were of two kinds: the agency that was set up for a special purpose, such as a milk or shoe fund;

or an agency set up with a number of diversified services, little related to one another and to other community agencies, but covering wide areas of service. The family and children's agencies of the nineteenth century were of the latter type, combining most kinds of social work under one administration. Thus, one family agency, started a century ago, offered relief, nutrition, day nurseries, convalescent homes, health services, sheltered workshops, and a home for the aged; and, when the era permitted, it added a mental hygiene clinic. Later, other family agencies supported, along with family work, housing and court reform activities, legal aid, social service exchanges, early experiments in work relief, such as wood yards and laundries, and even began schools of social work. A large children's agency founded the first convalescent homes, day nurseries, foster-care service, children's centers, homes for unattached boys, and so forth. The multiple-service agency was not operated, as is the medical center today, on the basis of an integrated, well-knit program for the care of the patient. Departments in these multiple-service agencies had little relation to one another. These pioneer agencies, however, not only laid the groundwork for the casework movement, but promoted community education, welfare councils, and stimulated preventive programs in most of the significant fields now embraced under the term of "welfare" today.

By the end of the century, early children's aid societies were not only stressing the needs of individual children but also thinking in terms of broad programs of child protection. In child placing, the practice was hardly less diffused than in the family agencies; from orphan asylums through indenture to foster care there was a formidable array of separate and frequently isolated approaches. Gradually the omnifarious services of the family agency began to be clarified and integrated, and the segmental character of the children's agencies became configurated and focused. In the large agencies, some of the services, such as legal aid or visiting nursing or convalescent homes, moved out from the family nest to become independent agencies or sponsored by other professions. Services such as the central index bureaus for information, for inventories of social and health resources, referral centers and so on, became common operations of welfare councils. Instead of separate agencies for intake, diagnostic clinics or "relief societies," study, diagnosis and treatment, making use of the appropriate social resource, became components in a well-defined casework process for all agencies.

Objectives as a Test of Function [7]

If one considers the concern of social casework with standards of living and constructive social relationships, one can see broad groupings of agencies around objectives which, in turn, suggest functions. One might enumerate such objectives as maintenance, counseling, therapy, protection, and correctional education. Maintenance is achieved through assistance funds and through foster care, substitute homes, or institutions. Accessory services, such as day nurseries, homemakers or visiting housekeepers, may be utilized. Guidance, counseling, and therapy are carried on in family and children's agencies, in clinics, in education, in the church, and elsewhere. A large portion of this work is done under sectarian and private auspices. Protection and supervision are aspects of child care, of casework attached to state hospitals, of probation, and of parole. In all such work there is a strong element of authority, and much of it is public. Correctional education—detention homes, schools, and parole for the treatment of delinquency—is rapidly being absorbed into the scope of social welfare, and casework and groupwork processes have been accepted. Prevention is a charge upon all social welfare, not a responsibility of one group of agencies or of any one profession. There is overlapping, for example, among maintenance, guidance, therapy, protection, and correction activities; nevertheless, it is possible to think of these objectives as furnishing one clue to function. Other clues which help define function are found in the scope, the resources, the characteristic complexity of methods used, professional competence, and jurisdiction. These are interdependent. What the agency wants to do and what communities want to do have in the past been strong determinants of function

[7] For further discussion of specific problems and functions see Chapter X.

in any given time and place. Today the trend is toward a responsible alignment of structures and functions in an over-all community plan of welfare.

With "the break-up of the poor law" there was a gradual emergence of the aged, the sick, and the dependent child from the all-embracing classification of "the poor." Classification is useful when it brings to the surface conditions which if given special attention lead to fresh knowledge and methods of treatment; classification may deter progress if its values harden into permanent categories and isolated procedures. Some of the good results which were brought about by releasing dependent children from the obscuring, inclusive poverty label were the deepened understanding of the needs of children, the recognition that childhood is not merely a preparation for life but also an important phase of living, and that the health, education, spiritual training, and economic security of children are the first concern of any society. Less beneficial results have followed whenever the study of children in foster-family homes and institutions has been divorced from the study of the family. Although originally it was assumed that each problem—unmarried motherhood, poverty, or dependent and neglected children—represented a special "field," requiring a special approach and skill, professional training soon began to make the worker's knowledge more inclusive, covering the common philosophy and techniques of social work. This has made it possible for workers to move more easily from one field to another. Child-placing and child guidance clearly call for specific disciplines, but not for separate versions of basic social work knowledge. Fundamental casework concepts are always subject to institutional adaptation, as for medical or psychiatric settings, for the administration of public assistance, or for other functions. Experiments in rural social work have shown clearly that urban caseworkers with a capacity for adaptation can be just as successful as those born or brought up on the farm. As the problems with which social casework is dealing are modified by cultural factors, so casework, in turn, modifies its own approach in terms of cultural and administrative conditions. The recognition of certain characteristics of each age range, such as the nursery years, adolescence, or old age, or of various social problems, such as unmarried parenthood, does not imply that a special "field" must be created to handle it, but that special aptitudes and knowledge are called for. Social problems, because of their very value, have not led to productive and dynamic advances when isolated. Social problems are so many faceted and social treatment is so varied and flexible that rigid categories have hindered as much as helped in the development of the requisite skills. Practice limited to any specific area, essential for the sharpening of insight and skill, tends to ritual and stereotyping not related to common professional processes nor contributing to a constantly tested theoretical base.

At the more primitive stages in the growth of the profession, a "commodity," such as a settlement, relief, a children's institution, is established, and a staff is trained to "administer" it. In later stages knowledge, concepts and techniques are formulated, and the worker makes use of various resources, tools, and skills on a diagnostic basis and as indicated by the problem and treatment aim. The basic services and resources for social work must thus be conveniently grouped and arranged for maximum availability and benefit to clients. The unifying principle is the characteristic professional process, not the good-natured or grudging cooperation of unselected department heads. When the social work agency is properly equipped and staffed, it is then ready to participate in collaborative effort with other disciplines. In the same way, the medical, court, and educational institutions must clarify and integrate their characteristic structures, aims, and functions before they can make good use of other professional disciplines. In some areas the public school system has so elaborated adjunctive departments and functions that its central business of education has been diluted. That every child goes to school should not mean that every kind of service must be offered at a school center. Today there is a tendency to make the school a sort of omnibus institution. The emphasis should be placed rather on characteristic educational processes and relevant supporting services and cooperation with other facilities.

Public and Voluntary Auspices

American social work is part of the social and economic movement which must determine future relations between governmental and nongovernmental activities. Social work can have no independent solution. The same forces operate in areas of welfare, education, health, and the business life of the nation. Western civilization has seen the dominance of church over state, the disestablishment of the church, freedom of worship, and recently, in the dictatorships, the absorption of the church by the state. To the American mind the private nature of religion remains unassailable, but the average citizen accepts the concept of an interlocking relationship between public and private efforts in all other fields. In welfare it is conceded that the community as a whole is responsible for meeting widespread and continuing needs, a responsibility which can be effectively discharged only through tax-supported agencies. The provision of a maintenance income for whole classes of the population, protection, public health, education, and the larger aspects of recreation are clearly functions of government. That there are supplementary services in private schools, voluntary hospitals, family and children's and groupwork agencies does not change the central assumption. The content is the same whether under public or voluntary auspices; education is the same whether in public or in private schools; golf is the same game whether played on the public course or on that of the most luxurious club; medicine is the same whether carried on in a university medical center or in a city hospital. Mass provision under governmental auspices may or may not affect the quality—but the professional processes must be fundamentally identical. The contribution of the voluntary agencies is in flexibility in treatment, experiments, and research and in the promotion of new projects.

Caseworkers trained under private or voluntary auspices and drafted during the depression by the hundreds into emergency relief administrations were at first bewildered and overwhelmed by the problem of mass case loads. What possible use, they thought, could be made of skill in individualizing when queues of applicants filled blocks or crowded the waiting rooms? The fallacy of relief as a "business" was then apparent in the minds of officials, because it was erroneously thought that the methods used in loading cars and producing shoes could be immediately transferred to the care of human beings in distress.[8] Social workers, resisting this concept, sometimes fell into the opposite error of assuming that an array of social services would be necessary to counteract the effect of routine and inadequate "business" policies. However, what emerged in the most efficient public assistance units were new skills and techniques in which large-scale administrative policy and reasonable individualization were found not incompatible. Caseworkers have learned what to "depersonalize," such as eligibility data, and what to personalize, such as the attitudes of a client toward his situation, the agency, the assistance itself. They have learned how to use policy as part of the process. For the meaning of the economic situation, like the meaning of illness in a health problem, lies in its emotional and social results. To devise objective tests of eligibility, rather than to judge the "worthiness" of the client, to encourage the client to participate in establishing his eligibility, to learn to appraise rights as well as needs, and to release capacities for self-direction and self-organization, even under the relentless pressures of unemployment and destitution, were challenges which served to increase, not to diminish, casework skills.

The family field was historically concerned with the maintenance and conservation of family life. Family well-being is threatened in two ways, *lack of income* and the *handicaps and asocial behavior of its members*. To overcome the first hazard, income can be provided through social security provisions, both insurance and assistance.[9] The great bulk of maintenance relief is now and will continue

---

[8] See Pray, "New Emphases in Education for Public Social Work," in *Method and Skill in Public Assistance*, p. 94: "It is clear that the subjects of administration are services, not elements of an organization nor wheels in a mechanism. The objects of administration are the protection and assistance of human individuals, not the management of items of statistics, or pins on a map, or lines on a chart."

[9] See pp. 199–205.

to be a function of the tax-supported family agency. For the second hazard—the handicaps and behavior problems of the adult wage earner and homemaker—responsibility has not yet been fully delegated by the community to the public agency, except in so far as the family or domestic relations court carries one phase of the problem. Child guidance clinics, formerly under private auspices, but now beginning in the public schools, courts, and elsewhere, get some of these difficult parents, although here the problem has usually been displaced by the parent upon the child and therefore is popularly thought of as a "child's problem" rather than an adult's behavior problem, which it usually is. Our whole probation system is public, but a very large portion of the family behavior problems are treated by voluntary agencies—churches, marriage counseling clinics, adjustment bureaus—essential in sound community planning. Since it is true that clients are helped to a greater self-awareness and responsibility whenever social services are clearly and definitively organized for their use, family counseling should be more clearly interpreted as a primary function within the well-equipped family and children's agency, whether under public or private auspices.

AGENCY STRUCTURE AND FUNCTION

As the agency or institution has become increasingly articulated in modern times, in social work perhaps more than in most professions, it is the recognized basis of practice. Particularly since the spread of social assistance, the fact that the worker is a representative of public policy and procedure has definitely set limits and defined responsibilities. While emphasis on agency structure and function [10] has proved clarifying and steadying to the casework process, agency reality should not be overelaborated any more than should inner emotional reality or the social environment or any of the basic realities with which we are concerned. It is the balance and interaction of all these realities which constitute the psychosocial process. The concepts of worker-client, agency-worker, and client-

[10] This has been the special contribution of the Pennsylvania School of Social Work.

agency relationships should be thought of as complementary aspects within a set of geared operations. In casework generically, skill has been developed in helping applicants, through the interviewing process, relate to and use the social services provided within the several agencies.

Policy and Procedure

Since social work is conducted through the framework of agency structure, the worker must be able to identify himself constructively with the agency and learn to use its services and procedures helpfully with the client. He is responsible to the community through these institutional and other resources. The worker interprets the function of his agency both to the client and to the community, adjusts work routines to carry his case load effectively, to handle priorities, to meet emergencies, to compile statistical and other reports. The caseworker must be alert to the effect of procedures upon clients, sensitive to changing needs and community developments and resources, which should be sensitively reflected in administration. He must be constantly on guard lest clients be fitted too closely—asked to come to terms too rapidly—with the techniques of the day. All techniques tend to become ritualistic unless constantly reviewed in the light of the client's needs and social changes. The integration of legislative framework, administrative policy and social work process on a high level is the challenge to the public social services today.

As a professional person the worker assimilates agency policy and procedures, yet retains his freedom to evaluate and question whenever it seems to him in the interest of client and society to do so. Indeed, if his professional conscience is in conflict with his daily practice, he has a responsibility to do this through appropriate channels, (see discussion of professional ethics below). If social workers do not believe in the policy of an agency for which they work and cannot modify it, presumably their obligation is to seek employment elsewhere. They are always under obligation to work for the prevention of social ills, as well as constructively to engage in activities necessary for the betterment of community conditions and services.

One difficulty is those limitations which theoretically one does not accept, but which actually do exist in practice. Thus, a voluntary agency may not have the funds to carry cases for long-term clinical research, or a public agency may not have emergency funds or funds for appropriate miscellaneous needs above the subsistence budget; it may be that neither agency is equipped with sufficient trained personnel or financed for the sort of treatment which the problem requires. Nevertheless, these fortuitous limitations of an administrative sort are inherent in actual, as opposed to a purely theoretical, division of labor. Even after an agency has clarified its main lines of service and decided on priorities, there will be marginal or twilight zones for which it is only partially equipped—or appropriate zones for which it is not adequately financed—thus creating functional problems which can only be met by shared immediate and long-range community planning. The public protective function includes elements of authority which limit flexibility. It has been found, however, that acceptance of administrative limitations or of authority itself is not necessarily a handicap, but is, in fact, essential in sound community planning and makes for an intelligent division of labor. It also seems to be true that a clear and definitive organization of social services helps clients to a greater self-awareness and responsibility, wherein casework assists them to make active use of all services instead of taking the role of passive recipients. That this can be true even in an authoritative setting is one of the encouraging developments for "protective work." [11]

"Functional Approach" [12]

The function of the agency conditions the client's use of relationship, since necessary restrictions affect the extent to which one can put oneself at the disposal of clients. While all social workers believe

[11] See pp. 287–93.
[12] As indicated earlier, the conceptual basis of this book is "diagnostic," and for comprehension of the "functional" approach the reader is referred to the literature sponsored by the Pennsylvania School group.

in clearly defined agency structures and functions designed within a well-planned community pattern, in so-called "functional case-work" agency function rather than client need becomes the pivot of "the helping process." The worker is said to carry the responsibility "for knowing the processes of helping only in terms of the agency setting," not "knowledge about helping in the mass or specific situations." "The caseworker's responsibility . . . must first of all be to the agency and its function." [13]

In the casework situation the helping process is thus said to be characterized by "moderate reality," and "a choice is left with the client" whether to meet agency limitations or to find for himself other solutions. The dynamic is the agency function which the worker represents, and in coming to terms with this it is assumed that the client will find a new focus for himself. The client is offered "a new experience in yielding himself to a fixed and limited reality," that is, the agency.[14] In the point of view of the writer, agency policy and procedures should subserve rather than become the center of the treatment process. It is unfortunate whenever theoretical reformulations tend to split into "schools" instead of clarifying and refining process. As has been often observed, the new contributions are, if valid, slowly absorbed by the older school, whereas the newer school tends to disregard the tested substance in the field, and become a cult.

[13] For functional limitations see Jessie Taft, "The Relation of Function to Process in Social Casework," *Journal of Social Work Process*, Vol. I, 1937, p. 8: "Certainly function is never completely static or inflexible, certainly it alters over a period of time in terms of changing social conditions or should alter, but relatively it is the known factor. . . . The worker sets up the conditions as found in his agency function and procedure; the client representing the unknown natural forces, reacts to the limitation as well as to the possible fulfillment inherent in the function, over a period of testing it out. He tries to accept, to reject, to attempt to control, or to modify that function until he finally comes to terms with it enough to define or discover what he wants, if anything, from this situation."

[14] As Kenneth Pray put it: "He is the representative of an agency which itself is a part of the fixed social reality within which the client must find his own satisfying solution and ultimate adjustment. The worker is limited in the nature and extent of his help by the choice the agency has made among many possible services and methods of service and by the conditions it has attached to its service." *Journal of Social Case Work*, XXVIII (October, 1947), 288.

Agency practice can be caught between the Scylla of a formless and ill-defined approach and the Charybdis of a barrier against a flexible and humane practice. Safeguards for a progressive, wise, and broad development are furnished by the integration of staff efforts through committees and conferences, emphasis on community as well as staff projects, the creative use of the services of volunteers, and the team, or multi-discipline, concept. It may be that, with the wide spread of public services, one of the specializations may be the integration of policy with casework, as today one of the specializations is the integration of therapeutic principles with casework. Obviously, generic professional education must equip the worker with basic clinical and administrative principles of treatment.

INTERAGENCY COOPERATION

The emphasis on cooperation, long a cardinal point in social casework, is derived from the fact that the typical social case is complex, has many facets, and indeed, usually has, more than one "client" in it. In rural work the public nurse, the children's court judge, and the public assistance or child welfare worker may all be concerned. In a large city not only the settlement worker but also several caseworkers may be involved with one or, more likely, several members of the same family. The practitioner learns to appreciate and to interpret not merely his own agency but also other agencies in the field of social welfare and health. In this way vastly better service to the client results. As Mary Richmond pointed out in an unpublished code of ethics, it is the responsibility of the caseworker to render or else to procure the particular aid or service requested by the client when the need is made apparent. If this need or service cannot be met by the immediate agency, the obligation of the caseworker is to help the client receive this service through another agency.

When agency A comes to the end of a course of treatment within its function and transfers the case, itself withdrawing, to agency B, this is not called a cooperative case. In most instances it is better to explain community facilities to the client and to allow him to make his own application to agency *B*. In fact, if agency *A* makes out the "prescription" for agency *B*, this "tandem" relationship never works well. To transfer a case properly means doing it with the consent of the client and, if indicated, sharing among the workers the diagnostic thinking as well as the treatment undertaken to date. A cooperative case means one in which planned treatment is carried on simultaneously by two or more agencies or two or more workers, as discussed earlier. Reporting promptly to the source of referral the disposition of the case is a professional courtesy conducive to good public relations.

It is an obligation upon both public and private agencies to make promptly a suitable written or oral report, with the client's consent, when an appropriate request for information is received. All selection of content for the report must be determined at the agency's discretion, always considering the client's interests, the relevance of the inquiry, the professional standing of the agency, and the highest good of the community. Cooperative casework can have little meaning except as there is common professional education, a functionally appropriate division of labor, and complete respect for and protection of the rights of clients within the framework of responsibility to the community. In general, since professional courtesy is a two-way etiquette, Agency *A* should not ask for confidential reports unless it is prepared to furnish them in return. Workers should not insist on reading records of other agencies. Record reading should always be carefully restricted; recourse to it is a responsibility for special purposes, accorded only to persons competent to make professional use of the material. While certain records are public documents, without the protection of confidentiality, it is a mistake to think that case records are ever public documents, even though kept in a public agency.[15]

Just as the client should know the nature of the social investigation and participate in it, so should he be informed and his

---

[15] Legal protection is not yet afforded social casework records. The whole question of handling subpoenas is too complicated for discussion here. For further discussion of confidentiality see pp. 38–39.

consent secured if reports are to be sent to outside agencies. Obtaining the consent of the client is still, one fears, honored more in the breach than in the observance, but the acceptance of this fundamental principle is unchallenged today. One can think of valid exceptions, when it might be unnecessary or unwise to consider solely the client's permission. If the client is psychotic, critically ill, delinquent, or a menace to himself or others, discretion must be conceded to the responsible worker. The client should know and be truthfully informed, if he asks, that records are kept and what sort of information is shared with the agency workers and consultants. The client readily understands the necessity of staff conferences and appropriate records and in what sense confidentiality is maintained. He rarely seeks to know the details, nor should anxiety about what is, after all, common-sense agency procedure be needlessly aroused. If special anxiety is shown which cannot be handled by a matter-of-fact statement, conditions are present which must be understood and treated individually.

The client has the right to count on the maximum of protection in the professional relationship. If other agencies are properly concerned, he should know the terms of their interest and the obligations to be assumed by the worker—to share or not to share the information with associated institutions. In many instances a professional agency having an appropriate reason for inquiry may be communicated with under the sanction of a sensible and reasonable interpretation of the rules of professional courtesy. It is assumed that the inquiring agency will use the information in the interests of the client, as the agency first concerned would use it. There is no formula for determining the amount and quality of information which may be shared. Irritations may arise because of ignorance and abuse of elementary considerations. Professional courtesy does not make it obligatory, as in medicine, that only one practitioner be in charge, but professional courtesy does imply the selective use of the Social Service Exchange and other forms of clearance and conference.

Social Service Exchange

The Social Service Exchange, or Central Index, is a device to help gear the work of separate agencies or departments in the interest of the client. Once a product of the charity organization idea, most of its registrations nowadays are cases under public social-work auspices. Each public service—assistance, child welfare, probation, and parole—must maintain a master file of its cases. Whether there is greater economy and efficiency in pooled than in separate files has not yet been determined, but meanwhile a central index facilitates the identification of cases known to two or more services. The "exchange" means only that one agency may on request be notified of prior agency contact. No other information is exchanged, since no form of "case" record is centrally kept.

There is some difference of opinion as to whether clients should be routinely informed of the existence of Social Service Exchange. I believe that this is a piece of inter-agency mechanics not easily grasped by the uninitiated; that the significance of such information, when volunteered by the worker, is usually not comprehended by the client and merely tends to arouse anxiety. If the client asks for information about any form of record he is entitled to a frank and truthful answer, the worker being sensitive to the probability of anxiety behind the question and so responding to this also. The chief ethical consideration is, not the attempt to describe a piece of useful but technical apparatus, but to gain, whenever necessary, the client's consent to comply with requests for information and make reports to interested agencies. It is not usually difficult for the skilled interviewer, with or without recourse to the exchange, to persuade the client to discuss previous agency contacts and treatment or to gain his consent to making any proper inquiries or sharing reports made in his interest. Voluntary agencies keep a master file of their cases and use discretion concerning the type of case to be cleared or registered in the Central Index or Social Service Exchange. In general, cases with numerous social agency contacts or showing gross social pathology should be registered. Agencies not carrying many cases of maintenance or chronic pathology may have less occasion for a 100 percent registration and clearance. Moreover, a discretionary procedure for registration is more feasible under voluntary than under public auspices, where procedures for mass caseloads are more uniformly applied.

Confidentiality requires that only a minimum of identifying data be on file, and a basic form is provided for this purpose. The fact that the family unit type of identification is used protects the individual known to courts, mental institutions, and the like. Whenever possible the unmarried mother and out-of-wedlock child are registered under the appropriate family unit. The real problem today is to devise an economical system for pooled indexing of large case loads in public welfare and the protective services.

CASE RECORDING [16]

In all institutional or agency practice the case record assumes great importance in the treatment of the client. This is partly because the factors in the psychosocial problem are extremely complex and it is difficult to recall them accurately and partly because of the group use of the document—more than one worker being involved concurrently or sequentially. In addition, the case record is used for the several purposes of practice, teaching, research, and, on the basis of its evidence, may contribute to social planning as problems are understood, described, and classified.

The main considerations in recording are: the need for sufficient relevant factual material, both social and psychological; the worker's professional analysis of the situation; the formulation of diagnostic and treatment evaluations; the preliminary outline and step-by-step reports of the treatment which is made available, and the recording of the final outcome of the case. All case records should include as minimum data: identifying information; the details of the psychosocial situation in which the client now is; the nature

[16] The content appropriate to various considerations in treatment will be suggested by the examination of the chapters in this book. See also Hamilton, *Principles of Social Case Recording.*

of the problem, its onset (appropriate, but not routine, history), the nature of the client's request, his feeling about his situation and his attitude towards using the agency for help; the details of the treatment and reactions of the client to it. Records are written to be read, and the contents, therefore, should be in a form to be readily grasped. The material must be accessible, clear, concise, suited to the situation and the nature of the treatment to be undertaken. One requires only as much data as will enable him to understand the problem to be solved and the main factors in its solution. In all problems of behavior and failure to adapt to society, whether the behavior is deviant with regard to an economic or a family situation, considerable study will be required to reveal the personality. When solution of the problem calls for a relatively uncomplicated form of social assistance, details of personality development and emotional relationships, including worker-client interaction in the interview, may be minimal and should certainly not be reproduced in verbatim process style. The client's reaction, whether to practical or to psychological conflicts, and his feelings about a course of action are always important, but if his feeling is appropriate, usual, neither a hindrance to nor an elaboration of ordinary behavior, one need not record it any more fully than other psychosocial facts. The old rule that one should always pay attention to the obvious—to see if it is what it seems—but not over-record it, holds true concerning emotional as well as practical affairs.

Presentation of Evidence

The record should contain both the relevant physical, social, and economic data and the primary psychological evidence as to feelings, expressed largely through attitudes and behavior. These data are reported in two main ways: (a) narrative, the "story" form, giving facts, and (b) summaries; or a mixture of these two styles may be used. The narrative form is the simplest and usually the best way to report material which deals with attitudes, feelings, and worker-client relationship, since this style best permits the use of primary evidence, that is, verbal material and observed behavior in the interview. The only way one knows how the client feels is from what he says about himself and what he does during the interview. The primary psychological evidence, therefore, requires selective verbatim reporting [17] within the interview situation, including the worker's role. Verbatim recording of important interviews or significant portions of interviews is indispensable for study and for clarifying psychological goals in treatment. It is seldom utilized for the more obvious social goals, or for offering concrete practical services, when condensation and summaries are preferable. Verbatim reporting of most interviews is indefensible. Verbatim should be used for significant portions of treatment interviews to show emotional overtones, subtle reactions, especially interchanges between worker and client which indicate feeling tones in and the use of the relationship, play interviews with children, where observation of the behavior and the child's response to the relationship are revealed, and so forth. Even in carefully selected verbatim recording of the interview situation, the emotional tone will not necessarily be caught and the worker, who, as participant, best knows what happened psychologically, has the responsibility to give his diagnostic or evaluative comments at the beginning or end of the entry as to what transpired. Verbatim, on the whole, which is a useful style for certain, especially for training purposes, should be sparingly used. However, the swing to an all evaluative form of record—recently called "process" (process used to be thought synonymous with verbatim, but is no longer generally so employed) has its own dangers. It is still advisable to caution that every record needs sufficient psychological as well as social primary evidence, but this must be rigidly selected and controlled or the whole will be unreadable. Frequent condensation is equally essential.

The summary form of recording is used for reporting social data, both eligibility material and in preparing an orderly history to show

[17] "Verbatim" is only an approximation of accurate reporting unless there is dictaphonic recording, which has its own limitations.

personality patterns, growth, development, and interrelationship. Treatment summaries are also essential. Social study (including eligibility and summaries and psychogenetic histories) is usually in condensed topical form, under the broad headings family background, economics, education, or unemployment data. Unit records in medical and other institutions lead to a maximum use of summary for the participating group. Supplementary records should always be sparingly used in agency practice, lest the main trends of treatment be isolated and dissipated. Usually a card form of supplementary record should suffice for the desk use of auxiliary units, and all significant material, in abbreviated form should be placed in the central file by the appropriate member of the group. Circulation of the record among those treating the patient or family obviates the necessity of anything more than an outline or rough note type of folder or card. If extensive use of carbon copies or major duplicate files are kept, it usually suggests failure to integrate the treatment process itself. In all cases in which the interview is the chief medium of treatment and emotional material is dominant, the associative context is more important than the arrangement, and condensed narrative is more appropriate than topical. However, diagnostic thinking provides short cuts.

Treatment summaries should be made at appropriate intervals, either in lieu of narrative entries or through condensation and evaluation of progress during significant periods, sharply to reduce the necessity for long narrative entries. Periodic summaries, for example, monthly or less frequently, may be made that administratively offer good controls, but it is theoretically better to have the summary cover a phase of planned treatment to be evaluated at the end thereof. Summaries are frequently required before a change of workers, and they, certainly better than nothing, are not so good as making appropriate summaries at the appropriate time, that is, social study, diagnostic or treatment evaluations when treatment demands. In child placing periodic evaluations made about every three months are effective both in condensing the record and in holding a clear treatment perspective.

Interpretation of Evidence

The professional record is the worker's tool. No mere reproduction of fact, no matter how detailed or discriminating, can be substituted for the worker's thinking—a professional opinion—his own or shared with supervisor, consultant, or as the product of staff conferences. What the client thinks and feels is shown through primary evidence of the interview; what the worker makes of the attitudes, the problem presented, the personalities involved, and pros and cons of treatment should be written briefly and clearly in forthright statements. A record cannot be said to be professional unless the writer is not only able to set down the relevant facts accurately and concisely but also to say how he interprets these facts. The diagnostic summary should culminate in a psychosocial diagnostic statement. Periodic summaries with evaluation of treatment should be required.

The chief forms of interpretation are known as the diagnostic process and the evaluation process.[18] The worker makes running comments from intake throughout the handling of the case as to the meaning of the facts—this is the over-all interpretation process. At intervals he makes formal diagnostic statements and diagnostic summaries, prognostic statements (evaluation), treatment evaluations, and such special summaries as evaluation of a foster home before and after use. Variants of special diagnostic and evaluative formulations are familiar and need not be cited here.

Some workers write the greater portion of the record in an evaluative style—thus: "Mrs. B. showed her attempts to control throughout the interview by constantly trying to set her own terms." This has the virtue of brevity, but is to be preferred only if the interpretation is properly supported with adequate social facts and verbal (selected verbatim) evidence. Workers must be vigorously trained towards effective condensation through habitual and careful reading of the record and making notes before each dictation, thus

[18] See pp. 214–19 and also Little, "Diagnostic Recording," *Journal of Social Casework*, XXX (January, 1949), 15–19.

avoiding repetition, by preparing for dictation in advance, not reacting spontaneously to the stimulus of the stenographer or the dictaphone. The fact that the client repeats himself is no reason for the worker to do so. Even when a change of workers occurs only new material—not new to this worker, but new to the record—should be introduced. New material and conflicting material, if relevant, should be introduced and pointed up as to its difference and probable meaning, but repetition of the same material by the client should warn us that the problem is unsolved and drive us to more thoughtful diagnostic and evaluative efforts to analyze its significance rather than to repeat it in the record.

We cannot remind ourselves too often that time spent in reading garrulous records is even more expensive than uncontrolled dictation time. Sifting of material should always be done before dictating either single or summarized entries. Regular dictation schedules, not more than twice a week, often only once, careful preparation of notes, practice in summary and interpretative writing, even rationing of cylinders tend toward effective recording habits and a more usable record. How much diagnostic and evaluative tests, such as Rorschach, thematic apperception tests, and others, may supply supplementary shortcuts to the diagnostic process is not known. There seems little reason to think that any medium will supplant the interview as the central tool of casework.

The following example shows modified process with some of the workers' evaluative comment:

Mrs. Cohen began this interview by discussing with me all the values there would be for her and for Gloria in a placement plan. She had or seemed to have a much more positive acceptance of what placement could do for them. She discussed her feeling about Mr. Curran (the man with whom Mrs. Cohen lived) and his continued irresponsibility, but she later explained that he was sick and could not work consistently. For this reason she questioned whether a permanent alliance with him would have any value in it for her or Gloria and thought that she was getting pretty disgusted as she got older about what her life meant. She felt that maybe it would be best if she got outside of the house a little bit and maybe even went to work herself. She talked about the

Dept. of Welfare too, and her disgust in not being able to get anywhere with them. She added a significant comment about its not making much difference whether Gloria was in the home or not, as far as she could see, to get relief. This has been something that we discussed before, and I knew that she also had talked it over with the Dept. of Welfare, but she had not accepted, until this point, the fact that Gloria could not be used as bait for home relief. Now she talked more about a job and the diversion and interest as well as the additional income that this would offer her. She added that if she were working she could not leave Gloria unsupervised. Apparently whatever job she was thinking of, and I did not get this quite clear, would keep her out in the early part of the evening. Gloria was the kind of girl who stayed home a lot, and she did not like the idea of her being alone with nobody to get her dinner, etc. She thought that if she could have Gloria in a good home where she knew she was safe, it would be much better for all of them.

I wondered if she had made up her mind to go ahead with placement then, and it was at this point that she turned completely about-face by letting me know that she supposed she had no other choice. She revealed having signed the application blank and that Mr. Curran had told her that she now could not change her mind. Mrs. Cohen came out with the conclusion that if the Dept. of Welfare would be ready to use the court, she would not want that and would instead agree to go ahead with placement. However, she did not like us or anybody else telling her what to do, and if she didn't have to go ahead with placement maybe that would be better. There was no point in reasoning with her, because the contradictions were obvious, yet she could not face them.

I pulled two things out of this discussion, which had been a very detailed one: first, her continued reluctance to face placement even if it would be in many ways to her advantage and to Gloria's; secondly, the relationship of this feeling to her need to have the placement decision out of her hands. There had been enough indication of this in what she said for me to bring it to her attention and to have her accept it. She had been telling me in a roundabout way that if it had to be placement it was all right with her, because they would both be better off that way. On the other hand, if nobody was going to make her go ahead, even though it would be better for them, she wouldn't do it. As I brought this to her attention, we finally got somewhere.

For one thing she was able to express what had happened in placement to her relationship to the other children. Bitterly she explained all the material advantages that placement had meant for her which enabled the girls to forget her and leave her out of the picture. She had been supplanted by the agency in their eyes. She did not feel any threat about new relationships that they had taken on, because she pointed to Iris' continued replacements and dissatisfactions in the foster home, and also the fact that Violet was in an institution took that threat away. She felt that it was just the idea that they could get what they wanted without her that had turned them against her. She had no recognition of her own inadequacies or of the strains in the relationship that had existed apart from whatever material values they gained from place-ment. Gloria had meant far more to her than any of the other girls, I pointed out, and she admitted readily that Gloria was really all that she had and she was not going to lose her, too, because of placement.

When we reached this point together, I asked her to consider what it would mean to have things continue as they were and whether she thought that would be a way of getting closer to Gloria or whether this would pull them even farther apart. She insisted that if Gloria did not know that she could be placed, the girl would make an effort to get along better at home. While this was the same deadlock that we had reached in our previous interview, there was now room for some-thing different. That is, Mrs. Cohen had also arrived at the fact that placement had value in it for her and for Gloria and that they might be best off apart. She also saw that she did not dare to take this step for fear of what it would mean to their relationship. If it came from some place else, she would be willing for it, but if the decision had to come from her, it would be as if she started what would have to be the ultimate complete break between them. Her expression of this was in a very superstitious fashion, as she brought in, in Yiddish, that luck would be against her because she was doing a bad thing. Mr. Curran had told her this over and over again.

Therefore, what I came to was having her go back to the Dept. of Welfare to find out exactly what their position would be about her withdrawal. She was willing, and when we reached that point together she seemed almost afraid that they would say that they would let her withdraw. This came out as she asked how long she had to get Gloria into a foster home. She was aware of the fact that once Gloria was 16, we could no longer place her and that we would need time preliminary to her 16th birthday to find a home. Since Gloria's birthday was in December, there was obviously a time limit when Mrs. Cohen would have to make up her mind. She added that if she withdrew the applica-tion and then Gloria acted up again, she would be stuck and there would be nothing further that she could do.

It was with this that I pointed to her recognition of the fact that the relationship was strained and that things were not satisfactory, far apart from the question of separation and placement. She acknowledged that that was so, but still held to her hope that something could bring them closer and that Gloria would come to her senses. She did not see her part in changing or in doing anything to make for that change in their relationship.[19]

Intake interviews, especially if a separate staff is used, are usually recorded in full, and longer, as well as more frequent dictation periods are afforded, always, however, with stress on selectivity and relevance. Beyond this, experimental techniques, such as adaptations of psychotherapy to casework, are usually recorded fully for study purposes. As soon as the worker knows the meaning of the data and has good control of the process, he will tend to diagnostic and evaluative shortcuts as far as practicable, with selective use of primary evidence to support his conclusions whenever indicated. A good rule is that whenever one *knows* what is happening psychologically in an interview one should record this meaning in condensed style rather than reproduce the conversation *in toto*. Selected verbal evidence may be adduced to clarify the interpretation. The trend to take more systematic pertinent history during the early contacts results in arranged and formulated data.

STAFF AND INTERDISCIPLINE COLLABORATION

In the urban setting intake is done by workers who rotate on this service. Accepted cases are then allocated to other staff workers according to their skill, interest, geographical area coverage, fair distribution of case load, and other considerations. It is not sound to retain certain workers exclusively on intake, as this tends to stereotyped attitudes and procedures. In the rural setting the worker, who may be taking interviews many miles from home and not likely to return soon, must gather more factual material and go further in the social study process than when the client is easily accessible. Not only is this a common-sense adaptation but also the relationship can be strongly established, since the same worker more often

[19] In some current practice indirect discourse is even less used for verbal evidence, but one should be cautious to keep a balance between fact and interpretation.

continues with the case. In hospital admission various patterns are used. The social workers may do one hundred percent intake for the hospital as a whole, or they may cover the intake of their assigned services, such as pediatrics, surgical, dermatology, or tuberculosis. Some take only cases referred by physicians.[20] Whenever the same worker continues from intake with his own cases, the relationship can be built up, and the intake process may go more rapidly than when the interview is taken for later allocation among the professional group. It is, however, a fortunate peculiarity of human experience that good will established with one worker through well-focused exploration of the problem and the request, can generally be transferred to another worker within the agency he represents. People are likely to form strong attachments to a school, hospital, or other institution where they have had satisfying emotional experiences. This is especially true in a treatment situation. The client comes to feel that everyone he meets is friendly towards him rather than that one person alone understands him; the agency, far from being a mysterious monster of impersonal regulations, becomes a human refuge, with procedures which he can understand and of which he can take hold. He may also take umbrage at some kindly figure and reserve all his positive feelings for another, but this will be understood as an aspect of "transference." Once a relationship of any intensity gets started, it may be desirable that it be continued with the same worker, as this imposes an obligation which cannot be lightly set aside. But this is also why skilled control of the relationship is so essential.[21]

The concept of "team" [22]—doctor, nurse, social worker, technicians in the medical setting, of psychiatrist, social worker, and psychologist in child guidance—is beginning to have wider application in the idea of a multi-discipline approach. Psychiatrists and physicians are serving on staffs of social agencies just as social workers serve on staffs of medical institutions. Home economists, lawyers, nurses, nutritionists, and educators find appropriate roles

[20] See pp. 293–95.   [21] See pp. 48–49.
[22] See team in the medical psychiatric setting, pp. 299–302.

in many types of social agencies. With the spread of public social work, not only must the social worker know the principles of social legislation and administration thoroughly but also the lawyer consultant will, no doubt, be more utilized. In making this progressive adjustment to the complex needs of modern society, confusion is obviated when the central professional commitment of the agency is kept clear; in the medical institution the nurse or social worker is there to further the medical purpose; in education, doctor, nurse, and social worker, the educational purpose; and in the court, the legal purpose. In the social agency, the lawyer, or other consultant, like the psychiatrist on the staff, must adapt himself to the purpose of social work. The most important consideration is that professional thinking should be shared, not authoritative decisions handed down or routine examinations made. The usefulness of a staff psychologist in a social agency is determined not only by his ability to give a battery of tests but also by his participation in determining when testing is necessary. He may not only aid in diagnosis, but also continue with cases for psychological therapy, such as remedial teaching, when indicated. The question of who shall participate in the day-to-day treatment of the client is a long-range one, to be worked out by examining the best trends in professional practice, the particular staffing of institutions and agencies, under a process of shared and enlightened self-study.

There are two schools of thought as to the future of social work. One sees it as a social component in medicine, industry, law, education, and the like, but without a separate identity. This would assume social workers, but not a definable field of social practice. The other sees it, as the writer does, as a gradually expanding and deepening profession, with its own body of transmissible subject matter, its own fields of skilled operation and usefulness, and its own disciplines and methods. In a great hospital there are doctors, nurses, technicians, and social workers; in public assistance there are social workers, accountants, clerks, and so forth. The hospital, however, derives its meaning from the practice of medicine, and, despite the importance of finance and business methods in the large-scale relief transactions, the public assistance agency derives its meaning from the practice of social welfare. Social workers are found today in courts, schools, churches, employment offices, but welfare agencies are organized and operated under social work auspices. It is true that social institutions change with changing structures, but the idea of a self-liquidating profession of welfare has never seemed realizable or desirable. Health, legal, and educational institutions also markedly change, but do not thereby become self-liquidating. Rather they offer wider coverage and greater skilled service, which contribute to a higher standard of living and a more informed and responsible citizenry. Certainly there is today greater clarity as to purpose and better integration of many fragmentary welfare activities into broad functional services. Yet there are still too many small or narrowly conceived activities isolated, duplicating, or competitive. The chief challenge to community planning is to clarify and consolidate the main social welfare functions within which the characteristic professional processes of social work are to be carried on. The multi-discipline approach in welfare can only be effective where the social-work function has been defined and accepted by the cooperating professions.

PART II

CHAPTER VI

APPLICATION AND INTAKE PROCESSES

WE HAVE SPOKEN of the psychosocial case as consisting of inner and outer factors, of person and situation, but that is only a way of expressing how it must be regarded by the practitioner. People need food, shelter, clothing, and safety in order to survive; and they also need affection and success, some capacity to love and be loved, security and also opportunities for growth and development in order to lead satisfying lives. In all walks of life, not merely among the less well-to-do, some find it easier to ask for concrete things— for advice about definite steps. Thus, out of many complex factors they select one area on which to focus attention. People do speak about generalized unhappiness, it is true—the adolescent who is unhappy is simply engulfed in unhappiness; but most persons pin their difficulties on something relatively definite before they ask for help. Some ask for help easily; for others asking comes hard; but whether hard or easy, to ask at all the person must be in a dilemma or a predicament which he no longer feels he can solve single-handed.

CONTINUITY OF STUDY, DIAGNOSIS, AND TREATMENT [1]

Social caseworkers describe the steps taken in identifying with the client—in accepting him as a person, in analyzing and clarifying the situation, and in trying to elicit or to supply what will help him to make the most of himself and his resources—by such terms as "study" or "investigation," "diagnosis and evaluation," "service" or "treatment." Logically one would study, diagnose, and treat in

[1] These technical processes will be analyzed in ensuing chapters.

that order; actually these steps are not performed in sequence, but are woven in and out, one process paralleling another. While we are asking a person about his situation, we are "treating" him—and later, when we are doing something with or for him he may be bringing out new values in the situation, so that together we study it afresh. Intellectually the steps are distinguishable; in life, the case-work process flows along in one single, comprehensive movement or unity. We make a tentative diagnosis at the outset; we "treat" in some fashion right away. Our minds go on drawing inferences; we are engaged in study as long as we know the client. Since one treats persons, not problems, while we are trying to understand (diagnose) the nature of the problem we are also trying to understand what sort of person has the problem, and as long as the treatment continues there are recurrent phases of study, diagnosis, and evaluation.

In another sense, the processes, though interwoven, should be articulated in orderly stages of procedure or the case may drift along inconclusively. In the diagnostic approach there is always a phase of fact gathering appropriate to the problem and the request initially presented. Out of this information understanding is gained as to the nature of the difficulty (diagnosis) and the evaluation of the person's functioning in terms of the service or treatment asked for (eligibility, treatability). On this diagnostic appraisal the aim of treatment is formulated with the applicant. Certain caseworkers believe that too much emphasis has been given to the "problem" and goal formulation in the application process and see in intake chiefly the opportunity, through defining the nature of the agency's service, to stimulate the client to move toward mitigation of the difficulty he presents, the case being focused throughout on the way in which the client is seeking to come to grips with his difficulty through the exercise of his will.[2] There should be no incompatibility between diagnostic effort, which assumes that needs can be objectively understood, and the stimulation of the client's ability to work on his problem. At its best, casework always strikes a balance between problem solving and mobilizing ego strengths, comple-

[2] See pp. 127–28.

mentary aspects of which are treatment. Both are fully utilized in the diagnostic approach.

THE "RIGHT" TO ASSISTANCE

The application process has been deeply affected by changing cultural attitudes toward security in basic income, health, and welfare services. The right to social assistance is both statutory and moral. In contractual insurance the right is so specifically defined that the benefit may be in many instances almost automatically granted. In welfare programs the right to assistance has to be established, and procedures thereto are clarified and channelized, largely by means of attention to the client's expressed and implied need. Even in the insurances, veterans' benefits, and so forth, recognition of the fact that not all requests lie in the uncomplicated area of contractual obligation is beginning to affect the training of personnel so as to conduct a flexible and enlightened procedure leading to collaboration with social workers when indicated. In all types of public welfare, eligibility, as defined by statute and regulations, imposes a framework for social practice. Clients' attitudes toward public assistance may be unlike their attitudes toward voluntary assistance—some preferring one, some the other—but since all clients in any relief situation have attitudes which must be understood, basic knowledge of human behavior will be required. In a modern welfare program both the concept of a statutory *right* and the diagnostic concept of individual *need* are incorporated into a clearly defined and communicable casework process of exploration and appropriate treatment. The public assistance case is always psychosocial, but if uncomplicated by related problems may fall into the category of "administration of a service" rather than other forms of treatment.[3]

Attitudes toward Seeking Assistance

If one asks a young college graduate how he felt when applying for a job or a patient how he felt when he went to an unfamiliar

[3] See pp. 243–46.

clinic, one will find that both have had similar feelings. There is probably a period of fear, worry, or increased tension about the problem, a struggle to make up the mind to do something about it and fear of the unknown agency, or shop, or institution. The applicant may be uncertain as to the best place to go. He often depreciates himself: "I guess he'll think I'm not experienced enough for this job" or "Maybe the doctor will believe I'm making a fuss about nothing," softening an expected rejection. Or perhaps he puts it to himself otherwise: "This job is really beneath me, but I need the money badly" or "I'm afraid the doctor will find me worse than I imagine." He may be afraid, that is, that he has too great a problem or too small a problem or that people will blame or reproach him, and sometimes he feels that he must justify himself in his own eyes because he anticipates rejection or lack of appreciation. Sometimes this fear of rejection is so intense that he has worked up reasons beforehand to let himself down easily—"My qualifications are first rate, but probably they're looking for entirely different training." The same kind of feelings and defenses are involved in applying to a social work agency, with the added possibility that our culture may have placed such a stigma on the kind of problem —failure in self-maintenance or illegitimacy or destitution, that shame and self-reproach may be acute.

The casework process is set in motion whenever someone becomes conscious that he has a social need and that he must have help. All indecision is a "search for a way to act." Once the client has decided to act, his purposes become unified, sufficiently at least to make him inquire about resources. Perhaps he has thought of help in material terms: "I need money for rent," he says to himself, or "I want to send my little boy to camp," or "I need a job," or "I cannot manage my children any longer." Probably he has vacillated, too, about where to go, since social agencies as yet do not have as clear a status as that of the hospital and public school. Certainly he will be mildly apprehensive or actually fearful of his reception. He may be angry at the way life has treated him; he may feel humiliated that he couldn't work out a solution for himself, but at least he will have done something about the problem by seeking assistance. It is sometimes thought that the self-sufficient person who struggles grimly on by himself without asking for aid is a nobler character, but asking for help may be quite as often an indication of strength as of weakness. The test of character lies not in whether or not a person seeks assistance when in difficulty, but in what a person does with the assistance when it is made available.

Now when the individual has betaken himself, to use the strong old verb, to an agency, a kind of sifting must take place. The applicant makes the request; someone must talk with him and find out what the general nature of the trouble is and whether it can be treated here. If not, he has to be referred to the appropriate agency. This procedure is usually called "application." In a hospital the administrative or agency side of application is referred to as "admitting"; in a social work agency as "intake." It is not usual to count a case as a "case" for statistical purposes until after this intake, or sifting process, has been completed. In the assistance field, as in others, "intake" has the objective of determining the question of "presumptive eligibility," by which is meant that through the initial inquiry it is determined whether the client's need is one which may effectively—and legally, if a public agency—be met in the place where the application is made. Applicants may be intimidated by unfamiliar surroundings and procedures, disconcerted by indifferent attitudes on the part of attendants, which make them feel inferior and therefore resentful. Professional terminology is also frightening. A woman who had gone to a medical center and had just been assured that her trouble was minor, but had also been routinely referred to "diagnostic clinic," heard only the phrase "diagnostic clinic" and came to the social worker in a panic of apprehension as to what was to happen next.

All such emotion surges *beneath the surface.* What the interviewer sees is a person who may appear shy, or inarticulate, or restless, or haughty, who shows an injured dignity, or one who may be aggressive and threatening and demanding. Sometimes the applicant is nervous and confused and cannot readily tell what his trouble is, and sometimes he has "a chip on his shoulder" and does not want to give the necessary information. The intuitive interviewer will recognize the feelings of insecurity, anxiety, and irritability. But most caseworkers have to learn the meaning of these attitudes and develop skill in reducing the fear, in restoring the damaged self-esteem, by giving the applicant undivided attention, privacy, and help in discussing the topic of greatest interest to him—namely, his situation and request. It is not necessary to "make conversation," although all skillful interviewers learn little devices of word and gesture to help particularly timid and nervous applicants to feel comfortable at first. Just as the teacher who is not conversant with mental hygiene is apt to value the good, timid, obedient child above the unruly and aggressive, so the unskilled interviewer may be misled by a liking for the respectful, appreciative applicant and be disconcerted, if not antagonized, by the touchy, demanding, ungrateful, or sarcastic one. The skilled interviewer knows, however, that the applicant tends to displace his feelings about other social relationships onto the application experience, so that as much can be learned by being attentive to disagreeable as to pleasant, first impressions. Behavior in the interview is often characteristic.

While social assistance gradually has become less stigmatized, there are residual attitudes which make asking for help in this area painful. Not only may the applicant consider himself a failure, but he fears lest the "investigation" may be damaging to his self-esteem, expose him to criticism, or control his actions. Life experiences may already have sensitized him to frustration and rejection and created a pattern of resentment or submission to authority. Making him aware of his rights and letting him participate in the study lessen his feelings of inadequacy. When he understands his rights under the conditions of eligibility, his initiative and judgment are encouraged, his freedom of decision as to what he wishes in the way of service is respected (noncontingent eligibility), the procedures cease to be alarming, and he regains his feeling of self-respect. Recognition of his own attempts at solution, discussion of his plans for the future, and encouragement toward self-sufficiency tend to maintain potential strength and energy. In making decisions which involve other members of the family [4] he will be encouraged to arrange for their participation as well as his own. Aged and ill and incapacitated persons may need active help in their applications, but they will be encouraged to do as much for themselves as possible. One might say that at one end of the application process one finds the "client-*citizen*," at the other the "client-*patient*," [5] depending on the kind of person, the kind of problem, and the nature of the treatment contemplated.

"A Full and Patient Hearing"

It is the first task of the caseworker to hear the applicant's description of his problem, catching not only the words but also their meaning for the speaker—what is said and what is unsaid are important. In *Social Diagnosis* [6] the "first interview" was described as affording an opportunity for a full and patient hearing and for getting an idea of the client's attitude toward life. Mary Richmond knew that the tonic influence of an understanding spirit could help develop self-direction and self-reliance. But although she did not think that the first interview should carry the full weight of factual information, she did see it chiefly as laying the factual basis for later inquiry. Interviews can be wrecked between the Scylla of covering too much factual ground and the Charybdis of such sympathetic listening that the client says, "No one has ever really understood my problem before," and becomes dependent on his listener. The overfactual interview can effectively screen one off from any understanding of the person, just as pouring out of the heart without direction can obscure the real situation and at the same time set up a most unmanageable relationship. Young workers, uncomfortable with emotions, may barricade themselves behind facts, or, unskillful with facts, may be tempted to plunge into discussion of the deeper emotions. A balance between preliminary fact finding and recognition of feeling is to be kept.

[4] See pp. 99–102. [5] See pp. 48, 294.
[6] Richmond, *Social Diagnosis.*

In application we notice and accept rather than explore the client's feelings, initiate a working, not an intensive relationship; clarify the situation; make sure that it is not more appropriate for another agency; find out what the applicant has done about his problem and what he wants to do or wants us to do about it and give him some idea, through interpretation of the agency's services, of our probable role. Application interviews should create a condition of mutual confidence, obtain sufficient data to allow for a tentative diagnosis of the area of the difficulty, a preliminary estimate of the client's and the agency's capacity to deal with it, and the formulation of next steps. The applicant is encouraged to tell his own story and describe and give his view of his situation. He feels understood because of the worker's respect for him as an individual with rights and needs, but particularly because of the acceptance of his feeling about himself, about coming for help, and about his immediate situation. When a client comes to a social agency it is not always easy to discover what the real request is or what the client is suffering from. Frequently the social situation is confused or the client is emotionally disturbed, and at the outset he may not clearly know what he wants and expects. The following two excerpts show an attitude of respect and acceptance.

Mr. Arnold [r] came for his appointment promptly. He was unshaven and carelessly dressed. His face wore an expression of deep resentment. I felt that he was very tense and troubled. He asked if I knew what he had told the receptionist and proceeded to repeat everything he told her. He said that things were even worse than when he came here yesterday, because he was going to be put out on the street tomorrow morning. He had received an eviction notice. He went on in great detail to tell how he got into this situation. It was all the fault of the foreman on the job, who discriminated against him because he was leader in the union. When the case came up in court this foreman said that there had not been an accident, but Mr. Arnold said he could produce enough witnesses. Everyone with whom he has talked has told him that he has a good case. He struck with his fist at his stomach as he told that he is wearing a cast. He was in the hospital from the middle of April until

[r] From a family service agency.

May 10. The foreman has a nerve saying that there was no accident. He won't be able to go back to work for maybe six months, and even after that he does not know whether he will be able to do his regular work. His voice grew louder as he told me all of this, and as he finished, he was standing up and shouting. He could prove this to me if I wanted him to. I could get in touch with the hospital and with the relief office, where he had been turned down. Can't they realize that he is the sort of person who would not come for help if he did not need it? I said that I thought there was some way I could help him work out this situation. *He sat down at that.* He began to tell me how he had gone everywhere before he came here. He has exhausted all borrowing capacity. He has pawned clothing, and he pulled from his pocket tickets to show me. I said that he seemed to have had to prove everything to a number of people. He said he could prove everything that he had said was true. I said that it must have been hard for him to come to us. He said it was terrible. He had never had to take anything from anybody before. Then he went on to build up the picture of his former comfortable circumstances. He had owned a house, which was lost by a foreclosure. He had given a great deal of money to charity. I said that it was hard when one had always been in a giving position to have to take help. *He seemed to notice me for the first time at this point.* (An accepting attitude combined with readiness to offer help induces the positive relationship.) He said he hoped that what he had been saying about agencies and other people was something that I did not think applied to me. No one seemed to understand how awful it was for him to be in this position. He had never talked with anyone as he was doing now. Often he has wanted to ask his wife what she is thinking, but she sits there and does not say anything. He thinks she realizes that he cannot work now and that he wants to provide for his family. (He apparently was wondering what the worker was thinking about him.) Nobody believed that he could not stand what was happening, and he would much rather be working and taking care of his family. Meanwhile he is facing eviction.

I suggested that we might talk about his present situation. I realized that he must feel that he was pushed into coming here by the fact that he has an eviction. (Specific facts would be elicited here.)

The load of anger or anxiety before help is sought may have piled up unbearable tension, which must be released before questions or explanation of our service can become effective. After an outbreak, the inexperienced worker may be frightened away from the topic, whereas the experienced worker can often move quietly in for the necessary clarification, since the discharge of tension often makes a favorable opportunity for rational inquiry into the facts.

Mr. Arnold then said that he did not know what he would have done if he had not come here. He wants to thank me for listening to him as I had done. Sometimes he has just thought that he would go mad. He has wondered what was the use of going on living. But then he thinks of his three children and his wife. He has such a lovely, devoted wife, and such beautiful, bright children. He cannot bear seeing them suffer the way they have. I said that he had done something about it by coming here. He seemed to relax somewhat after this, and said maybe this was the place where he could talk over plans for the future. Everything seemed to have been going to pieces until now. I said that this was the place, if he wanted to come. He said he would like to think about that, and I suggested that after he had, he might call me and I would be glad to arrange for an appointment. . . . He expects to get his compensation in a few weeks. But he said that won't solve his problem entirely, because he has to think of what will happen after he is well enough to go back to work. He is so afraid that he will not be able to do his old work, and that would mean starting all over again learning something else. I said that if he decided that he would want to talk those things over with the next worker here, he would have an opportunity to see what would be best. As he left my room he said he did not know what happened to him today, but he is glad he came, because he feels as if there is a load off his chest. . . .

In beginning a contact it is important to think whose problem the applicant is presenting. Did Mr. Arnold want help for himself in changing his situation, or was he putting it all off on his family or an unkind world? After his accident he saw everything going to pieces, and he did not seem able to take hold of anything. It is always important, when we find the applicant upset or disorganized, to try to estimate as soon as possible whether the response is chronic, a patterned reaction to life situations in general, or due to a temporary or immediate situation. Mr. A. seemed to have projected the responsibility for his trouble onto the whole world. The worker could not know at this point whether the projection was characteristic or not. Mr. Arnold was apparently feeling a deep sense of inadequacy, around which were all the fear, tenseness, and anger which he had shown in the interview, yet the experience of seeking help and of working on the eviction situation seemed to have given Mr. Arnold some feeling of being able to do things again. Whether Mr. Arnold's story is objectively true can be determined later. It is probably true for him. He can be, as here, accepted as a person, and his feelings as real feelings, without having his story accepted as fact. With a less defensive person factual clarification is always easier, but a factual basis, always important in starting, should have been attempted earlier than in this case.

One learns to see as well as to hear feeling tones, in behavior, in gesture, in appearance. One notices signs of anxiety, physical tension, hesitancy, irritation, annoyance, discouragement, and depressed moods. The student is first taught to notice the overt signs of emotion, but later to become sensitive to many shadings—ambivalence, defenses against feeling, resistance or the overcompliance which leaves the problem on the worker's lap in dependency or hostility. Often applicants show a great deal of capacity to manage even painful situations. A single interview in which the attitude shown is that of acceptance of the feeling with respect for the strength may be sufficient to set a person on his road.

An elderly woman, Mrs. Wilson, came to a voluntary agency because she feared to make application for an old age allowance on account of certain irregularity in her marriage status. She was encouraged to discuss her situation further.

Mrs. Wilson [8] leaned closer to us and said that we understood that she married only for companionship and she didn't feel like going through another court procedure. . . . She did not bother about legal documents. She did not care about it. In her application to the Old Age Security she had explained that she was a widow, that her present husband was a boarder. She also told them about the divorce. Mrs. Wilson explained that the gas and electric bills were listed under her husband's name and that the investigator would question her about it. What should she do? Worker explained the conditions under which old age assistance was given and that nothing would be done without her help in determining eligibility.

[8] From a family service agency.

Mrs. Wilson produced the various documents and displayed them on the desk. She looked absorbed and serious and said she wouldn't care if she didn't need the old age pension. Her husband doesn't care enough. He is a peddler. He barely makes enough for himself. He can stay with his son. She wouldn't want him to leave her. "You know how it is, not that I need him as a husband." Mrs. Wilson again asked what she could do to get the pension. The worker suggested that Mrs. Wilson must have given this a great deal of thought, and had she herself come to any decision about it? Mrs. Wilson said that she thought of explaining how the bills were not in Mrs. Wilson's way, since her rent receipts were in her own name. "Was there something else 'in the way'?" Mrs. Wilson said that she was worried about the fact that she had lied to the Old Age Division. When the investigator comes she'll have to tell her that the boarder is not her husband. She turned to us and pleadingly asked whether it was all right for her to "lie to the city." Worker said she was sorry not to advise her about this. What did she think? Mrs. Wilson smiled and said she understood. We couldn't tell her to go ahead and lie. She repeated, as if to herself, that she wanted the pension, that she needed it, and that she felt funny about deceiving the city, and it may come out. She repeated that we knew why she wouldn't bother about legal marriage. Worker smiled. Mrs. Wilson's face lit up as if in sudden inspiration. When the investigator comes if Mrs. Wilson decides to explain everything, what can they do to her? Her husband cannot support her. She has worked hard enough. She is a citizen and entitled to the pension. Mrs. Wilson reiterated that she had better tell them the truth, and when at the door she repeated in a soft tone of voice, as if whispering to us, "They can only say that I live in sin." Mrs. Wilson said that she had nothing to fear, and worker agreed with her. Mrs. Wilson thanked worker for her kindness and repeated that she appreciated the advice.

The worker said little in the above interview, partly because the woman was a self-reliant person who was headed in the direction which would get her out of her difficulty, and partly because in a conflict of this sort taking sides with the woman's conscience or against it would not help her make up her mind. Workers are sometimes tempted to reassure an applicant about a specific status before it is established. Thus, "I believe you will be eligible for old-age assistance," instead of explaining, as the caseworker did here, the conditions of eligibility in which the woman's marital status would not be relevant. Note also that the worker agreed that the woman had nothing to fear, rather than committing the public agency to a course of action. It is true that the caseworker could easily have given the woman more support, but that would have tended to tighten the relationship with the first agency, whereas the relationship should be firmly established between the caseworker in the public agency and the applicant. Caseworkers sometimes make the mistake of being too "understanding" when they are not going on with the case. The applicant here feels that she has been given valuable advice, yet is free to move along to a solution of her problem. If she needs further help with her marital problem, she will probably seek it later.

Focusing through the Request

On one hand, we focus by means of understanding and restating the chief *complaint*; on the other, we focus through the request—what the client wants to do and what he wants us to do about it. This, in a special way, makes the relationship a dynamic one because we meet the client at the point of greatest interest. We try to find out what was the client's expectation in coming. What brings him to us? Why today? Did someone suggest it? What crystalized his decision to make the move? Is he asking for a pension, or an insurance, or other assistance? What effort is he making to get what he needs? Does the mother think she wants to place her child or to procure a visiting homemaker when she enters the hospital for an operation? What does she anticipate in using the latter resource when we inform her of it?

As part of the discussion of the request, we interpret the services of the agency, but very simply and if possible in response to questions the client is asking, rather than in a routine general explanation. The request—the expectation—is thus related to what the worker, representing the agency, can do about it, and it introduces the client to the agency service in a realistic way. Clients do not easily grasp the function of a complex agency at first, especially if they are anxious and do not take in routine explanations of policy and procedure. Our initial interview should be in itself a demonstration of the way we work. Discussing the request to see what is in the client's mind and considering possible next steps together give the client an opportunity to "catch on," as the slang phrase has it. There was a time when the request was minimized in favor of discovering the "real" problem, but it is always wise first to explore the request and see where it leads. If the request is appropriate for the agency, one can move to meet it immediately; if the request is a disguise for hidden needs and feelings, exploration is more difficult, but in either event we take the conscious desire seriously and discuss it in a serious way. If the request should point to some other problem and to another form of treatment, this can be later formulated so as to see what the client wants to do about it. Many initial applications to a social agency are for some form of practical service. Such requests may have deeper roots, which may or may not need to be explored. Many are for help with interpersonal problems and behavior which involve long-range considerations.

A person may ask for an obvious service or for practical assistance because he does not know that social agencies offer other forms of treatment [9] for what bothers him. Since the overt request is usually the external aspect of the deeper problem, attention to it is the best as well as the most sensible approach. Whenever the request is presented as having two sides—if, for instance, the person asks and withdraws in the same breath or expresses opposing wishes—this is a fairly reliable clue to some sort of conflict: "I would like to place Johnny, but my husband doesn't want to": "I need a job, but I can't seem to find one I am suited to." Here, as part of the exploratory process, the worker *verbally recognizes the conflict*—restating it as the client has phrased it, but with the added emphasis of: "So where shall we come in to help you decide on this or that course of action? Perhaps we had better arrange some interviews to discuss this further." If the request is met, how much will it improve the real situation, or is the client asking for something which will not be a solution? This reservation may not be shared at the outset.

[9] See pp. 249–52 for counseling and therapy.

If the case has been referred by another agency, the client may not be sure why he has been sent, so that it is important to find out from him what he had in mind. This is often presented in terms of what he was "told at the other place." We need be less concerned as to what he was actually told than what he thinks he was told, since to us his version may express his wish or his fear. The worker must then discuss what he thinks he was told to see if it is what he himself wants. It may be presumed that since he has come here he did have some idea in his mind. Especially, knowing the functions of the other agency or worker, one must guard against making assumptions that one therefore knows all about the referral and how the client feels about it. Usually one lets the client understand that one knows there was a previous agency contact because of the importance of tying up the present experience with the past and finding out the meaning of the previous contact. The danger of working in the dark is in not knowing whether or not one is handicapped by the past experience in handling any significant reactions. If the client says resentfully, "but Miss X told you all about it in that letter or on the telephone, didn't she?" one may still say casually, "Yes, but I wonder if you and Miss X had the same impression as I" or "Tell me again so that I shall be sure to understand," being careful not to introduce leading questions. The worker does not try to force a request either by a dogged silence or a suave, "What can I do for you?" but actively tries to assist the client to express his preconceptions. There are exceptions, as when we have been already prepared for the reception of a sick or disturbed person and must take immediate action to help him, but in general the attempt to get the client to verbalize at the outset some aspect of his own ideas or request is sound. When clients have been ill-informed or have had fantasies about the agency and its services, their expectations may be out of proportion to what can be done for them either in general or by this agency in particular.

In applying for child guidance or child placement the parents are helped to see how the treatment will involve them and what their role will be. Advice as to the handling of the child is inhibited.

Instead a process of thinking, feeling, anticipating, and experiencing will be started. One should not harbor preconceptions against placement, but begin with the parental request, exploring this carefully enough to see what factors are really involved in this step and from what motivation. If this is done, we shall see fewer instances in which parents seem to start off cooperatively and then ease out of the picture or become destructive during the placement experience. If placement is the appropriate solution, one must be ready for skillful work with the parents. If placement is not the solution, there must be available sufficient resources to offer realistic solutions acceptable to the parent, for example, adequate financial assistance, homemaking service, or day care facilities, to relieve pressures.

Essential Social Facts

The client feels understood not only because of the attitude of acceptance and willingness to help shown through attention to his request, but because of relevant questions which convince him that the worker is taking an "intelligent interest" in his situation. The minimum essential is to get enough social facts to grasp the nature of the problem, establish "presumptive eligibility" for the service, and enable the next worker to carry on without having to ask obvious questions all over again. Clients will rarely resent, although they may occasionally resist, sensible questions in close connection with the problem they are consciously bringing up. If a problem of family relationship, one is likely to encounter areas of sensitivity quickly. We interview first in the areas of the client's expressed interest, noting painful spots as we proceed. Later, we can interview in the direction of psychological preoccupation, but at intake one asks about the psychosocial aspects of the problem which the client brings up, rather than encourages the giving of emotionally charged material. In getting specific facts the worker learns to use responsive interviewing techniques,[10] but unlike the questionnaire, which also aims to get specific facts and opinions. The worker must follow

[10] See pp. 57–61.

what the client is saying and explore in these terms. He must have acquired in his training and experience a body of knowledge about the things he probably needs to know, depending on the type of problem presented; he does not interview according to a pattern, but picks up the clues from what the applicant is telling and from the emotional overtones to get an adequate statement.

It takes a great deal of experience before the worker is able to ask the little relevant questions. "Housing is so expensive nowadays," says the client. "How much rent do you pay?" asks the worker, or "How are you meeting current expenses?" "I persuaded Bobby to come here with me." "What did you tell your little boy about bringing him here?" When the client has made some such vague remark, unconsciously or consciously designed to block further discussion of difficult subjects, the worker picks it up. "How was that?" "What happened then?" We explore around the "complaint." If a school problem, what has happened at school, the program, the teacher's attitude, what has the parent done about it; if a disability, when did he first notice it, how does it bother him, symptoms or pains, what has he done about it before, where has he been getting treatment or is thinking of getting treatment; if a financial request, relevant economic questions, status of employment, how has he been getting along, debts, to whom and how much, and so forth. One does not first establish a relationship and then get the facts. Getting the relevant facts tends to help establish the relationship, and vice versa. To ascertain the focal point of difficulty does not imply the application of pressure, and the client usually feels a sensation of relief when he knows that his problem is grasped at the outset. After a period of drifting (*circa* 1930–40), in which workers thought that the relationship would be inhibited by factual inquiry,[11] there has been a sensible return to a preliminary intake "outline" appropriate to the purpose of each particular agency,

[11] It is just as important to get a clear preliminary history in a child guidance clinic as in a public assistance agency; the content will vary to correspond with the nature of the problem, function of the agency, and so on, but a certain amount of psychosocial data will be needed for almost any type of agency and for any competent referral, purely "steering" and information excepted.

which the skilled worker uses flexibly in the first interview or two to achieve a factual base of operation. The client is encouraged to tell his story but the interviewer clarifies, elaborates and points it up.

While all application interviews are a joint enterprise in which worker and client try to determine the nature of the problem and whether the service asked for can be appropriately given, the public welfare agency, or the state hospital, or some other unit may have to get a considerable amount of information at intake in order to determine the status of "presumptive eligibility" and so reduce the number of unnecessary examinations. This is particularly true in rural areas, where long distances have to be covered. If an adequate inquiry is not made at once, the succeeding worker is burdened with pending cases and the client inconvenienced by the delay. In public welfare [12] agencies the intake process has two aspects: (*a*) sifting or screening, the purpose of which is to redirect those who have come to the wrong place and to record preliminary identifying data, and (*b*) the intake interview, or interviews, in which requirements are explained and needs discussed as part of, or usually in connection with, an application blank. Documentary proofs of eligibility may be furnished. In a small agency, these two procedures may be combined in the duties of a single interviewer; in a large agency, several interviewers will be concerned, following linked procedures. It is conceded that reception, clearance, and supplementary interviews, with resource or other technical consultants, if indicated, should involve as few interviewers as possible, so that the applicant need not repeat identification or eligibility data or feel that he is on an assembly line where no one treats him as an individual.

Whenever a restrictive requirement has to be explained, the worker accepts responsibility for the denying or limiting aspect of the agency's function, but recognizes any frustrated feeling on the part of the applicant. Limitations, flexible or arbitrary, exist in various degrees in all agencies. If regulations are too depriving,

[12] Illustration of public assistance intake is difficult unless one knows the statutory conditions for eligibility in each state and how the division of labor is allocated in case load. See Social Security Bulletins, Federal Security Agency, Social Security Administration, Washington, D.C.

perhaps they may be changed by appropriate joint staff and executive recommendation, but until the worker is able to face pressures and rigidities as part of his job he will not be free to help angry, resentful, or critical applicants.

Readiness to Use Help

Readiness to use help may be determined in part through discussion of the request together with our explanation of possible service. It is through discussion rather than through exposition that degrees of readiness may be ascertained.

A county institution had agreed to place Russell Blake, through a voluntary agency, and had sent a summary. The mother, who was unmarried, was anxious for a placement as soon as possible so that she could go to work. A careful explanation of what the agency could and could not do seemed to awaken real interest and effort in the mother, who had been described by the county office as erratic, casual about the baby, and not much to be depended upon.

I [13] had to take most of the responsibility for starting the interview. I told mother that I understood from Miss Brown that she was considering placing her baby with us. She immediately agreed. She did not ask any specific questions or volunteer anything regarding any feeling she might have about this plan. I asked if she understood what arrangements we made for children, and said that I was not sure just how much Miss Brown had talked to her about this. She said she thought she did know something about it, but she was interested in hearing more. I gave her a description of placement arrangements in general, bringing in our visiting the home and the purpose of that. She said she had known we kept in touch with the homes. The manner in which she said this indicated some understanding that this was a protection to the child. I then asked her if she thought that she would be likely to visit very often. She said, oh yes, she would want to keep in touch with her baby. I said that I thought that was something we would want to work on together to some extent, that for instance, we felt it was better to have some regular plan for visiting, particularly when a parent expected to be visiting frequently. There was another thing that we might want to talk about a little—we had found it worked much better for the child to have been in the home for a while before the parent visited (a brief

[13] From a child-placing agency.

explanation). She said that she could see that. I had mentioned two weeks as being a good time to elapse before a visit. This seemed a long time to her, in fact weekly visits seemed infrequent to her. She did not stress this point, but only mentioned it.

This was the first time that she had given any indication of beginning to understand what placement would mean, the separation, and having other people involved in planning for the baby. In the discussion of the reason for regularity in visiting she began to think about what it would mean to have a child related to a foster mother. There is a current trend to let the parent go with the child to the foster home in certain instances, much as parents stay with anxious children in school or nursery. Techniques in the process of separation must be flexibly adjusted both to the realities of the foster parents' situation and the psychology of child and parent.[14]

She said she certainly would not want her child not to know his own mother (the tone of her voice indicates dislike about this arrangement). I asked whether she had thought how long she might like to leave her baby with us. She said that she had not, that she certainly would like to have him some time, and wondered whether there would be any difficulty. I explained that we would take him only on the basis that she had asked us to do so, and that when she was prepared to care for him the thing for her to do would simply be to get in touch with us and the child could go directly from us to her. She was vague about our agency, and I illustrated the difference between arrangements with us and any sort of legal arrangement. She seemed to be satisfied.

There was careful discussion of the board rate and what she would be expected to pay on the basis of her wages. The support agreement—like the application blank it often helps to clarify responsibilities on both sides—was gone over with her and the procedure for medical care. Throughout this interview the intention was to try to involve the client responsibly in the process. She was able to react to this and became more "related" to the agency.

She asked when I thought we would be ready to take the baby, and I told her we would do that this week. She then thought for a moment. "Then

14 See pp. 281–83 for the separation experience.

I won't see the home before the baby goes into it?" I said no, that this was one of the areas where she would have to trust us. She smiled and said, "Well, I guess that's all right, you couldn't have all the parents look over the homes before the children are placed." I said that we did put a great deal of thought and care into the choice of a home for a child; that we knew what was available to us and tried to pick the best home for a particular child. She said, "Well, I guess that's your job." I told her that if, after she visited and got acquainted with the foster mother she had any questions she wished to discuss with us we would always be glad to see her. I then suggested that after we took the baby she write us when she would like to visit, and we would at that time make arrangements with foster mother and send her the address and directions for reaching the home. As she was leaving she said, "Then I'm to get in touch with you after the baby goes?" I said yes.

Willingness to discuss reality aspects of the problem is often a clue to the client's readiness to use help, to work on his problem, and the like, but there are many allowances which must be made if the client is dull, ill, frightened, has a language handicap, or is otherwise slow to give information. But if an experienced worker encounters unusually severe blocking in answering relevant and common-sense questions, if there are discrepancies, excessive phantasy, or defenses, one must assume that there are special problems of ambivalence and resistance, immaturity or other complications.

Verbal reassurance in general platitudes is rarely effective. The worker who says to the applicant, "I think you have been wonderfully courageous about your troubles, and I am sure you will win out," doesn't help the person who, under a compensatory brave front is feeling small and helpless and tired of trying to be brave. Likewise, if one says to a lad who has been committing anti-social gang acts, "I know you are the sort who wants to do right," the boy is effectively stopped from telling us how badly he behaves or sometimes wants to behave. It isn't easy to live up to people's good opinion of us, and it is no easier to live up to the caseworker's. Part of the treatment objective is greater acceptance by the client of his "real self," as well as of a real world. But it is the make-believe self or some role assumed by the self that is often put forward when one is in difficulty. In early contacts reassurance should in general be limited to letting the applicant know of our interest and willingness to help him resolve his difficulties, to reserve time for later appointments with him, and to plan specifically for the next steps to be taken together. In fact, there has to be enough tension to stimulate the client to go on. A drop in tension occurs at best from experiencing a gradual release of feeling in successive interviews and in making headway with one's own efforts at a constructive solution.

A boy nine years old, with conduct problems at school, when asked what he thought he was coming to the agency for, replied anxiously: "I have fallen arches and as soon as they are treated they will be all right." He insisted that he got along well at school, at home, and particularly with other boys. The boys all like him; he has a wonderful time playing with them. When the worker, careful not to puncture these defenses, asks him gently what he does with his time at home, he reports a full day listening to the radio and reading by himself. Catching the faint admission of loneliness, she asks how he likes spending so much time reading, or is he perhaps unhappy, too, sometimes, it comes out with a rush that he is terribly unhappy because the other boys don't like him, never ask him to play with them. He expresses a desire to be helped, and eagerly makes another appointment. Yet when he comes in the second time he again says there is no problem; his fallen arches are better because of his new shoes, so that he need not go on. The worker has to begin, arches and all, to help this fearful child edge slowly into treatment, yet the important thing to encourage at the moment is that he should come and so be helped to venture further.

Reassurance implying the worker's willingness to try to understand and to help, which is sound practice, should be distinguished from attempts to allay the anxiety the client has about himself and his problems. At intake we want the person to use the anxiety to go on with treatment, and the first move is to channelize it in our direction so that his concern will become fused in our concern for him. Children, like adults, may show initial resistance which must be understood clinically and culturally by the worker, not approached in a controlling manner.

RESISTANCE AND DEFENSES [15]

Emphasis has shifted from giving a practical service to *involving* the client in using the service or the treatment. One is not offering a commodity to a recipient, but sharing a service or an experience. One might say that the characteristic aspect of social casework is the skill employed in mobilizing the client's strengths for an active, participating role. This is reflected in the efforts to encourage him to tell his story and to discuss his request fully and frankly with him; to enlist his cooperation in establishing his eligibility; to explain and discuss the services, policies, and procedures applicable to the occasion; and so forth. The client's wish to do something about his problem is accredited rather than his reason for doing so challenged; further activity is encouraged, and next steps are worked out together. Learning how he has managed his life heretofore is helpful in appraising his current strengths. But although it is recognized that application is a way of starting to do something to solve one's problem, some need much more help than others in "putting it through," and the possibility of ambivalence—the client's both wanting and not wanting to move ahead—must be allowed for. Some clients, indeed, do not want what they ask for and, especially if they have to put anything into the solution, will tend to withdraw. The phenomenon of resistance must, therefore, be considered. It may occur early or be aroused at any point in the treatment.

The normal ego uses many defenses [16] both consciously and unconsciously, to protect itself from harm or criticism or anxiety —such mechanisms as displacement, identification with the aggressor, reaction formation, denial and evasion, projection of the blame on others are familiar. "Resistance" means using these and other defenses against yielding to the treatment experience. Often a person must be willing to lay aside some of his defenses in order to be helped. Resistance may be mobilized the moment the client glimpses what is involved in solving his problem. He may not

[15] See also pp. 266–67.
[16] Freud, Anna, *The Ego and the Mechanisms of Defense.*

want to meet the conditions of eligibility; still less may he want to change his behavior toward spouse or child. Often parents who come with a great sense of failure about a problem child, as soon as they notice how they are to be involved in the treatment, will withdraw saying that the child is behaving better, or giving some other excuse.

In marital or parent-child counseling the first phase may appear as "Something is wrong with my child, or my husband"; later, "Something is wrong with me; help me to behave differently"; but when one really embarks on a course of treatment, a counter-current is set up in the client which pulls to keep the worker away from the problem and fights to keep the problem or the symptom intact. This is because the situation would not have been created if it had not answered some need of the personality; and it is hard to relinquish immature satisfactions and secondary gains. This occurs more often when the complaints are neurotically tinged than when they are objective physical or economic needs. Sometimes a single interview or a few interviews prove genuinely helpful, but quite as often the push toward early termination means resistance against going on with the struggle. Resistance may die down and flare up again. Verbal recognition of the client's negative feelings is occasionally helpful, but this can prove unfortunate if it is attempted before one is sure what the resistance means. Neither false reassurance nor "bringing out the negative" in early phases seems as useful in general as a friendly and matter-of-fact assumption that he has come for a purpose with which we are disposed to help. A good rule is not to guess at resistance or negative feelings, but find out through sensitive, well-timed interviewing about the quality of affect accompanying the words or behavior—that is, of conscious desires and attitudes.

Initial resistance is usually born of insecurity, fear of the unknown or of the terms to be met, and may be increased by cultural unfamiliarity with the procedures. For the most part, attention and friendly interest suffice to resolve initial resistance, unless it has far deeper roots. Initial resistance may be personal or cultural or both. The person is ashamed to admit what seems to him to be failure to manage his own affairs. Moreover, many of the problems with which social workers are concerned are culturally stigmatized. Poverty, unemployment, unmarried motherhood, mental illness and neurosis, inability to manage one's affairs or one's children, delinquency, are to one degree or another frowned upon by the community. Being one of a minority group may have aroused fears of and defenses against the dominant group. These factors, added to the common fear of the unfamiliar, make applicants falter and give information with extreme caution. Courtesy, quick attention, explanation of necessary delays, recognition of the right to apply, privacy and quiet for the interview tend to reduce early defensiveness and resistance. Genuine kindness and consideration shown by the personnel, from the switchboard operator to the porter, give clients that first glimpse of "acceptance" which is so fundamental a part of the whole treatment.

Although any application is a step in starting to do something about one's problems which should be encouraged, the motive is certainly not unadulterated desire; the worker must be ready to handle ambivalence and other difficult initial attitudes. Applicants are likely to be resistive. They have no reason to trust the worker's good will, his sincere interest, or his readiness to try to help. They have many defenses against their own impulses and feelings. One may blame the situation on others, or one may anticipate criticism by excessive self-blame, or one may be very submissive or actively on the offensive. As a person comes to trust he will gradually lay aside these and other defenses and reveal more of his true circumstances and himself, since there are no "rules of evidence" to which he must conform, and he finds his defenses are not challenged or punctured, although obvious resistance will usually be commented upon. Resistance and defenses, however, may make a person inaccessible, as in the following illustration:

A settlement house referred a 16-year-old girl, to determine whether sending her to work camp for the summer was a suitable plan. The girl was disturbed, a truant, talked and walked in her sleep, had nightmares, was provocative toward her mother, was unhappy, had run away from home, had sex conflicts.

Her mother came in first, gave some history, showed uneasiness about the girl and her problems. Her father was said to be somewhat resistive about coming in, asking "who will she blame."

The girl came promptly for her appointment with the intake worker, bringing another girl with her. She is an attractive adolescent, casual but friendly in manner. She showed indecision, at first had thought she wouldn't come in, and wanted to know what it was all about. Could she talk freely, or would caseworker repeat everything to her mother? "Whose side are you on, mine or my family's?" She was given reassurance that caseworker was interested in her, and told that all material was treated confidentially. She then told that her mother "has a tongue like a shrew, but she gives her as good as she sends." Everything at home provokes controversy, especially between her and her mother. The difficulties with her mother used to trouble her, but not now. It was obvious that she got considerable satisfaction out of telling her mother off. She expressed pity for her father, saying he is a weak person. . . . She says she often feels insecure at home; thinks of running away again. The caseworker says it looked as if she needed to come to terms with herself and to find security; we may be able to help her with this.

The girl then tells something more of her hesitation about coming in; had quarreled about it with the family the night before; expresses fear that worker will take sides and tell parents what she says. "Now if you come and talk with me, what do you think I would do? Whom would I tell?" the worker asked smilingly. The girl smiled, but still doubtfully.

The girl then asked if she could bring her friend into the interviewing room. The caseworker smilingly explained that she would be glad to see her friend, but that she would not work that way in further interviews, pointing out the fact that she had brought this other girl to cover her fear and mistrust. At the end of the interview both girls appeared to want to come in again. Caseworker reverts to discussion of girl's resistance, asks if she wants to come back. She says that she does, but says that she will probably continue to bring out objections. The worker says that very likely she will at first.

In the second interview with the caseworker the client starts by being passively resistive. She says her mind is a blank; that she finds it difficult to talk of things that matter. This is why she brought in her girl friend before.

Actually the friend was brought for protection against revealing herself, and resistance continued to be mobilized against treatment. Since she was reinforced by the parents, treatment could not be successfully undertaken here.

Often relatives of mentally ill patients are so guilty that it is hard for them to accept help with their own feelings. The defense of being a good parent is unconsciously used. One does not want to reduce all the guilt at the outset, as it is necessary for them to work at the problem of changing their attitudes toward the patient. Only long practice makes the worker at all sure-footed in keeping the necessary balance between tension and relief from anxiety.

The mother of a schizophrenic adolescent came to the hospital and began to talk about her feelings surrounding patient's illness. (She wanted to get assurance from worker that she actually was not guilty for patient's illness.) Mother stated that she never had the faintest inkling that there was something wrong with patient. He used to play baseball, football, was a counselor at camp. However, his fears did not come till the evening, and then naturally mother was not around. Mother blames herself for having been too close to patient. All her life she has been wrapped up in her two children. She had so many problems of her own that the children were her only consolation. She now knows that was very wrong (self-accusation as a defense). She never gave patient an opportunity to grow up, because whenever he came to her for advice she gave it to him. However, now she has decided to let patient make up his own mind about various things.

Worker said that she probably did at that time what she thought was right. However, now she has changed somewhat and perhaps does not want to act that way, but it is not easy for people to change. Mother nodded her head and said that it has not been easy, but she is now convinced that she has to let patient free, because he is grown up and has to be an individual on his own. It was not even so much a matter of the patient as a matter of the girl he would some day marry. Unless she is a good mother to him, he will never be a good husband.

The patient was a very good boy. He did not drink, smoke to excess, play cards, or use bad language. She was brought up that way and wanted her son to have the same high standards. Didn't worker think that was correct? Worker asked mother why she asked that question? Mother said that she has been wondering whether maybe she had not been too strict in some areas with patient.

Such a conscientious but managing mother will need much support from the worker before she can face the hostility which is underneath her "good intentions." Her guilt can easily prove overwhelming to her. A violently negative attitude initially does not always mean inaccessibility or poor prognosis, as in the following example.

An eighteen-year-old boy, John W., was referred by the high school because he was unhappy at home, had few friends, always had a chip on his shoulder. He was said to be bright, but very hard to reach. The boy requested to be referred to a residence club and let alone. When the intake worker gently explored the request, he said it was his father who wanted him to get out; that there was constant quarreling between them, as each had a very bad temper. When the club regulations were explained (the requirements were immediately resented as a frustration) John became very angry, saying that he did not wish any investigators to snoop into his business. As the boy continued to be resistive, the worker asked in a friendly way about his school interests and drew out his hopes for college, his fear of failure, of his father's pressure, and of his desire to earn money so that he could go to night school.

He asked about recreational facilities at the club, which were discussed. John said that he did not know whether he would be interested. He did not want to be forced to join them. There was something else he did not understand. Miss Chase had told him that the Board at the club reviews all admissions; why was that done? This was explained to him in terms of determining to what extent the club might help each individual boy. John could not understand how a Board could pass on applications when they did not know the boys. Worker said that was the reason the boys were referred to us, and indicated that although John did not have to come here for help, she would like to see him get help, since he was quite unhappy. He stated that Miss Chase had told him that he ought to go to the club, where he would find friends and where he could be more gregarious; that he ought to be more gregarious. Why should he be gregarious? John demanded. Worker said, smiling, "Is it always so important to be gregarious?" If John is happier living with himself, then nobody should try to interfere. John fairly shouted, "This is not so, I like people." The worker asked why, if he likes people, does he not find friends? John replied that he does not get along with people because he is shy and afraid that they will not like him; for that reason he fears to approach them.

He then stated defiantly that he is not a delinquent, and asked why he should come here? Worker asked him to explain what he meant by this. He replied that his mother had read in the newspapers that the organization was a place for delinquents. Worker explained that we also helped young people who are withdrawn and shy. John stated with feeling that his mother had said that we would send investigators around to the home, snooping into their private business. Worker told the boy that boys and girls were seen here at the office, that parents were seen here, and that homes were not visited unless someone made the request. John seemed to accept this explanation and suddenly said that he did not know exactly what to do; what did worker advise him to do? Worker told him that he ought to come here, that he needed someone who was interested in him to whom he could talk. He was entitled to such a relationship. It was very difficult for him to go along without someone who would give him friendship and understanding; that he, like anyone else, needed someone who would not let him down.

After some hesitation John stated that he thought he might try it for a while. He really did not need help in finding a job, he could figure that out for himself, but he thought he might try help with "the other things." Worker told John that we would be very much interested in giving him this help, but suggested that he go home, discuss the situation with his mother, tell her about us, and return to the agency the following week.

John returned a week later. He appeared to be quite depressed. His defiant manner had disappeared, and he gave the impression of being a very disturbed boy. He talked in a low monotonous voice as though he had little energy. After a short talk he was informed that his own worker would get in touch with him very soon. He asked who his worker would be and how soon he would be able to see him. He was then introduced to his caseworker.

John accepted a program of regular appointments with a caseworker and made headway with his problems. He assumed some responsibility for his part in the home difficulties, which was hopeful. The defensiveness and anger which he showed against "investigators" (the intake worker) who would "snoop into his business" was his habitual reaction to the pressure put on him by his father. John is a withdrawn boy with deep-rooted fears, who does not easily relate himself to others so that the intake worker must go out to him. Anger and critical reactions are not necessarily an indication that the applicant is rejecting help. In fact, quite the opposite, as here, may be true. The worker, perhaps too quickly, touched an area of great anxiety—John's withdrawal and fear of "gregariousness," his defense that he liked to be alone—but the boy's need to be helped was even greater than his fear of being helped. Another worker might have let it go with a gentle, "this gregarious idea worries you," and the defensive reaction might have been lessened. We can assume from the outcome that John responded to the worker's reaching that part of him which was well enough to use the services, once he understood what was being offered him, and that the response was made possible by the genuine sympathy with his suffering.

Resistance may be shown by refusing to give the necessary information or by a rush of talk which overwhelms the worker; by specious reasons for delay; unusual difficulties in finding time for appointments; criticism and doubts about other agencies; and so forth. The intake worker has to be skillful both in disarming initial resistance and in accepting the client's right to withdraw after discussion if he wishes. Even when the worker's handling has been skillful, a client may not continue in treatment, because his anxiety drives him away. Denial that a problem exists (when patently it does) often means that the client does not wish the worker to go too far into the situation, extreme helplessness and hopelessness in the face of proposed alternatives, extreme projection onto others for the difficulty or for the need to change, repetitive presentation of obstacles to inquiry or treatment, constant intellectualization, barriers of garrulous talk or empty terminology, and clichés of the "once bitten, twice shy" variety may warn the worker of the strength of the defenses. Confronted by such evidence it is often better to focus directly on the resistance. "What do you think anyone can do about this?" "How could such a situation be changed?" "How do you think I could help you?" Otherwise, attempts to get relevant history and to explain possible services will fall on stony ground. If the client gives any indication of what he thinks might be done,

one is more likely to be able to proceed in the usual way to discuss the immediate request and if feasible to offer further appointments to take care of the concrete realities involved—the request. The first frame of reference is usually a social service, if indicated, or appointments to discuss the problem and complaint so that the client may know clearly why he comes here. Only such resistance phenomena are actively handled as will block the client from going on at this time. Sometimes extreme self-blame or self-reproach is used defensively as resistance—the person wanting to be assured that he has no responsibility at all for the problem. If this is understood as resistance the worker will be more likely to help moderate the totality of the enveloping self-protective attitude.

Emergency and Urgency

An early diagnostic expedient is to appraise how severe the reality situation is and how troubled the person. Almost everyone piles up a certain amount of tension about going to an agency for help, and once there expects the worker to do something about it at once, being greatly frustrated by a waiting period. There is no easy answer if case loads are heavy and assignment of pending cases necessarily slow. Except in times of overwhelming distress the feeling of frustration can often be reduced by frank discussion of the agency's limitations, by definite rather than indefinite arrangements for later interviews or, if feasible, for care through another community agency. Real emergencies and cases of psychological urgency must be distinguished from the general run of applications, and more prompt intervention must be attempted.

Young workers are likely to think of situations, especially when they involve practical deprivation, as emergencies. There are, of course, emergencies, but in most applications the matter is more likely to be urgent in the sense that something should be done than to be emergent, in the sense that something must be done instantly. Even when emergencies do occur, the caseworker who has been in the habit of stopping to find out what the client has done or wants to have done is more likely to take time to do the right thing. A young worker learned something useful from the following experience.

A man being discharged from the hospital, when he was still quite weak after a serious illness, was referred late in the afternoon to a caseworker. He gave a most dramatic and pitiful account of his troubles. He had been living with his sister, and they both were working. He had developed this present illness, which had used up all his savings. His sister had also, at the same time, become ill with appendicitis, and while he was in one hospital she had been rushed to another for an operation; and while they both were in the hospital the apartment house where they lived together had burned down. The caseworker, appalled by all their calamities said: "Well, we can send you to one of our convalescent shelters. I'll call up and see if there is room." She came back in a minute and said, "They are all full, would you object to such and such a place? It's pretty late to make arrangements tonight." The client said, "No, madam." The caseworker arranged for his care in another shelter and sent him off with $5.00 in a taxi. The next week another worker saw him by chance in the follow-up clinic. "How did you like X House?" she asked conversationally. The man hesitated, "Please, madam, I do not like to tell you—that worker she was so kind." "Was it as bad as all that? I'm sure we'd want to know about it." "Oh, no, madam, but you see I did not go there." "You didn't go there? I thought your house had burned down!" "You see, madam," said the man apologetically, "I do not like any of those institution places." "What on earth did you do?" Still more apologetically, "I went to my brother's, madam, but the other worker was so kind, I did not like to tell her that I did not want to go to her place."

It is possible to do too much and to act too quickly, just as it is possible to reassure too much, or to interpret too much, or to precipitate too much. It is in so-called "emergencies" that the temptation to take the problem away from the client is greatest; just as when emotional needs are great, the applicant may project them upon the unwary worker because the needs are so appealing. Yet the experienced caseworker who has learned not to "play providence" will be able to take responsibility for quick decisive action or vigorous emotional support whenever necessary. When applicants are acutely ill or frightened or otherwise incapacitated, we must take active responsibility until they are well enough to take over the problem and themselves go on with it.

ALLOCATION OR REFERRAL [17]

At intake the worker is cautious about committing his own or another agency, if the case is to be referred, to a course of action, but rather clarifies the nature of the problems as initially seen, restating or reformulating what the applicant has said, designating an area in which the treatment or service can be offered, and defining clearly in specific ways so that the client can easily grasp the next steps in procedure, data needed, time and purpose of further appointments, and preparation for another worker or agency. The caseworker may hold over certain cases at "intake," but when assignment is made, the client is told that he will be seeing someone else. This statement should not be perfunctory, and if transfer is to be helpful there should be a link between the caseworker and the one who will subsequently carry the case. The connection is evident to the client because of the way in which the appointment is made, the second worker's grasp of the information already given, and his knowledge of where to begin his initial interview.

In the intake interview or interviews a process of study and exploration is started which, by establishing with the client a relationship, helps him mobilize his energies and resources to do something about his situation. The worker secures relevant factual data, clarifying to him and meaningful to the client, so that the predicament is understood, at least in part, by both the caseworker and the client. The worker explores the nature of the situation which brings the person to a particular agency, what the person wants to do about his problem, or what he wants us to do, and whether it lies within the scope of the agency's function to care for the request. The worker makes also some preliminary estimate of the person's ability to help himself—that is, whether he has any ability to use what the agency has to give in meeting his problem. Intake has a tentative diagnostic and evaluative function, and it is common for agencies to place

[17] See also pp. 129–31.

experienced and competent workers in charge of the application procedure, because thereby so much time, energy, and emotion can be saved.

The content of initial interviews should not be so exhaustive as to make the client overanxious or to seem to settle the matter so that he will have no impulse to maintain contact unless, as is sometimes true, the problem can actually be solved simply and quickly in an interview or two. Thoughtful exploration at intake is in itself a skilled brief, "short-contact" service through which the client's need may either be met or result in a carefully based referral to another institution or facility able to cope with the situation. If the sifting process justifies the acceptance of the case by the first agency rather than a referral to another, further study will be necessary. Such study may be carried on by means of a series of interviews with the client and his family, or it may be effected in part by observational visits and the use of references and collateral sources of information. In this way we may see more clearly what complications, if any, are involved in the initial situation and which of them must be worked through in order to meet the need the client has outlined. Sometimes the need is simple and obvious and can be met directly on the basis of the worker's immediate recognition and quick diagnosis.

Fortunately casework can treat some problems which are not fully understood, although the method characteristically does not dispense authoritative directions. Many needs, obvious and concrete, can be dealt with by the client himself after resources have been made available, but most needs, perhaps, are not. The purpose of further observation and study is quite as much to tell us what not to do and what to leave alone, as to tell us what to do. Methods of subsequent exploration will be discussed in the succeeding chapter.

CHAPTER VII

METHODS OF CASE STUDY

ALL EXPLORATION or investigation is for the purpose of coming to a better understanding of the person who has the problem, as well as of the problem itself, in order to engage in effective treatment. Since the term "investigation," which means "steps inwards" (toward understanding), has come to have unpleasant connotations we prefer "study" for the over-all concept. In the situation, significant people and events in the client's life experience and his feeling toward them constitute the unit of attention.[1] These circumstances and the client's chief emotional attitudes may be studied as condensed and refracted through the facets of worker-client interaction, as well as through objective observation and inquiry. In casework all investigation is a psychosocial process. Before interviewing was mastered as a primary technique for study and treatment, workers, after taking a comprehensive "first interview," visited the home, the neighborhood, and various independent references for facts and verification. Later there was a tendency to minimize objective inquiry, deriving facts and impressions from the face-to-face interview alone. Currently, however, we try to keep a balance between the client as primary informant and other reliable sources, enlisting the client's participation in such investigation.

In one sense "intake" may be regarded as the first phase of social study, but in another, intake, as we said in the last chapter, is a microcosm of the whole casework process. We listen with interest and attention to the client's own story of his situation; we work with the request to see where it will lead and whether it is appropri-

[1] Sytz, "Unit of Attention in the Casework Process," *Journal of Social Casework,* XVII (June, 1946), 135.

ate for our agency; we explain to him what we need to know in order to understand his problem; we acquaint him with our services, our limitations, our methods of approach, and notice and respond to his reactions. Through these and other devices we make him feel more comfortable and "related" to us in our professional role; we focus with him the principal area of difficulty; we estimate in a preliminary way what sort of treatment he wants and needs and to some extent his readiness to use help. As the exploration is continued, whether with the same worker or another (since a different worker is often allocated to the case after intake),[2] the procedure is extended and the relationship deepened. Careful perusal of the recorded material, however, guards the worker and the client against repetition of the same information.

TOOLS AND TECHNIQUES IN THE STUDY PROCESS

The means of exploration are: interviews with the client and those significantly involved in his situation, contacts with selected aspects of the client's economic, cultural, and social milieu, such as his home, his occupational, educational, religious, and recreational associations and with medical or social agencies and institutions (as indicated). Records and documents have a special place; tests and examinations may be valuable instruments. "Collateral" sources are those aside from the client himself or his immediate family group. As a casework process, social study rests upon skilled use of the relationship to involve the client and his family, when appropriate, in a shared experience, and always with their consent.

At intake we prepare the client frankly for the succeeding procedures and help him to engage actively in the subsequent steps. We are afraid neither to ask specific relevant questions nor to propose further inquiry, because the client wants us to understand him and his problem and is usually gratified if we can grasp quickly what his difficulty is. True, the client will at some points show reluctance or resistance, but in the main he tends to respond positively to genuine interest and appropriate exploration. At the outset

[2] See pp. 48–50.

most persons respond well to a clear explanation of procedures designed to clarify the problem and so put us on the road to a solution together.

Situation and History

Especially at first, it is important to get enough factual material to facilitate understanding the present situation and what the person has done and now wants us to do about it. Whatever groupings of facts relevant to the particular problem and request are to be elicited, we always want the current situation elaborated by specific details—the immediate onset and precipitating factors of the difficulty; how the client has managed in the past, and something about the significant persons involved in the problem. The method of study, or rather the combinations of methods, must be adapted to these considerations. The skilled worker who has mastered the main approaches will make whatever adjustments are necessary, but short-cuts should be reserved for the experienced.

Case study includes as an essential component how the individual is affected by and affects his cultural milieu. Diagnosis becomes clearer and more penetrating as socio-economic, psychological, and cultural factors are analyzed in relation to their interrelated meaning for the individual and the family. Treatment plan and activity flexibly geared to this total understanding become possible, and the worker is freer to move with the client, meet his needs, and help him make choices and act toward the achievement of his goals. Knowing what the client has already done about this problem, how he has managed before he came to us, not only saves the interviewer from missteps but also furnishes valuable hints as to the client's capacity or incapacity to manage his affairs now. Appropriate history-taking not only is essential to sound evaluation but also may keep one from getting involved in premature or wrong treatment.

The interview *can* motivate, *can* teach, *can* secure information, *can* help clients to bring out things which are bothering them. The interview provides one of the best ways of observing a person's behavior. It is a good way to get facts about a particular set of circumstances; it is almost the only way to achieve an understanding of attitudes and feelings—the unique reaction of the individual to his situation. Because the case is made up of inner as well as outer factors, the person's ability to talk about his feelings, as well as about the objective facts of his situation, heightens the importance of the interview. It would be hard for the caseworker to differentiate what he learns through the ear from that which he learns through the eye. Although one can observe without interviewing, one rarely interviews without observing. Motivation is often unconscious, but the client admits us to at least partial understanding of his emotional problems by his tone, his attitudes, his behavior, and by his manner of telling about his experience; by his silences, denials, projections, and other defenses. Interviewing and the accompanying observation, therefore, are relied upon to provide much of the case data. Repeated interviews offer reliable data which the single interview can rarely achieve. The well-trained eye and ear become astonishingly accurate, not only in noting significance in the objective situation but also in catching the inflections of the emotional tone. Observation of the client's behavior in the interview itself, his feelings of adequacy or dependency, his fears and irritations, compliance or aggression, his way of relating himself to the worker and the agency, and signs of strength or weakness are means toward appraisal of his social functioning and capacity for adaptation.

Part of the discipline for achieving a "social level of perception" lies in practicing the art of history-taking. Just as it is difficult to write a good short record before one has learned to write a good long one, so it is true that students who have not learned to elicit patiently and accurately the details of a cultural economic picture, developmental and early childhood material, work and health history, family and other natural-group associations are poorly equipped to evaluate experiences when the client gives them piecemeal. The worker whose professional education has specialized in psychiatric and psychological disciplines, with good understanding of the motivation of behavior and attitudes, may yet be little in touch with social realities. The worker who can budget with skill and accuracy, who knows economic conditions well, may not have sufficient grasp of personality growth and development. Familiarity with norms, both in the areas of standards of living and personal and cultural behavior, must underlie any real skill in the eclectic taking of history. It is, therefore, as important for the student to master outlines for taking history and charting the main courses of social functioning, as for the biologist to know the blood stream. There are two aspects or phases in history: (a) initial history for diagnosis and focus, which is readily obtained in the first contacts, and (b) history as abreaction or reliving certain emotional experiences, which comes much more slowly and should be regarded as within the treatment process.[3]

The keener one's diagnostic sense, the more relevant and economical will be history-taking and other means of social study. We interview responsively, moving from the surface to deeper levels, from now to what happened to bring "now" about, and do not begin with the lives of the grandparents in the style of "once upon a time." Specific details related to the problem for which the client is seeking help may be actively sought and are, in most instances, readily given. Some knowledge of a person's early experiences, family and group associations, and general mode of life may or may not be necessary in order to understand even the immediate problem, but whenever the problem appears to involve lack of adaptation in behavior and relationships a fuller inquiry is usually indicated. Social history is important because life is not a matter of disjointed and fragmentary episodes, but a continuous flow [4] in which cause-and-effect relationships may be found. In social problems the worker must determine how much can be explained by present conditions to which the person's behavior is a normal reaction, and how much

[3] It is not necessary to illustrate a psychosocial history, since there are now publications which give extensive case material.

[4] In Doctor and Social Worker, p. 29, Richard Cabot opposed the "catastrophic," or "accident," with the historic point of view, pointing out that the supposed accident "belongs in a long sequence, a chain of events, so that it is impossible to understand or to help it without knowledge, as extensive as our time and wisdom will allow."

is part of the life pattern in which the main trends were shaped early and so become part of the character.

In problems of disturbed emotional balance an accurate account of the main events and the most significant persons in the life history must be secured. A central point of inquiry is always the family constellation, especially the parent-child relationship, since many of the causal factors are to be found here. Often both "partners," parent-child, or spouse should be interviewed to evaluate their positions in the situation. Recognition that everyone has an organic and systematized life experience and knowledge of personality should not prevent us from obtaining data about the immediate events so we shall at least know where to begin. But unless the problem is quite obvious and simple we shall need further facts to aid our understanding. If the problem is to establish eligibility for some form of social assistance, the exploration may be directed largely to current practical and economic facts in the social environment. If the problem appears to be uncomplicated by conflict, anxiety, or overtones suggesting personal involvement, the "history" may be mainly questions aimed to clarify the precipitating factors. Other brief histories may be topical—work history if job placement is asked, health history if medical referral is sought, technical migration data if the client seeks advice about entrance into another country. In remembering that the person accumulates experience through facing one situation after another, one should not overlook that most significant situation which brought him to us—the situation in which he is now seeking help.

Home Study and Observation

In many instances an observant interview in the home may help us understand the circumstances better than in an office setting. Men live in a social world—they have homes; they go to school and to church; they lie in hospital beds; they have employers and friends and companions, neighbors and relatives. It is difficult to have interviews about people, and the difficulties are by no means all concerned with unreliability. Anyone who has gone home with a school acquaintance to spend the holidays knows what a new impression one is likely to get of one's friend. It is not always necessary to make home visits, but for certain objectives there is no real substitute for seeing a person in his home. As always, the nature of the problem and the needs of the client condition the selection of method of study. For instance, it is more pertinent to observe the home conditions of a chronically ill patient or a young child than those of a self-directing adult with an employment problem. Prior to discharge from an institution, particularly an institution for delinquents, it is customary to observe the kind of home environment and associations which the client will enter.

Since it is valuable to observe patients in their normal settings,[5] if a rounded approach to the appraisal of social capacity is important for the physician, how obviously essential it is for the social worker to maintain differential, but also a wide range of, approaches to environmental study. Home visits are sometimes specified under the law in public assistance or parole, and sometimes not; but the number and timing of visits should be a matter of regulation, not of law, with sufficient discretion allowed the operating agency.[6]

When placing a child, the prospective home will be carefully studied and evaluated,[7] including social data, cultural data, and the attitudes of the foster parents. In granting assistance, a voluntary agency will have more latitude about timing a projected home visit than is possible for the public agency, but each should be allowed reasonable discretion. Home visits may be embarrassing to clients, since neighbors can almost always "spot" the investigator. Explaining to the client the reason for the visit and, whenever practicable, getting the client to invite the worker and set the time for the appointment mitigates the discomfort. As the socializing of assistance as a right is gradually accomplished, the visit of the investigator will finally carry no more stigma than that of a doctor, a

[5] G. Canby Robinson, *The Patient as a Person,* p. 390 *et seq.*
[6] It is generally considered best for the law to confine itself to the principle—leaving the procedures for administrative regulation.
[7] See pp. 281–87.

county agent, or a trained nurse. Beginning workers tend to make too many hasty or unplanned home visits either at first or in a follow-up investigation, confusing effort with effectiveness. At one time even in voluntary agencies the practice of visiting every month was common, "to see how the family was getting along." But such routine follow-up is seldom justified. There was a time when case-workers had to examine every phase of the client's relationships—home, school, employment, church, social life; then, as a reaction, studies were conducted almost entirely by the device of the office interview. Neither extreme was successful. Among the various devices, such as direct interviews with the client, collateral sources, contacts with the "client-group," with experts, and through correspondence and records, the most desirable should be selected.

The office setting offers advantages for certain interviews, and the tendency to equip the agency with private booths and proper interview facilities is spreading. Most adults find discussion of their more intimate concerns easier in the impersonal atmosphere of the office—confidentiality is assured, interruption by family and friends prevented, and in general a professional objective level is maintained. There is no rule about this, however, and rigid adherence to office schedules may suggest that more attention is being paid to the convenience of the worker than the convenience of the client and the needs of the case.

There has been a growing tendency to observe the interaction of a mother with her baby—to notice the "group process" in families at home, or children in a play or a school group, or the interaction of patients in a ward. In many instances it is more fruitful to observe behavior in a group than in the individual play interview, but much can be learned about the personality by close attention to tone, gestures, and behavior in the face-to-face experience. For obvious reasons, interviews with children are only incidentally concerned with "history," and many interviews with young children combine some features of planned play activities as an aid to diagnosis. Although caseworkers commonly observe children in their natural settings, such as home, foster home, school, day nursery, playground, or institution, for little children the play interview is one of the best means of discovering his feelings and his home problem. The objective is not to "interpret" the symbols used in play, but to understand the child through experiences supplementary to the parents' story or description by other adults as he reveals himself directly in dramatizations in the presence of the worker. The worker, skilled in this type of interview, enters into the phantasy by assuming play roles at the child's behest. The child-worker relationship, as in all treatment experience, is what gives the interview significance. The child's behavior may be observed without the worker's participation in the one-way screen device, observation thus being kept at the objective level, much as history can be obtained at the social level, or may move into a treatment emphasis in what is commonly called "play therapy." [8] Here the worker may engage in aggressive games, darts, pillow fights, setting fires in buckets, or in the complications of the doll-family drama. Acceptance, opportunity to release anxiety and aggression, verbal recognition or recognition in the play role of the child's feelings, pointing out patterns and helping the child to make connections, are not different in aim from other therapeutic efforts. Unless, however, workers are trained in psychotherapy,[9] it is wise to confine their observations of children to the home, the group experience, the waiting room, and other unstructured observation posts. For young children, play, which is their natural medium, is carried on as a substitute for the interview; older children are encouraged to verbalize their feelings. Conscious feelings are picked up; motivation is rarely interpreted.

In the following example [10] the observations were made in an agency playroom—the chief purpose being observation for a psychiatric consultation.

Manuel's mother was referred to a family agency by a play school because Manuel, aged 6½, was unmanageable and excitable. The father

[8] See pp. 268–69.　　　　　　　[9] See pp. 303–4.
[10] From a Family Service Agency. Condensed from text in first edition. Some of the techniques are questionable, but will serve to show the main approach. For fuller discussion of observation and play in the study and treatment of children, see writer's *Psychotherapy in Child Guidance.*

had deserted when the boy was three. Although Manuel was excluded from play school in July, Mrs. Romano did not seem concerned about how it would affect the boy to be sent away, but only that she would not have to take care of him all day long. On the basis of her resentment she was willing to bring Manuel to the office with the vague purpose of relieving her own discomfort by getting him help, preferably away from her. She had made several attempts to place him.

The mother described Manuel as "unmanageable." He runs away from her constantly. She always has to run after him. He doesn't want to go to the park with her. He runs away from the park and plays on the street with older boys. He tries to be tough like them. He pretends to smoke "to make her angry." He began to be "bad" after his father left her. He had obeyed his father, but would not obey her. Mrs. Romano stressed how much he loved his father, and says he talks about him frequently. He calls her vile names. It is impossible for her to do anything with him, and he will grow up to be a gangster. She has heard that all gangsters were like Manuel in their youth. She has tried to discipline him on the basis of personal appeal—"do this for Mama." She punishes him by sending him to bed. Without much conviction, she said she didn't beat him very much. In school he struck children and teachers, ran screaming and yelling through halls, and could not be induced to participate in any activities. If approached, he would threaten to kill everybody. He seemed also unhappy in camp, did not take part in any activities. After some weeks he tried to run away (taking three other children with him) because "he was afraid his mother was dead." He had to be sent home because of the disturbance he caused. In September he started in first grade at public school. After a week or so he was excluded because of extremely unruly and wild behavior. The assistant principal and teacher reported that it was impossible to have any discipline in a schoolroom with Manuel there. He ran around wildly, was aggressive toward other children, and also incited them to disobedience. He did not seem to mind any punishment he got.

Observation of the Child

Manuel is a well-developed, good-looking boy, tall for his age. When caseworker called him into the interviewing room he followed without hesitation and without the slightest sign of fear. We suggested he take one of the games with him, and he chose a game consisting of a cork plate, hammer, and little pieces of colored wood and nails. (He was not too disorganized to start playing constructively.) As soon as he was seated, he took up this game and worked on it with remarkable skill. He was friendly and smiled at caseworker, saying he liked that game, and he was building something. We asked him what he was building, and he said he was building a truck. We asked whether he would like to be a truck driver, and he said with enthusiasm, "Yes!" Then he hesitated awhile and said he thought he would rather be a fireman. He had to wait until he was big enough. We said that was true and that he would go to school to learn a lot of things. He knew that. He started school this summer. We asked him how he liked it, and he said he didn't. When we asked why, he shrugged his shoulders. We asked if he liked the other children. He did not answer, but wondered whether his mother was waiting for him. We assured him that she was, but suggested that he could look for himself. He did and came back immediately and said, "She is still there," but added sadly, "My father's dead." (The caseworker perhaps prematurely here touches off the mainspring of anxiety.) Then he corrected himself and said he wasn't dead, but was away in South America. Would he like to be with him? He nodded. His mother had told him his father would come back and they would all live together. Throughout the conversation he was hammering and concentrated intently on putting the pieces of wood together. He included caseworker in the game, gave her nails to hold, and then bought them from her. He counted the nails he wanted to have and was absolutely correct in that. He seemed delighted with the game and said again he liked it here. He wondered whether caseworker couldn't come home with him. I said I could not today, but I could some other day. He said it was nice and quiet in here, and the caseworker let him alone. I wondered whether other people do not let him alone, and he said with feeling, "No, my mother yells at me all the time." Why did she do that? He did not answer, but went on with the game. He asked if we would come with him, that there was room enough at home for caseworker. I promised I would come and see him some day. (Since the mother does not love him, perhaps another would be better. It might have been better to keep this gratification within the office interview.)

There was a noise outside and a child's voice. He opened the door, looked out, and said it was a little boy. Then he closed the door, took up the game, but seemed less concentrated upon it. He said that caseworker might like to play with the little boy too. This boy was about three years old and much smaller than Manuel. I said I was playing with Manuel now, but if he wanted the little boy to come in it would be all right. He could do whatever he wanted to. He said quickly that caseworker might like the little boy better than she liked him. I shook my head and said that I did not because I did not know this other little boy at all, and liked Manuel. He looked at me very suspiciously and seemed irritated. Then he went out of the room and brought in the little boy (further to test the worker who had failed him by partially accepting the other child).

He took the boy's toy away and played with it, but did not show much aggression. His face darkened though. The other boy was peaceful and didn't mind having his toy taken away. He talked in a friendly way to Manuel. Manuel didn't pay much attention to him, but suddenly seemed angry and pushed the little boy out of the room. The boy was astonished and peeped through the door, but Manuel pushed against the door and caseworker did not interfere. Manuel had closed the door and was alone with caseworker again. His expression had changed completely. He did not talk to caseworker for a while, but went on playing with the game, hammering violently. I remarked that now we were alone again and I didn't have to have any other little boys in if Manuel did not want to. He took the hammer, swung it toward caseworker and said, "I hate you, I hate you." Then he showed almost manic behavior, breaking the little pieces of wood, hammering the cork plate. The pieces flew around and he said that he was going to kill caseworker and he was going to kill everyone. He ran around in the interviewing room, throwing things on the floor and nearly breaking the telephone. He showed caseworker his tongue several times and called her vulgar names, mostly with sexual meanings. I was sitting quietly at the desk writing. He took my pencil, threw it away, and said with a frightened expression, "Why can't you leave me alone? Why can't you leave me alone? Shut up, shut up, shut up! though I hadn't said a word.

He began to curse and said it was the most terrible place he had ever seen and that he hated the room. I told him that he wouldn't have to stay here, that he could go to his mother and go home any time he wanted to. He said he didn't want to have caseworker come home with him. I said he could go alone, and he began to quiet down a little and sat back in his chair, hammering furiously on the wood and breaking the pieces. I asked what he would do today when he went home. Would he play with the other boys in the park? He seemed quite calm again and said he didn't know, but on Sunday he would go to the beach. Did he like to go to the beach? At first he said yes, then he said no, he didn't like to go into the water. Again, with a raised voice, he screamed, "I hate the water, I hate the big waves!" He made a movement with his hand indicating that he wanted to kill the wave. "I hate them because I am so afraid of them. They push me down, and my mother makes me go into it." I said I could understand that he didn't like that, many boys like Manuel and boys much bigger than he do not like to go into the waves.

Such reassurance is of questionable value, but tension has mounted till out of control and the need for immediate psychiatric advice is obvious.

Here the observation of behavior reveals an anxious, destructive, and thoroughly disturbed little boy, which is confirmed by the history given by the mother and the collateral sources. The fact that the behavior has been unremitting (occurs everywhere—home, camp, school) suggests a more serious condition than if it were found only at home. The behavior in the interview suggests actual psychopathology also.

Collateral Sources

Consultation by visits, letters, or telephone to churches, schools, hospitals, employers, trade unions, courts, social agencies, relatives, and banks are colloquially, often called "collaterals." Social work, more than most professions, makes use of documents, case histories, interagency reports, consultation with experts from other fields, tests, and examinations of all kinds. Social work, which in practice has long favored the interdiscipline approach, has an equal investment in the cooperative agency idea.[11] Because social problems are complex and many faceted, it is often necessary for the client to receive different sorts of help from more than one agency simultaneously. Workers consider it their responsibility to see that the client gets the best possible treatment for his problems, and to this end work closely together. The Social Service Exchange is a device for facilitating the exchange of information among professional agencies for more effective service.

In social study the worker explains candidly to the client what we have to know in order to help him and what methods will be used to verify necessary data. Professional ethics require that the client's assent or consent be gained for such collaboration. Occasionally

[11] For discussion of the social service exchange see pp. 132–33.

there are situations, however, in which professional consultation across agency lines must be undertaken without the client's expressed consent, and more rarely without his knowledge. Cases of acute physical or mental illness, delinquency, and other reasonable exceptions, readily suggest themselves. But even for the mentally ill, frankness and participation are encouraged as far as possible. It is better for a child, too, to know what is going to happen to him and be prepared, whether for placement, or a psychological test, or a tonsillectomy. For minors the consent of the parent is essential, and for runaway children a communication must be sent whether the child wants it or not, but long experience in all fields of casework suggests that time spent in preparation, explanation, and gaining assent for a difficult examination or inquiry is rarely wasted. The question of interviewing legally liable relatives is a delicate one, and the older practice of doing this in a routine way, frequently without the client's knowledge or consent, is giving place to a thoughtful discussion with the client of key relatives, leading to a selective and discriminating use of them.

On the one hand the person's privacy must be respected and protected, and extreme care must be used in all interagency reporting.[12] We try to communicate nothing which is not in the interest of the client and nothing without his knowledge. On the other hand, we want him to let down his defenses enough to agree that various resources may be joined on his behalf. They are not promised "No one shall ever know," but are asked, "Would it not be wise for us to share this information or planning with those best able to help?" If the client refuses, his wish is to be respected as far as possible. There is no way in which social study can be guaranteed to be entirely painless, but we try to avoid unnecessary discomfort. Frankness in discussion, consulting the client about future steps, considering feasible alternatives and choices, explaining our purpose in difficult procedures or in asking painful questions, gaining assent or consent for interprofessional or interagency collaboration tend

[12] See pp. 129–30.

to conserve the elements of respect for the client and his ability to take responsibility for the solution of his own problems.

Special Examinations and Tests

Caseworkers utilize experts in other fields, supplementing their own inquiries so as to arrive at more accurate understanding. The caseworker must know not only where but also when to turn to experts in other disciplines. Social workers used to hurry most of their clients off routinely for medical examinations, including Wassermann tests and "IQ's," and thus annoy hospitals with thousands of ill-considered requests for old and useless medical reports; but as knowledge and skill have increased, selectivity should obtain. The value of periodic health examinations under appropriate auspices for everyone is unquestionable, but not as a requirement of each social case study irrespective of the problem and the request. Both within and without the medical institution the social worker may unify and coordinate various clinical data so as to help integrate adequate medical and social treatments.[13]

Before child-placing and adoption a thorough physical and if indicated a psychological examination is undertaken, although today child-placing agencies do not use these tests so rigidly as formerly, and often they wait until the child feels secure in his new setting. At one time routine examination of all applicants for a mother's allowance was practiced in order to be sure that the mother was "physically and mentally fit" to have charge of her children, but such procedures are no longer followed. When physical disability is part of legal eligibility, as in aid to the blind or certain classes of incapacity under the recent social security provisions, medical diagnosis is obviously essential. In child-guidance clinics it has been customary for the child to have full medical, psychological, and psychiatric, as well as social, studies, but practice tends to increasing flexibility. If a "battery" of examinations and tests are used, they must be guided by the nature of the problem, the wishes of the

[13] See pp. 293–94.

client, the responsibility to be discharged by the agency, the preventive value, and the availability of such resources. With disturbed children preparation is always important, and care should be taken in timing and handling reactions to the test both for parents and for children. At one time, before the unified character of the casework process was fully grasped, it was thought that there could be specialized agencies which would do nothing but investigation, or nothing but diagnosis. The seeking of tests [14] should always be related to the treatment purpose and should not serve, as regrettably it sometimes does, as the worker's escape from taking responsibility for psychosocial diagnosis as a guide to treatment. Except in emergencies, cases calling for examination by a psychiatrist should be carefully evaluated, and a psychosocial and intra-familial diagnosis [15] formulated by the social worker before consultation. Conference with the psychiatrist and decision as to appropriate treatment is likely to be thus on a sounder footing.

CLUE AND PATTERN

Many applications for social services and counseling do not call for prescribed areas of exploration as in eligibility determination; but the worker feels his way in largely on the basis of the request, which is often a vague or disguised approach to the problem. Applications in which the personality problem is displaced onto a practical matter are common in all forms of family service to adults. A veteran is upset because he cannot get his compensation; he is in poor health, but he fears that the medical authorities will find his disability is not "service connected." When the worker offers to help him get this matter cleared up so that his compensation claims can be adjusted, he shifts his complaint, saying that the trouble is mostly with his wife, who blames him for not supporting her. When the worker expresses interest in talking with the wife, he shifts again and says he is, after all, most worried about his step-

[14] The Rorschach, which has provided illuminating material in personality diagnosis, may be used along with thematic apperception and other projection tests.
[15] See Chapter VIII.

daughter, who is running around with boys. One of the characteristics of the psycho-neurotic is just such diffused complaints, and
these or similar applications are common in social casework. The
first phase, through clues consciously and unconsciously furnished,
is to try to locate the chief complaint with which the client wants
us to help him, and often this is best accomplished by enabling him
to verbalize a specific request which can be discussed and around
which we can begin to collect the relevant facts—in short, to focus
the case always requires some basic data. Dr. Adolph Meyer cautioned his students against the dangers of routine history taking,
reminding them of the importance of the present "complaint" (the
immediate situation for which the patient is seeking help). We put
the "complaint" in the center of our interest because, as he said,
it is always "the center of the interest of the patient," but we inquire
into its context in the current situation.

Many times, however, a person asks for an established social service, for which the determination of eligibility is the immediate consideration, or he may wish referral to a hospital, for which a certain
amount of health history is essential, or to an employment agency,
for which a certain amount of work history would be secured in
order to make the appropriate referral; or he may wish child guidance, for which a good deal of family and developmental history is
required. In requests for marital counseling which are often quite
vaguely presented as marital tension, a good deal of special data
about the circumstances—marital history and sexual adjustment—
would be sought, as well as the economic and social facts of the
marriage.

I believe that there would be general agreement on the following:
that we should always begin with the difficulty which the client
presents—and take such history or conduct such exploration then
or thereafter as may seem relevant for understanding the problem.
The amount of psychosocial data needed varies with the amount
of active interference called for and the difficulty of arriving at a
diagnosis. Concentration on certain data and selective approaches
are determined by the problem and kind of request, although profes-

sional knowledge as to significant stages in life history and the common aspects of cultural and economic experience serve as guides to relevant inquiry in each individual case.

Although there are many more or less patterned studies, such as preparole and preplacement studies—which survey the environment into which the client will be returned or introduced—the two most standardized prototypes of a psychosocial study, of which there are an indefinite number of variations, are the eligibility study in social assistance and the psychogenetic history in behavior disorders or emotional disturbance: the one tends to focus on the socio-economic life of the individual; the other, more on the life development and family relationships. Obviously this is a matter of emphasis, since data concerning family relationships are usually part of eligibility requirements, and economic and cultural factors are significant in the personal history.

ELIGIBILITY PATTERNS

While it may be said that there are practically always conditions which have to be met in offering treatment, it is in the public agency that the statutory requirements set a framework for investigation.[16] Voluntary agencies, operating within certain limits, are freer to adjust conditions of eligibility to changing community facilities or professional trends. Such shifts should not be made suddenly merely because of the interest and desires of the staff, without sufficient regard to the needs of the community as a whole, nor should the public services be slow in responding to cultural and professional factors which should indicate the need for a change in eligibility procedures. While there is always danger that any formula may be followed so meticulously that one cannot see the client for the procedures, the trouble is not with having a framework, but with the rigidity of worker or agency.

Statutory requirements, or a body of regulations which have the

---

[16] There is a trend to take "need" out of the requirement for eligibility in old age assistance, but whatever the trend toward pensions, whenever need *is* an eligibility requirement, investigation is a highly skilled process.

force of such requirements, necessitate specific inquiries, such as the degree of handicap or disability of blind or of crippled children; residence or domicile when settlement is a condition of eligibility; income and resources when need is a condition of the grant; age or marital status, and the like. There are shifts in statutory requirements from time to time as more provisions for income and medical care move into the insurance scheme under the social security program. The trend which has steadily been toward more liberal financial assistance, with ever-widening coverage, has also suggested simplification of eligibility procedures.

Eligibility Data

The eligibility study in public assistance rests, as all casework studies must, on a sturdy, direct relationship with the client and his family; but if the law requires that he shall be "in need," the interview is not the only, if still the best, approach to an appraisal of resources. Certain methods, standardized for the social eligibility study, are understood by worker and client alike. The commonest devices are the use of an application blank, proof of residence and settlement, home visits, resource clearances, the budget or other measurement of income and outgo, and a pay-roll or employment check. Eligibility data [17] connected with age, residence, citizenship, degree of blindness, even marital status, though calling for ingenuity, patience, tolerance, and care, do not usually require as much social judgment as does the establishment of need. The fact that the methods are objective and impartial on one hand, like an income tax return or a credit investigation, makes them easier to tolerate; the skillful handling of the relationship is, however, the consistent casework factor. The client may have quite unreasonable and unnatural objections to the application blank or any part of the procedure or real objections—either of which must be psychologically understood and technically well-handled.

[17] Acceptable documentary evidence of age, residence, citizenship, etc., will be found in public assistance manuals, federal, state, or municipal, and also in Young's *Case Workers' Desk Manual*, 1937.

In most agencies, however, with relatively set requirements of eligibility for admission, such as an institution or a public-assistance structure, application blanks have standardizing and time-saving value. The "impersonality" of the procedures suggests to the client impartial and fair examination. The application blank does not in any sense take the place of the client's own story at intake, but its questions do serve as a guide by which he can come to understand what conditions he must meet, since he thus knows the specific points which the agency must cover. Every item on an application blank should be designed to identify the client and to clarify his eligibility status. The trend toward general public assistance, supplementing a wider insurance coverage, and the lowering of regional barriers will presumably continue, but whenever requirements are specific, the form should cover these data in a specific, intelligible manner.

In large administrative agencies, "resource consultants" may be employed to clear and appraise property, insurance, and other liquid assets. The use of the asset is, however, within the budgeting function of the caseworker. Under the terms of eligibility it is assumed that the client's realizable assets in savings, property, insurance, and the like, must be substantially utilized before public funds are given. This is consistent with the principle of self-maintenance, but difficulties in practice may come from two extreme points of view. One, the worker may, according to his social values, resenting the economic system and the usually inadequate rate of relief, be reluctant to use the client's resources at all and so overlook their existence; the other is that because of a depriving attitude toward those in need he may turn to arbitrary, harsh, and coercive pressure methods to make clients cash in on their assets. If the staff is encouraged to participate in the formulation of administrative policy in appropriate ways, resistance to its operation is decreased and a reasonable consistency is followed. How far the citizen-client can also be involved in policy making has not yet been determined. Certainly he should be encouraged to express his opinion on matters on which he is competent, and his reactions to the administration of the service should be sought from time to time.

"Resource adjustment" is ceasing to be used as a deterrent and may be accomplished in such a way as to impose no hardship upon the client; indeed, in skilled hands insurance and property adjustments are genuine services. Insurance adjustments, in fact, could be beneficial to many people not actually in need. Through the judicious use of liquidated insurance savings, families may be made partially or temporarily self-supporting. Casework considerations, such as cooperative analysis of the values of the policies and full discussion with the client of the circumstances, obtain here as always. Rigid regulations requiring the liquidation of all assets are costly to everyone concerned, as most enlightened administrations have come to see. There should be flexibility and room for individual decisions, as in ill health or old age; or when need is temporary the decision should be made in the light of usual income and normal earning power, with as little dislocation of proper coverage as possible. Small resources that cannot be liquidated without unreasonable loss, should not be liquidated. The protection of rights assumes that exceptions be made for the person who qualifies for the exception or special category, but in any professional public service room for social judgment of a responsible person is given due weight. Exceptions too, however, follow a responsible procedure for review and determination.

A "pay roll check" may be carried out by a clerk, but obtaining employment references and estimating work ability call for individual and expert study. Public assistance is not considered a permanent source of income, unrelated to the person's ability for self-support or self-maintenance, and the question of employability with relation to job refusal is vexatious.

In most localities ability to support oneself is considered a potential "resource" and therefore part of eligibility. Older coercive practices are being slowly modified, by both enlightened labor and casework thinking; clients will not be ineligible to receive relief because of strikes or lockouts; clients will not be required to work under substandard conditions of hours or pay or personnel practices.

In short, the caseworker respects fair labor practices as conditioning the use of the "ability to work" asset. If the refusal seems to be due to physical or emotional rather than industrial factors, careful medical or psychiatric diagnosis is usually required. Again, a caseworker's understanding of economic and social reality on the one hand and of disability and the meaning of behavior on the other should together make for a flexible and constructive use of an otherwise arbitrary set of regulations. Interpretation to the client of the agency's policies and procedures and respect for the client's integrity as a worker and understanding of him as a person can make this approach to work capacity a skilled and constructive service to client and community alike. Even when a plea for assistance must be denied, the client's integrity and self-respect need not be damaged if he is made to understand the basis of the decision. Only as the insights of psycho-somatic medicine are brought together with the best thinking in employment, compensation, and placement services, will the question of ability to work be intelligently solved in a modern society.

Another highly developed aspect of social judgments is involved in the liability-to-support feature of eligibility. One cannot decide, without appraising the ability to support of a legally liable person whether or not income is to be supplied to a family. Whether a parent can pay for his placed-out child or whether a working youth should contribute toward the support of his parents is not always easy to determine. Experience both in public assistance and in the socially developed practice of modern domestic relations courts has shown that pressure tactics as regards the support function may increase the difficulty without materially increasing the assistance. Although the court has authority here, as in other anti-social behavior, the caseworker should be able to distinguish among those conflict situations which can be worked out constructively and those which call for legal adjudication and those which are best left alone.[18] Liberal construction on the responsibility of legally liable relatives is a factor in reducing the number of coercive actions.

[18] See pp. 287–92.

Requests from young people, especially young couples, for separate maintenance must be examined in the light of psychological as well as economic and cultural factors. Public agencies should not grant separate maintenance for vague "personality" reasons, but when separate maintenance contributes to greater personal and social efficiency it is within the jurisdiction of the administrative agency to grant it. These intricate judgment values in family economics are bound up with what might erroneously appear to the inexperienced as simple matters of mobilizing resources in the determination of eligibility.

In most forms of public assistance, but especially when there are employable persons, it is assumed that appraisal of status is "continuous." Clients should understand the basis of continuing eligibility and whatever form of recertification is necessary so that they may participate responsibly. How people are managing or have managed their affairs is a good question in any form of social study, but in the economic area it is especially useful. Regulations concerning the reporting of work income should be reasonable and act as incentives both toward suitable work effort and to encourage the client's will to cooperate with the administrative policy. Time limits for the grant proposed and for review should be stated in advance to the client, and renewals and termination should be discussed and realistically adjusted to new considerations.[19]

Although need is in some places gauged by a fixed monthly sum —"grant-less-income"—the budget deficiency method is a more accurate measure when eligibility depends upon need. We may, perhaps, note as an exception to the lack of objective measurements in casework, the tool of the budget. The technique borrowed from the field of home economics is now "naturalized" in social work. As a measure of need, the budgetary method has limitations as at present applied, but it is an improvement over per-capita allowance, relief scales, or the purely subjective judgment of the investigator. Cost-of-living studies [20] are now regularly made, which furnish ac-

[19] See pp. 236–67.
[20] See studies made by the Bureau of Labor Statistics, the Bureau of Home

curate data on the prices of food, clothing, rent, light, heat, and household supplies, and so forth. Nutritionists have computed the approximate amount of food required for subsistence according to age, sex, occupation, and physical condition. One reason that budgets do not seem to measure need accurately is that in so few agencies are even subsistence items properly allowed for. When necessary items are not covered, the family must take money from the food allowance or some other basic allowance. It is an advantage to make out budgets as blueprints, even if one does not always succeed at once in getting the necessary appropriations made. Variable needs, such as medical care, replacement of essential household equipment, and the like, cannot be measured in the same way —although expenses incident to work or illness or education are measurable to some degree; and no one has devised measurements for differential standards of living—whether, for instance, it is more important for the carpenter to buy a low priced car or to send his boy to high school—since they involve value judgments. From another angle, the budget reveals the nature and amount of the gratifications which a community permits to its dependent citizens and the nature and amount of the deprivations which it imposes. The budget range thus reflects the cultural patterns of a community.

The provision of basic income, like essential medical care, follows social security insurance and administrative practice, but for supplementary forms of aid, and whenever temporary or occasional financial assistance or ability to pay for a service is concerned, the budget [21] remains one of the most effective and reliable instruments of practical and psychological value. Impersonal, yet flexible and capable of individual adaptation, it is not only a measure of cost of living but also with skilled counseling becomes an excellent educational device for better income management.

Psychologically, also, the budget presents a well-defined reality

---

Economics, and studies by home economists in family social work. See pp. 87–90 for use of money.

[21] See pp. 87–90.

against which the client reacts. The budget serves then, in some degree, as a measure of the intensity of the client's responses. By the test of consistency and appropriateness it helps to locate the client's problem both within and outside himself. One must guard, however, against a decision on the basis of only one tool, the budget, instead of evaluating the client's reaction to other and possibly more significant experiences. As a test of eligibility for public grants the budgetary method of determining need is no longer the main device. And, indeed, with a wider coverage in the social insurances techniques for establishing eligibility will no doubt tend to follow modified actuarial lines, with the budget retained more as a measure of psycho-economic efficiency in specialized problems.

The concept of right to social assistance [22] has infused the whole process of establishing eligibility. Workers should not be apologetic about eligibility requirements. If they are not just, right, or efficient in operation, efforts should be made to have them changed, but an eligibility study well done is a challenging and even a fascinating task. Accuracy, imagination, resourcefulness, genuine love for people, and a deep understanding of human behavior will be called into play.

PSYCHOGENETIC HISTORY PATTERNS

The twin concepts of history for diagnosis and as reliving or abreaction must always be kept in mind. The use of history to gain understanding of the growth of the personality in a specific environment assumes inquiry into familial history and relationships, developmental and health data, symptoms, defenses and behavior patterns, attitudes and emotionally charged experience. Such information leads to the formulation of psychogenetic diagnosis. On the other hand, the reliving of emotionally charged experience is, as we have said elsewhere, an important aspect of therapy. Orthopsychiatry not only clarified the dynamics of the parent-child rela-

[22] See pp. 90, 149.

tionship, but in its study of the "total child" has thrown light on causal factors in the family constellation. These new insights as to the meaning of the "family drama" affected the study and treatment of delinquency and of behavior and symptoms in general. Knowledge concerning the evolution of the personality necessitated new skill in the art of history-taking.

The child-guidance movement, which from its inception hoped to modify behavior, stressed the psychogenetic approach, since it had been found that the earliest years are deeply influential in the formation of personality. A reaction against full developmental histories set in, partly because of the heavy case loads during the depression (*circa* 1930 and thereafter), when people had little time or energy to look beyond the stark realities of unemployment and destitution, partly as a reaction against the exhaustive and stereotyped inquiries of an earlier decade and partly because of clearer insights as to the relation between history and treatment. Schematic histories, the purpose of which clients did not understand and consciously or unconsciously resisted, often proved unreliable because the client's feeling was so little recognized and therefore inhibited the start of a treatment relationship. Actually a well-focused inquiry promotes the beginning of "relationship"; although the initial relationship of good-will is, at intake, to the worker as he is a representative of the agency.[23]

A weakness of history in social work practice is that its picture of cultural conditioning is incomplete. The family role has always been accredited in casework, the more so with the reenforcement of psychiatry, but the influences on the family because of cultural factors has been usually too little understood. Dollard's statement that we should always think of the cultural "group plus one," the "one" being our client, is arresting. As anthopological material becomes better adapted to social work practices, concepts of the acculturation process will be clearer.[24] The idea of cultural pluralism,

[23] See pp. 162–65.
[24] See Dollard, Criteria for the Life History, p. 8, for discussion of the development of an individual's organized and systematized social life.

the enrichment which comes from the acceptance and enjoyment of cultural differences, should increasingly affect all disciplines concerned with constructive human relationships. We do not have to pull growing things up by the roots to assure ourselves that they have roots, nor do we have to deny the existence of norms because it is true that each case is different and must be individualized. Needs are created by the totality of psycho-biological, cultural and interpersonal interactions.

In the growth of the individual within the culture, patterns become functions, and vice versa. It is in culturally approved and disapproved situations that we feel emotions. General understanding of cultural conditioning is important, but even more important is learning to take a cultural life history. Security in one's culture is an essential part of self-acceptance. Because each individual uses his culture in terms of his psychological needs it is important to be sensitive to caste and class, to understand that the defenses, conditioned as they are by familial influences, inevitably are modified or reinforced by social cultural forces, which the person has learned to use.

Today there is reemphasis upon appropriate psychogenetic history as there is support for a well-directed psychosocial study. The chief improvement derives from greater skill in the method of inquiry, as well as in clearer focus and aim for the exploration required by the problem. That one may not always need to obtain thorough history or a complete social study in no wise changes this fundamental realization of life patterns. The psychosocial concept of the case must be the disciplined acquisition of any professional worker. For history, as for social study, patterns belong under the blotter or, better still, at the back of the head, but not in the interview process. Categories lead to conformity and rigidity only if we strive to push things into them. The doctor who concluded his lecture with the remark, "Now, gentlemen, you know all about cardiac disease, and now you will never see cardiac disease," was reminding his medical students that they would be treating persons, not categories.

In many mental hospitals and clinics it has been customary for one person, usually a social worker, to "take" the psychosocial history [25] according to a preconceived outline designed for the use of the team as a whole. Data on relationships, attitudes, and behavior are always important features. Areas of inquiry commonly include *the present complaint* and the history of its onset—how long the present behavior has been going on, when it started, where it occurs, against whom is it directed, and what is being done or has been done by the family about it; *developmental facts*—birth, weaning, sleeping, feeding, body habits, mobility, toilet training, outstanding behavior and incidents in the nursery years; play, aggressiveness, fears; *defenses, traits, and symptoms; school progress*—learning difficulties, special attachments, and reactions; *history of traumatic experiences*, such as illness, accidents, and handicaps; *family background; cultural and economic status* (similar data here as in eligibility study); *significant family relationships, attitudes, and events*, such as early separations from the parents, conditions in the home, relations to brothers and sisters, other companionship, marital relationships, recreations, interests, and talents. For convenience, historical data obtained fluidly in the successive interviews should be arranged for the record in a topical pattern which will thus tend to clarify the main findings and precipitate the diagnostic conclusions.

In most child guidance clinics today the outline for history emphasizes the current behavior of the child in the interview and in the life situation as well as in the genetic development. For the adult one must depend on his verbal evidence supported by other social material, if indicated; for the young child, observation of what he is actually doing is so important that the play interview is extensively used. The child will reveal in his play situations at home, at school, and elsewhere which have disappointed, frightened, or otherwise emotionally affected him. Through his selection of play incidents he may show his personal experiences in nursing, in being weaned, and in toilet training, rivalry with siblings, struggle for the possession of his parents, traumatic illnesses, and other events.

[25] See pp. 293–94 for the medical setting.

Not all children play freely enough for accurate diagnosis, and whether they do so or not, the worker will have taken pains to get a careful history from the parents.

To obtain such a history from a parent about a child, or from a relative about a patient in a hospital, is a procedure that differs in some respects from obtaining a reliable history from a person about himself, but there are certain considerations which must be borne in mind. In the first stages it is important to help the parent to tell the child's story without shifting focus toward himself so that one may get as clear a picture as possible of the child and his relationships. Some parents will tend to turn toward their own problems and conflicts in other areas—the parent prematurely wants to become the "patient"—moving into the center of the stage. This may also occur, although less frequently, in obtaining histories from relatives of ill persons in hospitals. It is almost impossible to take a good psychogenetic history unless one focuses on a chief "patient," around which the family constellation is elaborated. To keep a child- or "patient"-centered focus means simply that the main person is for a given period of treatment accorded central attention, investigation and diagnostic processes being constantly directed toward him. Related problems, however, are allowed to come up and interactions clarified. That is only to say that all significant interrelationships are noted, but from the angle of the disturbed or ill person. The resulting diagnosis may be clinical or interpersonal, or both, but because the purpose is essentially that of treatment it will be person-problem centered. In most eligibility patterns the focus is psychosocial and interpersonal; in psychogenetic histories the focus is patient centered throughout, the interpersonal and social data being constantly referred to the child or other ill person about whom the exploration is made. The material is thus recorded from the "patient" angle, and additional histories are taken if other "patients" in the family subsequently emerge.

In taking a history from an adult about himself, we may easily elicit feelings about the social situation, but access to the more significant emotional experiences must wait until the relationship is deepened and a release is induced by the therapeutic attitude and attendant transference phenomena.[26] In less emotionally charged situations the client is conscious that the worker knows his job, means him well, wants to help him clarify his eligibility status and put him in touch with the right resources, and so forth. Usually clients are willing to give the necessary information when it is to their interest to do so. They will reveal their economic circumstances when the purpose is clear and the questions relevant, but this is less often so with regard to the more intimate concerns or when the facts are felt by the client to be discreditable. One must be prepared, therefore, to meet the client's resistance. In general, as we have said earlier,[27] resistance is less mobilized when the interviewer is sincerely interested and friendly, and explains the reason for asking difficult questions. But if resistance continues one usually has to recognize it frankly—"It is hard for you to tell me this," "Perhaps you really are uncertain about going on with us." The giving of history is a way some clients take to establish themselves with the agency. Sometimes the too-willing giving of history is the client's way of avoiding a discussion of his immediate situation, and he must be gently brought back to face it with us. Usually clients do not resent either appropriate questions or relevant inquiry, if they grasp our purpose and are convinced of our genuine concern to help them. Anxiety-arousing procedures should be specially timed, and specially phrased explanations and desensitizing are required. If the problem indicates an area of psychological preoccupation, as we move in this direction the pace may be slowed down, and we can only wait, aided by responsive questions and comments, for what the client is ready to give us in a deepening relationship. We encourage and help him by accrediting his efforts. He will offer more when he finally believes that we can accept him as he is, good and bad, that we will not turn against him no matter what his disclosure.

In the more obvious forms of exploration the professional relationship remains characteristically "real." The focus on social reality tends to inhibit, just as the very nature of the revelations of emo-

[26] See pp. 256–58.   [27] See pp. 266–67.

tionally charged material tends to encourage, transference phenomena. To a considerable degree the worker must be able to dilute transference or permit it to develop as indicated by the role to be assumed, the goal of treatment, and the skill of the worker in therapeutic procedure.

In a recent article [28] it is said that an "administered service demands ability: to develop and apply administrative policy; to operate effectively through an orderly administrative structure and . . . to exercise skill in the relationship with the client." To cover a clearly defined area, whether of financial need or developmental history for a child-guidance clinic, does not mean that the client should be treated impersonally or routinely or that his cooperation should not be enlisted. There is danger, perhaps, in too sharply distinguishing the economic services, such as public assistance, from the "clinical," such as child placing, marriage counseling, child guidance, and so forth, but it is equally risky not to keep the goal or purpose of the investigation clearly in mind and not to hold the data closely to its purpose. In addition there may be said to be forms of "psychological" eligibility which enter into any treatment process. If a person is incapacitated, eligibility may be largely, or even wholly, established on his behalf, but in so far as being helpful may depend on the client's ability to mobilize himself to use the service, other considerations enter in. However, it seems to us less confusing to consider psychological readiness under treatability than eligibility.

Frankness on the part of the worker and the assumption of responsibility on the part of the citizen-client for his use of the community resources result in a policy of "open covenants openly arrived at," to quote a famous political phrase, with the client's participation. If he is not able, because of illness or infirmity, to establish his eligibility alone, the worker will help him, or even do it for him, but always with an abiding sense of the client's right to manage his own affairs as far as he is able. In all casework the emphasis has shifted from the offering of services or income as commodities toward

28 See also pp. 243–46.

helping the client use the service responsibly for himself. In the pattern of psychogenetic study the area covered stresses the more intimate family-person interaction in the growth process, although social, cultural, and economic data support the central theme as called for, much as in the eligibility pattern. We shall now see how psychosocial data of all kinds are interpreted through diagnostic and evaluation processes.

CHAPTER VIII

DIAGNOSTIC AND EVALUATION
PROCESSES

IN ORDER to understand the meaning of a case, as we have shown in Chapter VII, sufficient psychological and social facts, gained through appropriate methods of study, are indispensable. Knowledge of the client's environment, both immediate and historical, the present cultural and social situation, the degree of social pathology, the adaptive patterns, attitudes, and feelings of the client, with some recognition of probable areas of disturbance, are the usual subjects of observation and inquiry. These are, however, always approached in terms of the specific problem and request. The worker's professional opinion as to the nature of the problem and the strengths and assets in the client should be formed as soon as possible; in most instances within three or four contacts—earlier if the case is obvious, later if more obscure, but even in complicated family involvement not later than a few weeks after study has been commenced. The impressions gained during the study should be brought together to aid the intuitive focusing of interpretation, and this formulation carefully recorded. The meaning which the practitioner derives from incidents, history, and behavior, as these are presented, is called "diagnostic thinking" or "impression" and, in its formal recorded version, "diagnostic summary" or "diagnostic statement." [1] Incorrect or incomplete diagnoses should be restated whenever indicated.

[1] For further illustrations of these types see Hamilton, *Principles of Social Case Recording*. Pp. 70–76.

Diagnosis and Evaluation are Concurrent and Related

Study, diagnosis, and treatment occur in the natural progress of a case, each problem as it arises demanding a specific point of view. One must always remember, however, that the arbitrary division of the casework process into steps is an intellectual device to help us comprehend the nature of the total process. While to live is always more important than to know, one must become conscious of the components of any discipline through "discontinuous thinking" as well as through intuitional identification with a case "in pure duration" as the chronological shared experience allows.

Diagnosis, understanding the psychosocial problem brought to our attention by the client, and *evaluation,* understanding the functioning of the person with regard to his problem, his capacities, and the availability of outer as well as inner resources, are so closely related that some prefer to use the phrase "diagnostic evaluation." We shall, however, describe separately these two complementary ways of eliciting the meaning of a case. The thought process directed to the nature of the problem and its causes is called *diagnosis*—"knowing through," or recognizing, or understanding thoroughly; it attempts to answer the question "What is the matter?" If one assumes the responsibility of a treatment role, then it is essential to understand the client's problem. Essentially, diagnosis is the worker's professional opinion as to the nature of the need or the problem which the client presents. It is not a "secret labeling of the client"; it is not an uncontrolled adventure into the mysteries of life; it is a realistic, thoughtful, frank, and "scientific" attempt to understand the client's present need, which is always a person-in-a-situation formulation, including inter-personal relationships.

Diagnosis and evaluation are social perceptions, or, more correctly, psychosocial perceptions. In order to know what to look for, to understand deviations and failures in adaptation, the student must have acquired a considerable body of knowledge about social functioning in a normative sense although it is always easier to say what is "abnormal" than what is normal. He must know something about character structure and work conditions, about family relationships, about education and play and worship, the roles in supporting or being supported by others, about neighbors and friends and group associations. Unless professional education teaches workers this basic subject matter, casework is merely a skill resting largely on intuition and opportunism. Without a body of technical knowledge including thorough training in the social sciences one cannot take an intelligent history, determine eligibility, or construct useful, accurate diagnoses.

Both diagnosis and evaluation are professional opinions. From the moment the client makes an application he is invited and stimulated through the interview to express his own feelings about his situation. How is it that when one encourages the client to tell his own story and give its meaning for him, the result is not "diagnosis"? His life experience is a configuration for him as well as for the worker, and it is to his own view of his situation that he habitually reacts. The client chooses the agency on the basis of his own "diagnosis" and preconceived ideas as to the remedy, usually with little awareness of the psychological factors involved. If for no other reason, then, the worker should unquestionably start where the client is and explore his problem with him as he sees it, but he should always be aware of the possibility of displacement in the client's view of it, aware of the natural defenses, and should not commit himself too early to the correctness of the applicant's interpretation. There is no reason why one should not call the client's subjective version of the situation "diagnosis," except that it is confusing to use the same term for the lay opinion and for the professionally disciplined process. It is always important to find out what a person thinks is wrong with him, for this is part of the total meaning, but it is not necessarily what is discernible to a trained observer. As the client gives the meaning the situation holds for him, this becomes the starting point for treatment, because when the worker accepts the feeling and shows attentive interest, an initial relationship is set up.

In other words, no matter what the client's objective life story or what he subjectively feels about any phase of it, the caseworker must try to elicit fuller meaning, to make sense out of the various elements which are presented. Sometimes one does little except confirm the client's interpretation. "I am," he says, "a case of involuntary unemployment." After studying his situation with him, one may agree. On the other hand, one may see his problem as involuntary unemployment complicated by an occupational handicap, or one may see that he is constantly getting himself into difficulties with his employers and fellow workers so that he unconsciously contributes to getting himself discharged.

Evaluation implies a disciplined capacity for making social judgments. Social workers are interested in the establishment of an adequate standard of living, good income levels and conditions of work, protection by social security systems, and also in the quality of human relations, sound family life, social justice, civil rights, nondiscrimination, constructive labor relations, and group collaboration for the common welfare. Diagnosis is concerned with causal interaction; evaluation with social purpose. The latter comes rather more naturally to us in our own life experience, whereas the attempt to define the problem and its causes presents special difficulties. Skill in diagnosis rests on the mastery of a large body of psychological and social sciences; skill in evaluation, perhaps, depends more on the freedom to think and feel without personal bias, with a minimum of prejudice about this or that kind of individual or this or that course of action. These two fundamental disciplined ways of thinking perhaps most clearly distinguish the professional personality. Personality evaluation and characterization are usually related to treatibility, success or failure, constructive and destructive factors in prognosis. In characterizing one does not approach personality in the abstract ethical sense of "goodness" or "fineness" or "ignobility," but with regard to the capacity to perform certain functions, for example, the support role, the marital role, the filial or parental role. Although such judgments seem arbitrary, they are inescapable if one is to treat within the field of human conduct and relationships. One must know not only from what limitations but to what ends capacities and energies are to be released.

Reflective thinking, therefore, involves not only description and definition, which we call diagnosis, but consideration of treatment ends and possibilities, which must include the appraisal of resources and the evaluation of the client as a person. All character is to the practitioner "acceptable," but within any given cultural framework certain character trends will appear more favorable to social adaptation or achievement than others. Personality is a social activity rather than "a thing," and although the set of limits and rules which the world has imposed seem very confusing there is still a good deal of agreement on essential values. It has been said that civilization has "gone off the gold standard" because the Ten Commandments are not taken seriously in the culture of today; but civilization must always have its "gold standard," and experience continues to teach that some acts are "better" than others and that the fundamental and enduring assumptions of mankind must be moral and social.

Diagnoses and evaluations have as their goal making treatment effective. What do we need to understand before undertaking to help anyone? In what areas can we treat? What does the client expect of us? In all history taking we are looking for clues to meaning, giving particular attention to the client's reactions to himself, to others, to his immediate problem, and to what he has done and seems to want to do about it. We explore his request with him to see where it really leads. If it leads to problems other than the one initially complained about, the worker must be able to discern this, but the client may or may not see these deeper problems or want them treated. A good diagnostic hypothesis helps to explain phenomena, in a limited way to predict, and it should contain indications for treatment. For professional diagnosis is essential to understand the problem or complaint for which the client is now seeking assistance. Other complicating factors may emerge; the problem presented may not turn out to be the core problem; supplementary diagnostic formulations directed to other problems or persons may become necessary later; and so forth. Despite all this there remains the necessity for initially defining the problem at the point where the client senses the difficulty and trying to estimate now and later his capacity to deal with it.

THE DIAGNOSTIC PROCESS [2]

Knowledge and skill in the social diagnostic process include familiarity with the interaction of inner and outer experiences and, in addition, certain logical concepts and relationships such as facts and inferences; findings and interpretations; the theory of causality; case definitions and classifications. Underlying the diagnostic process is the professional commitment to help the client if possible. Diagnostic thinking strives to arrive at causes because this means a more precise definition of the problem. The fact that the client himself may be a contributor to his own social problems complicates the formulation, but does not change the aim of diagnosis. Descriptive definitions, often a preliminary step in diagnostic thinking, are also useful. When the client tells us that he is not able to get along with his wife and we note this as an instance of "marital friction," we are using a descriptive diagnostic phrase. Later we attempt to find the causal components. In casework diagnosis is essentially a psychosocial formulation—its relation to clinical diagnosis we shall discuss later. Within the psychosocial (person in situation) concept we shall place the interpersonal diagnostic configuration, especially the intra-familial problems of balance and interaction.

Diagnosis as Gestalt

Every diagnosis is a configuration, or Gestalt, which derives its meaning as a whole from the fact that as practitioners we are going

[2] See pp. 137–38.

to do something about the client's request for help—to "treat" him. The situation has particularity for the caseworker which is not the same as that for a lawyer, or doctor, or engineer. The total configuration is made up of the individual interacting with his environment (person-in-setting), a whole of interdependent parts. The indispensable element in the configuration which makes it typical for social work is that there must be a social problem causing, or being caused by, some breakdown or failure in social adaptation. This particular problem, of which the client is aware, must be examined to determine the nature and extent of the disturbance in the living experience. Whatever may or may not be done about the basic problem, it is our essential grasp of it which makes us able to attack realistically the difficulty, and intuitively the client will know whether we understand or not, and our understanding contributes to initial rapport. The personality reacts to a series of stimulating situations, to the impact of a total culture, to inner urges, as well as to external stimuli, so that psychosocial diagnosis is concerned with the whole situation, inner as well as outer, the relationships of person to situation and of person to person. The simplest psychosocial unit might be that of an unemployed person with a physical limitation as to available jobs; a behavior problem would suggest a probable intra-familial causal connection also with psychosocial repercussion.

If the complaint is about a child's stealing or destructiveness, then the diagnostic formulation will attempt to give the meaning of this behavior; if a child is to be placed, what is the nature of the family situation which necessitates it? If a person is unemployed, what factors of health, personality, or the job market seem most likely to cause the difficulty? Whatever complications may be found or whether or not other problems more interesting to the worker coexist, the first essential is to understand the problem consciously presented by the client for solution, and the diagnostic formulation is the worker's, or staff's considered explanation of this problem—its structure, its etiology, the elements in relationship.

Casework has substantial content derived from the social and psychological sciences, and although the application of these disciplines is still more art than science one need not assume that this allows only for trial and error. While the unit for casework has not yet, and perhaps never will have, so exact an anatomy and physiology as underlie medicine, charting has been done in the realm of personality and social forces against which individual life histories can be studied. In an ultimate sense the human being may be unknowable, but diagnosis is not concerned with ultimates, but with practical working hypotheses. Within recent years study of emotional or inner factors, as expressed through attitudes, behavior, and verbalization has brought into casework an understanding of the person who has the problem as well as of the problem itself, so that "the Gestalt" always shows the person-in-the-situation relationship—through conscious feelings, needs, and desires.

Causality in Diagnosis

In social phenomena cause and effect are so complex that it is not easy to establish exact causal relationships. It is helpful, nevertheless, to express even partial connections—that is, this family is in difficulty because the wage earner is unemployed, or this girl does not enjoy parties because her sister gets all the attention, or this child is truanting from school because his program is unsuited to his capacities, or because his mother's being at home with a younger sibling makes him jealous. Social diagnoses are commonly descriptive, indicating such obvious interrelations, even when it is known or suspected that additional factors must be operating. Causality may be indicated in approximate, not absolute, terms. One could say, for instance, that this child's aggressive behavior was due in part to his early rejection by his mother, and this rejection was because the pregnancy interferred with her stage life, and her need to go on the stage was determined by—and so forth, but not indefinitely.

Historical causality is like an inverted pyramid—the current behavior or situation is represented by the apex—and the nearer one gets to the base of the pyramid the more causes appear. In the same way, if one searches for causes sociologically instead of psycho-genetically one encounters remote and extremely complicated causation. This man is in need because he is unemployed; he is unemployed because of overproduction in his line of work; the overproduction is caused by—well, no two economic experts will agree beyond that point. By causality, then, we mean merely that certain factors are found operating together in a given situation in such a way as to suggest a causal connection.

As we have said elsewhere, we do not seek to know the past because we are going to treat the past, but because the past is structured in the present. Failures in adaptation in the past are usually carried over and may be seen in the client's functioning in the current situation, even in the interview itself, but cross-sectional pictures, which are, indeed, important clues, should not be substituted for a careful personal history, especially in cases of "behavior problems." Since social causality is extremely complex, to know a single social situation fully is practically impossible. One clue is found in the fact that despite the complexity of the organism, its function may be relatively simple. It is possible to know something about society in general, but it is even more possible to understand how the individual is utilizing or reacting to his social situation. If it be true that behavior is purposive, then how the individual behaves is at least one key to understanding him, even in a complex situation.

Students practicing diagnosis are often confused when trying to sort out a "difficulty" from "liability" and a "cause" from either. They may be helped if they abandon schematic designs, not trying to assign a specific cause for each difficulty, but making a configuration, in a simple flexible diagnostic statement, of those problem factors which seem to hang together in time and space. One should also remember that "assets and liabilities," in the Richmond [3] phrase, are not part of this problem definition, but are the raw materials of evaluation for the purpose of treatment. Assets and

[3] See *Social Diagnosis*, pp. 361, and 226, below, for diagnostic statements.

liabilities may be physical or external, or they may lie within the personality of the client, or both.

Discrimination in terms of the actual problem to be treated is essential. We do not need a developmental history of the client in order to enter him in a home for the aged, and we do not need to subject the client to an exhaustive check-up unless his symptoms and complaints warrant it. A person who would test low in a psychometric examination may be socially competent to earn a living and may manage very well in noncompetitive situations. When a person applies for a practical service, even though the worker may recognize deeper problems, unless the client wishes treatment in these areas one should not probe into them. An initial problem in family economics or marital tension may be further elaborated, and a new "patient" may emerge, for instance, a child who may be said now to have his own problem or his own version of the family problem. This new configuration should then have its own diagnostic formulations, with this "patient" as central figure.

Diagnostic thinking, the drawing of purposive inferences, begins with the first interviews and observations and continues throughout the case. All diagnostic skills rest on knowing what to look for, what to disregard, and how to review the findings in the light of subsequent data. No interpretation of the living human event can be final; no diagnosis can be complete. As one moves along with the client to explore his request, the meaning of elicited facts becomes clearer. When one asks relevant questions, helps the client to bring out the necessary data, whether by telling about his current situation, his life experience, or his purposes in using the agency; whether he assists by producing documents, consents to a medical examination, arranges with us for a home or collateral visit or for an interview between the worker and another member of the family, one comes inevitably to some understanding of the problem and the person who has the problem. Casework, as method, is most effective when there are social components to be manipulated, as well as psychotherapeutic objectives to be achieved.

Classification and Diagnostic Statement

A complete definition of a case is scarcely possible, and it can rarely be final. It is, perhaps, best to think of the explanation arising from complicated case data as a diagnostic hypothesis or supposition. Although diagnostic thinking continues in the sense of a deepening understanding of the problem—and especially the person who has the problem—for all practical purposes one does not go on making diagnostic formulations unless one appears to have made an incorrect hypothesis at the beginning or the situation itself is radically changed. The client does not ask us to treat his whole life, so that after the problem which he has brought to us has been cleared up, his discomfort reduced, or the problem found to be too complex or insoluble, we do not necessarily make a new "diagnosis." On the other hand, diagnoses should be reviewed from time to time and altered if new insights have occurred, and new phases of treatment are to be undertaken.

As one perceives social reality, it is a grouping, a design for living, with qualities of its own, each case being unique, yet related to similar cases through common attributes. One cannot describe and define without classification any more than one can evaluate without norms and goals. Everyone who thinks at all must classify in one way or another. One cannot accept a dinner invitation without thinking whether it is a formal or an informal dinner, since the classification, together with other social value concepts, will suggest how to dress. In the same way the classifications "unemployment" and "sibling rivalry" and "unattached and homeless" and "marital friction" help workers to marshal substantive knowledge of pathology, to supplement one's knowledge of the case specifics. Classification is indispensable to thought, an essential part of the diagnostic process, its validity depending on the noting of real, not chance, resemblances. Classification is a key to meaning, not the total meaning. Complete diagnosis requires definition within the class, showing the differentiating factors. Students who have learned that each case is different often forget that they know it is different because of conscious or unconscious classification. Both definition and classification, therefore, are involved in all diagnostic thinking.

The use of a diagnostic term or label, for example, "cardiac valvular" heart disease or "anxiety neurosis with behavior disorder," as is found in medicine and psychiatry, is not common in social work. It would be helpful to have a system of phrases by which problems might be indexed, but such a classification has not yet proved to be as satisfactory as the diagnostic statement. It has become fashionable in some quarters to disparage diagnostic categories, although these are actually indices to stored professional knowledge.

In a "child guidance" type of case the summary would accent family background and relationships, the economic and social picture, onset of symptoms, developmental history, psychological and medical findings if tests were made, description of the child's attitudes and behavior, together with significant attitudes and relationships at home, at school, and elsewhere. The conclusion would then pull together these essential findings in a diagnostic paragraph. Such a paragraph may be detached from the history proper and stand alone as a psychosocial formulation. The social worker's special contribution to diagnostic thinking is the picture of the family dynamics or the person-situation configuration, neither of which is easily expressed in one label or phrase.

Our objective is to define the central problem which the client presents and his feelings about it in terms of the chief interacting causes, which may be physical, psychological, economic, or cultural in any weighting. In reactive behavior problems of children, since inevitably family relationships are causally involved, such interrelationships should always be expressed in the diagnostic statement. The worker must have a good comprehension of the main syndromes of illness with their effect on social functioning; he must be familiar with the meaning of neuroses, psychoses and character disorders, and with the implications of more refined clinical interpretations arrived at by the psychiatrist.

Findings and Diagnostic Statement

Findings are the raw materials of diagnosis, but they are not diagnosis. Facts and inferences are not the same. It is important to be able to distinguish findings from diagnosis, just as it is important to distinguish diagnosis from treatment. Findings are the analyzed breakdown of the essential factors in a case. They may be listed separately or grouped under headings, as in the conventional diagnostic summary; diagnosis, however, requires the synthesis or interpretation of these factors to give the psychosocial meaning of the case as a whole. While in a logical way one would say that first one gathers data, then derives from these data certain significant items (findings), which when configurated give one the meaning (diagnosis) of a case, actually the inferential process is continuous and one can see fragmentary interpretative thinking related to an incident, an interview, or even a piece of behavior or attitude within a single episode.

In the early stages of a case, as one carries on successive interviews or assists the client to take the necessary steps to gather social evidence, one becomes aware of the significance of certain factors as over against other factors in the situation—their relative weightings for reasoned explanation become clearer. To the carefully trained worker a person's characteristic patterns of thinking, feeling, and behaving begin also to emerge as he gives his history or relates himself to the agency functions and procedures. The facts which seem to be most significant for understanding the problem or the person are called "findings." Sometimes workers write down their findings, sometimes they carry them in their heads, but in drawing inferences they go through a process of selecting, weighing, and giving special attention to certain data as against other data.

Findings are arranged in several ways, depending partly on what we are being asked to do. The findings below have been selected with an eye on Nicky, the chief "patient," referred from school as a behavior problem.

The family income is $12 a week, earned by the seventeen-year-old son for a family of four. The father has recently been deported. The mother has chronic multiple arthritis, with almost total incapacity. A thirteen-year-old girl does most of the cooking and housework. Nicky, aged seven, is not his mother's favorite, and she rarely shows him affection. Two months after his father's deportation Nicky began teasing and hitting the children at school, fighting with his sister, and breaking things about the house. Physical examination of the children shows them to be underweight and undernourished. The older children are constantly held up as examples of dutiful behavior to Nicky.

Relating these factors—drawing inferences—we might arrive at the following interpretation.

Diagnostic Statement: Nicky, an undernourished and neglected child, is showing aggressive behavior, which, deriving in part from his being unwanted and rejected, is now accentuated by the additional deprivation involved in the loss of his father. The home setting is one of general financial strain, together with impairment of the mother's child-caring and home-making roles. Nicky's resentment of his sister may be explained by the marked approval now given her by the mother for her household activities. Both good children are now allied with the mother against him, and he alone is bad.

Perhaps further study would show that Nicky feels his father had been sent away because he was bad, and we might discover evidence of many fears or other symptoms. If so, we might make a fuller interpretation adding the phrase "neurotic anxiety" to the diagnostic statement. This diagnostic picture would be reviewed with the consulting psychiatrist, and a plan of treatment worked out which would include both child and family. If the family had been referred for financial assistance the study might have been initially more weighted with economic and eligibility material, residence, and so forth, the findings would have reflected this selection, and consequently the diagnosis, when made, would be accented to that end. If and when Nicky's problem emerged, a new formulation centered around Nicky as "patient" would be made.

We have indicated in Chapter VII [4] patterns for social study or

4 See pp. 198, 205.

psychogenetic history. Following the eligibility study a statement defining the need situation should be made as a basis for determining the grant. For instance:

This is the case of a man, wife, and three young children, in which financial need is created by the man's incapacity to support, due to severe and possibly terminal diabetes. As the mother must remain home to look after the children and there are no financial resources either in assets or in relatives' contributions, there is a condition of complete economic dependency of the family unit.

The statement should be followed by a recommendation of the type and amount of assistance to be granted.

A good diagnostic habit suggests the questions: How severe is the social reality? and How troubled is the person? Certain problems show a primary conflict with the environment, and suggest making an effort to modify the unfavorable environmental pressures as the initial step in treatment, for example:

This problem of insufficient income is the result of the relative unemployability of an over-age person in the job market.

A mother complains that her five-year-old daughter fights with her and with other children, is defiant, destructive, provocative, and generally out of hand. Study shows that there were signs of feeding- and toilet-training difficulty, scenes and temper tantrums at nursery age, an indulgent grandmother; that the mother has a marked preference for the younger brother. The child is intelligent and precocious, and although a handful at nursery school, not half so bad as the mother makes her out. The grandmother both spoils the child and criticizes the mother. The background material shows that this mother felt rejected as a child and resented a much preferred younger sister. Although there is some attachment between father and daughter, he "tries to keep out of it," and the problem remains focused in a battle between mother and daughter.

This may be regarded as a primary behavior disorder. The aggressive behavior is a reaction to the mother's controlling pressure, which has a strong element of hostility in it. The situation is made more acute by the presence of the grandmother, who openly indulges the grandchild and criticizes the mother's handling. In this we see a reactivation of the mother's feelings of rejection and sibling rivalry, now displaced upon the little girl. The child's behavior pattern is one of provocation and retaliation against the mother, and the disappointment may be said to be mutual.

In casework, when the request or complaint is a multiple one, or if there is conflict, confusion, or anxiety shown, or concern to get "straightened out," or the like, the worker is usually justified in assuming that the problem involves a disturbance of personality functioning, and treatment will be in the nature of emotional readjustment, that is, "therapy." [5] In child placing there should always be an initial diagnosis of the family situation which necessitates the placement, including significant attitudes and relationships affecting the child, as these will constantly reappear in different guises throughout foster placement. For instance:

The placement of Bobby, six, and Sally, five, is necessitated by the hospitalization of the mother for manic-depressive psychosis. The father, who has assumed little responsibility for the support of the family, while expressing some affection for Bobby, rejects Sally as not being his child, more, it appears, as a way of avoiding payments than because he really believes it. Both children are reacting to the traumatic separation with acute behavior, Bobby with bursts of aggression, and Sally by refusing to eat.

Such preliminary diagnoses will have to be individualized for each child later and further clarified, but the original family dynamics should not be lost sight of in subsequent planning. Actually, such a diagnostic statement should follow a careful family study summary similar to those made in a child guidance agency, the interpretation becoming the culminating paragraph of the summary. Ideally, each child's social and psychological situation should be well understood before placement plans are undertaken. This does not mean that parents who want to place their children should be persuaded against doing so. As in all casework, the request is fully discussed and the parents' responsibility for the decision is recognized. The current tendency to prepare both parent and child for the "separation experience" affords an excellent opportunity for a

[5] See pp. 252–69.

stronger diagnostic formulation than used to be possible when placements were too often treated as emergencies.

Diagnostic formulation of an unstable marital and child-parent situation might be as follows:

This is the case [6] of a young couple intermittently separated after a forced marriage. Unemployment and the economic strains of living with in-laws increased the friction. Moreover, the man seems tied to his mother as a source of assistance and moral support. Mr. M. takes very little responsibility for the failure of the marriage. He appears to be a self-centered person who projects all the blame upon others, instead of trying to work things out. He is just another child who wants to be taken care of by his mother, and would need a maternal wife, which Mrs. M. is not. He has a sense of inadequacy and fear of a rival, which makes him suspicious and jealous. Now he seems greatly detached. With his inferiority feelings and effeminate make-up he may want a wife more as proof of his own masculine respectability than on the basis of affection. His role with his little girl has been a maternal one. Because of unemployment and low income, the wife assumes a wage-earning, masculine role, and she apparently is a poor housekeeper and manager. She seems to want the child occasionally, but not to take full responsibility for her nurture. She is not maternal—liking Sarah most as a little pal. She is interested in her work and her social contacts, and is rather casual about her domestic relations. The child is a pawn in the struggle between the parents, and her current relinquishment by the mother to the paternal grandmother may be regarded as a partial rejection.

Or an instance descriptively formulated of marital and financial interacting factors, classified as "desertion" and "nonsupport":

The husband is economically unstable, turning to women for support. In the psychosexual area, it is apparent that living in a marriage situation is difficult for him. He is wholly asocial in this area—deserting, negating the existence of his child. He is alcoholic and has severe temper outbursts. He repeats situations over again and again. In terms of the real situation, he is of no value as a husband. The wife has strong dependency needs, as illustrated by her failures through life. A strong masochistic drive, with a tendency to self-destruction, provokes situations in which she is always the loser. To the persons closest to her she shows great

[6] This is an extract from the Monte Case given in the first edition of *Theory and Practice of Social Case Work.*

ambivalence. She lacks personality integration to enable her to use her past experiences in her present situation. She acts out rather than permits herself to feel tension. She seems to have only a small amount of guilt over failure of the marriage.

In regard to the neglect of the children the interpretation might be:

Mrs. B. shows minimal ability to carry out her motherhood. Her illegitimate child may have been the working out of a phantasy about her own birth and throughout she has had a tendency to neglect her severely. In her own life experience Mrs. B. was "boarded." Her father died; her mother worked. Left to the care of the grandmother, with her first child she repeats and then undoes what was done to her. Her inability to handle her youngsters adequately stems from her resistance to facing what was done to her. Because of her basic dependence, she cannot face what she is doing to her children, and the outlook for a stable home is discouraging, as she can neither permit it to function nor break it up. (The last sentence is prognostic.)

Collaborative Diagnoses

On the whole, clients come to social workers because of a failure in social adaptation, which may be a simple reality, that is, reaction to pathological environment, or may be the result of neurotic conflict acted out through the family or some other social situation. Medicine and psychiatry get chiefly those cases in which problems are presented in the form of suffering or of symptom formation and disability. In cases of illness, physical or mental, or in severe emotional disturbance the diagnosis is made by a physician or a psychiatrist, since medical treatment remains in their hands. In many instances the caseworker, in consultation with psychiatrist or physician, may carry out whatever social treatment is needed; in still others the social worker may assume full responsibility for psychosocial treatment. Social workers, however, need careful and full professional disciplines in order to recognize which diagnoses lie within and which without their competence.

In casework we are not yet able to base interpretation on objective tests and measurements; the caseworker must find his data largely through observation and interviews and structured living experiences. Considerable research has been done in psychological laboratories on aptitude tests, but it is not yet clear how useful they are in treating the person in trouble. No mechanical instrument has yet been invented to measure the extent of sibling rivalry or hypertension in marital relations. Besides the intelligence tests, there are many valuable measures, especially in the so-called projective techniques, such as thematic apperception, and Rorschach tests used as aids to clinical diagnosis and to evaluate personality. So far the individual Rorschach coupled with the interview seem to offer the best methods for appraising potentiality for emotional controls and abstract thinking, freedom from childish dependency, a reasonable tolerance for life's anxiety, and so forth. Even the projective test, however, like the psychometric, must not be regarded as absolute, but as one element in clinical diagnostic procedure.

There is no truer sign of professional maturity than knowing where one's own boundaries lie. As caseworkers achieve greater security in their own observations, they are less tempted to route their clients hastily here and there in search of oracles or, through mistaken pride, to refrain from sharing activities. The better the caseworker's training, the more deliberate will be his use of experts, for he will first make a careful preliminary diagnosis. This does not mean that in the face of obvious disease the caseworker does not at once seek medical consultation, but most cases present themselves to a social agency with the psychosocial configuration uppermost—the problem as acted out through familial and social functions. For these the social worker, with and without medical consultation, will probably continue to be assigned by the community major responsibility for psychosocial diagnosis and treatment.[7] Since group or team practice is already well established in social work, staff consultants from various specialties should be available.

The caseworker who is engaged in therapy should be sufficiently grounded in the dynamics of personality to understand such classifications as "neurosis," "behavior problem," and "character disorders" for each "patient" in treatment. In many agencies case-

[7] For discussion of psychotherapy see Chapters IX and X.

workers are encouraged, as an aid to precise thinking, to make more discriminating classifications, and since psychotherapy should be carried on in collaboration with a consulting psychiatrist, this would seem to be a progressive step. In other words, the caseworker should be qualified to make the person-situation (psychosocial) and interpersonal or interfamilial diagnosis and should, therefore, be able to participate in the formulating of the diagnoses for the more common "clinical" types of neurosis, psychosis and character disorders. Familiarity with clinical concepts is essential in family and children's casework, as well as in the child guidance clinic. The treatment of disease remains the responsibility of the physician, but the treatment of medical social problems, of patients and their relatives, and the treatment of ill patients with disturbed social functioning must be shared with social workers and members of other professions.

THE EVALUATION PROCESS

Diagnosis and evaluation are complementary intellectual processes directed toward eliciting the meaning of a case; both begin at intake and continue to be used with varying emphasis throughout treatment. At intake we make a rough decision as to the nature of the problem presented through the "complaint." "What is the matter?" calls for a diagnostic formulation. At intake, also, we make some estimate of the person's capacity or incapacity, readiness or unreadiness to use help, cultural factors, and so on, and these social judgments are known as "evaluation."

When the interpretation is directed, not toward defining the problem, but toward analyzing how the person is meeting his problem, the result would appear to be an evaluation rather than a diagnosis. Emphasis on the assets, the potential strengths of the client in taking the step of helping himself by seeking help has been, perhaps, a useful corrective to the tendency to become preoccupied with problem material; but we should recognize that the evaluation of a client's potentialities to help himself in a treatment relationship has not the same purpose as the descriptive defining process we call diagnosis, although diagnostic and evaluative skills are equally indispensable in the "unity of the casework process." Since social work utilizes so much this estimate of the person as an essential part of the meaning of the case, it is important to understand the clinical picture in relation to specific social ends. If one were to express this in a sort of mathematical formula, one might say that diagnosis is to problem and situation, as evaulation, both of personal potentiality and social resources, is to treatment.

Evaluation is a balancing movement which weighs assets and liability, strengths and weaknesses, constructive and destructive courses of action. It begins in the first interview when we try to decide whether the case is suitable for our agency; whether we are the best resource for the help needed. It appears again when we appraise the client's strength to work on his problem, his reliability, his practical assets, and his character. Understanding what a person feels about his situation and what he wants to do to correct it, what he wants to become, is as important as understanding causal factors in the socio-economic environment. In a first contact with a client and thereafter one is appraising the current functioning of the personality in terms of adequacy or inadequacy to deal with the problem, willingness to cooperate, to take some part in the solution, how well he has managed his affairs heretofore, how realistic is his request, how well can he withstand limitations, delays, frustrations of any kind without undue tension or aggression or anxiety.

Eligibility as a casework process has in it more evaluation than diagnostic emphasis.[8] Our chief question in determining eligibility is not so much "What is the matter?" as whether the person is entitled under the statute or other conditions to this assistance or this service. The emphasis throughout is largely weighing of assets and liabilities, mobilizing strengths and resources, determining whether the client does or does not meet fixed conditions. In public assistance, for instance, in initial stages at least, a problem-solving approach is not necessary—the assumption being that the citizen-

[8] See pp. 199–205.

client is a self-directing person who is applying for a known benefit.

A common form of evaluation is related to the selection and use of a foster home. We do not say "What is the matter, and how did it come about? but "How good will this home prove to be, or how good has it proved to be, for this child?" What is evaluated in a foster home is less the economic aspects, although minimum economic security must be assured, than those less tangible, but essential human elements on the part of the foster parents—a positive love for children, "common (that is, a good "reality") sense," firmness, tolerance, and willingness, because of general maturity, to work along with agency and parents.

In adoptions, the whole process is speeded by improved methods of diagnosis and evaluation. It is possible to determine much more accurately than formerly the unmarried mother's psychological and social situation as regards potential parental functioning; to distinguish the psychopaths, psychoneurotics and character disorders from more normal personalities and, therefore, better to appraise the wisdom or unwisdom of plans for keeping or giving up the baby. Because of greater accuracy in the testing of young babies, constitutional defects can be discovered earlier and attitudes towards children appraised. Since modern culture still stigmatizes, though less than formerly, both the child born out of wedlock and its mother, casework plans often are not ideal but only the best that can be made under the circumstances. Some day, when mental health for children and parents is approached in a wise and tolerant culture, the program for the child born out of wedlock will take on fresh aspects. This shows that evaluation is always relative. We can evaluate only in terms of a given standard, a norm, a goal for a course of action—in terms, that is to say, of something else. Under certain conditions dependency is normal and regression to be expected. When retardation is noted, one can only apprehend its meaning with some reference to norms of behavior and development for this age level. In consultation with the psychiatrist one tries to account for the deviation—physical or psychosocial—whether likely to be transitory or to interfere with growth. Well-focused diagnosis and evaluation of young children afford the possibility of far-reaching preventive elements. Children are observed minutely, both currently and in sequential behavior, noting the immediate factors in the environment to which they are reacting, gaining a careful history from the parents, and thus estimating the level of maturation and possible fixation or regression. Since a child's development is known to be extremely fluid, evaluation proceeds with caution.

This is an unusually gifted pre-adolescent girl, with a keen sensibility and some originality in her fancy. She has already reached her social adjustment in so far as she has accepted her feminine role. Her sensuality, which is strong, is no matter of guilty feeling, but is, on the contrary, a way of stressing her artistic sensibility. She is also selfish, vain, and exhibitionist; she knows that she is bright and clever and wants to make everyone know it. She is not well-trained for hard work; and since she is quick to learn and everything appears easy to her, she is superficial, and certainly more bright than efficient. But nevertheless she is definitely superior to the average. No real deep problem is to be found, as she is resolving her infantile complexes in an artistic mood.

Consideration of the client's current adaptation or social functioning supplies some diagnostic clues to the person-problem formulation, but more typically is part of the evaluation process. Also, family pathology (diagnosis) should be distinguished from how the members are functioning in spite of their problems (evaluation). The family constellation must be evaluated, its strengths and weaknesses and balance, as a unit. We cannot arrive at a plan just by knowing the type of problem or the severity of the problem; we must also know how one is tackling his problems. The clinical principle suggests that it is not the amount of anxiety that counts, but how the personality is tolerating the anxiety. So it is important to get an impression of anxiety in relation to the ego defenses. Is the anxiety diffuse, stimulated by many situations, or stimulated by a particular situation? Does it come from within with a definite form, or does it seem to be free-floating, unattached to a specific problem? Anxiety results from repression of impulses, which leads to symptom formation, thereby draining off emotional energy by means of displacement. The degrees to which neurotic symptoms impair functioning differ greatly, but if anxiety is pervasive and it continually impairs activity, it suggests psychoanalytic procedure.

In considering the maturity or immaturity of a person's reaction one observes the person's attitudes toward and handling of reality both within the interview and in the outer world. How reasonable is the client's idea of himself, his problems, capacities, achievements? How much self-esteem or inadequacy does he show? What is his level of self-control, his need to control or dominate others? How rigid or flexible, responsible, adventurous, reliable, or unreliable does he appear? Is he able to express his feelings—appropriately, inappropriately—or does he seem to be unable to express feeling spontaneously? These and similar observations supply a clue to the functioning of the individual. How well the family manages with respect to its particular culture can also be evaluated, although the multiplicity of factors makes estimation more difficult. The position of the client, his status and role within the family, is an important consideration.

Careful recording is essential for evaluation just as it is for diagnostic formulation. Some impression as to the client's readiness, capacities, and ability to use treatment, which appears at the close of an intake interview, is often helpful. The first formal evaluation recorded after the diagnostic summary appears in the statement of prognosis and treatability. Evaluation of the client's progress in treatment, which is a matter of constant review, may be shown by running comment and by evaluation summaries in which the course, use, and results of treatment are discussed.[9] Evaluation in regard to the progress of treatment and the pros and cons of termination should be set down. The goal of treatment is always to help the person return as soon as possible to his natural channels of activity with relationships strengthened so far as possible. This evaluation is, of course, shared with the client and tentative arrangements for termination of treatment agreed upon. We shall now consider the goals and methods of treatment in more detail.

[9] See pp. 133–41.

CHAPTER IX

METHODS OF TREATMENT

SINCE THE GOAL of treatment in casework is to stabilize or to improve the functioning of the client in terms of social adaptation or adjustment, especially in the balance of inner and outer forces, the psychosocial approach in study and diagnosis is also the characteristic of treatment aims and methods. The distinctive characteristics of the casework method have been described earlier: [1] the conscious, controlled use of worker-client relationship; skill in the interviewing process; knowledge of and skill in the use of social resources; skill in the use and interpretation of agency policy and services and interagency collaboration. Treatment is always conditioned by culture, by the mores and opportunities of the community, and by the aptitude and skill of the individual worker and his participant associates.

THE CONCEPT OF ADJUSTMENT

Critics of social work may suspect in the word "adjustment" an attempt to make the client accept—in the sense of acquiescence— a harsh, depriving, and unjust society. This is not true. The caseworker may, however, help the client to identify what is real in the external world, whether he or anyone else acquiesces in it or not. This may be more easily understood if one thinks not solely of economic affairs, but of other situations, for example, a child, in an unfavorable parental setting. The caseworker will first approach this through the parent-child relationship and will try to modify parental attitudes and behavior toward the child. If successful in this, parental pressures will be reduced, the child will behave better,

[1] See Chapters II–V.

and perhaps nothing further need be done. If the parental incapacities are too great, or the rejection of the child too deep-seated, some form of foster care, either substitute parents or an institution, may be offered, to insure the child a more favorable environment.

Sometimes this radical change of setting will work out well, and the child will make a happy "adjustment," but not always. If a child has been subjected to a depriving situation with which he is in conflict and the struggle has remained directed against the environment, shifting the factors and reducing the pressures may enable him to handle them better; but if the deprivations have set up a personality conflict—because of his own angry, retaliating, and anxious feelings—altering the external factors alone will not help him. The caseworker may then have to try, through direct treatment, to modify the child's feelings. When the individual, whether child or adult, cannot accept himself or others, when his social behavior and attitudes are affected, when his feelings are complicated, confused, or contradictory, psychological treatment is usually indicated. In intrapsychic conflicts creating symptoms or severe behavior disorders or suggesting a disease process, a psychiatrist should be consulted, but if the problem is not too diffused or the struggle too severe or of too-long duration, the caseworker may by "direct" treatment, help the child to cope with his own family.

It will be clear that these considerations obtain also in economic social situations. When the need is purely external and the struggle is to make a living under unfavorable circumstances, there is no problem of "adjustment" which a job or financial assistance may not satisfy. But if the struggle with a hostile world has been internalized—even though the difficulty seems to be displaced on unemployment or other concrete situations—a job will not necessarily remove the dependency or economic benefits reduce the hostility or the anxiety. Personality adjustment may be attempted by direct treatment, environmental treatment, or a combination of both, the requisite conditions being that the client himself wishes to change and that he will pursue whatever course of treatment will help him either to change his situation or to modify his attitudes and behavior patterns, and that to a greater or lesser degree he will accept his responsibility to effect a change. The goal of emotional readjustment is usually equated with therapeutic aims and techniques discussed in the latter part of this chapter.

Objectives and Focus of Treatment

One way of expressing the objective of psychosocial adjustment would be to say that the caseworker is interested in preventing social breakdown, in conserving strengths, in restoring social functions, in making life experiences more comfortable or compensating, in creating opportunities for growth and development, and in increasing the capacity for self-direction and social contribution. A person's ability to maintain himself depends on his constitutional equipment, his acculturated personality, his self-awareness, and the resources and opportunities available to him.

The psychosocial objective is implemented by attempts: (a) to change or improve the person's situation either by supplying a social resource, such as financial aid, or changing the environment, as in child placing, or modifying a school program; (b) to help a person change his attitudes or behavior within the social situation, either by "environmental manipulation" or direct interviewing treatment; (c) or in combination. Sometimes the objective is only to keep the situation from further deterioration, to sustain the *status quo*—maintain whatever the current level of personality functioning may be, through psychological and practical support. Social action directed toward improving general economic and cultural conditions is the responsibility of social workers along with other groups, but such social action is not part of the "casework process," as such, which always refers to the balance between inner and outer forces in a particular situation.

The caseworker asks himself in what areas and with what means he can best meet the problem presented. Parents may come to the agency to complain about a child's tendency to steal or his retardation in school, and may ask for psychological tests. What they may actually want is to rid themselves of the burden of a troublesome child. To some degree they must be helped to come to grips with their real objective as early as possible, not in terms of unconscious motivation, because inevitably defenses will prevent this, but in terms of a progressive formulation of possible treatment aims and alternatives.

To be helpful, all treatment must be based on careful diagnosis. Blanket plans and opportunistic methods without a knowledge of the person, his behavior, motivation, and situation, have little value. Needs may be largely environmental and socio-economic, or personal and emotional, but usually they are mixed, so that differential treatment must be planned with respect to psychological and social components. The caseworker considers the whole situation as a living human event, in which emotional, mental, physical, economic, and social factors interact in various proportions and are not peculiar to agency settings. Therefore, treatment may possibly embrace or touch upon all these factors. A medical worker does not deal with a physical problem alone, a public assistance worker with an economic problem, a psychiatric worker with an emotional problem, an X worker with an X problem, but each is concerned with a human being, and in every situation numerous factors operate. On the other hand one does not offer omnibus services divided into parts, so many economic, so many emotional, so many health; but the direction of the treatment will, in part, be determined by the preponderance and weighting of factors in any given situation. The treatment aim is directed initially toward the client's main complaint, always remembering that its connection with the core problem may later emerge.

"Focusing" means deciding what to do in the light of the presenting request, the diagnosis, and what the client seems able and willing to undertake. Focusing means determining the direction of the treatment and periodically reviewing it with the client, since the focus may be changed because of new factors not earlier apparent. Normally, focus is possible only when there is a good relationship with the client. Where there is poor *rapport*, the client will be unwilling to help focus the treatment aim.

SPECIFIC MEANS OF TREATMENT

In any area of treatment one assumes that there are appropriate clusters of basic techniques depending on the problem, the aim, treatability, agency function, and other factors, such as: the establishment of confidence; the reduction of anxiety by acceptance, support, and measures undertaken to assure an understanding of the problem and to help the client meet it; the maintenance of focus on specific goals desired by the client, through shared steps in exploration and the mobilization of inner and outer resources; the support of constructive defenses and work with the relatively non-conflicted part of the intrapsychic aspects of the client's personality; the introduction of practical resources; structuring situations to stimulate growth and sublimation by arousing interests, aptitudes and talents. The worker undertakes to clarify obscure feelings and attitudes which, pre-conscious or partially conscious, vaguely disturb the client, so as to enable him to have a better understanding of the role he is playing. Usually such clarification has the intent to permit the expression of more feeling by the client within the relationship, reducing the tensions of uncertainty, and thus to enlist the healthier parts of the personality in the struggle.[2]

Classification of Treatment Methods

A number of attempts have been made to classify the chief methods of treatment; for example, executive, enabling (leadership); direct and indirect; direct and environmental. All social and personal combinations shift and overlap. Any of them may be used in one particular case, but weighted differently in another. In this connection the terminology is not precise. "Treatment" is the word most commonly used, but one also finds "social services," "the helping process" (in functional casework), and "therapy," the last too often incorrectly offered as an equivalent for "treatment." The word "treatment" is used in medicine, but as it is also the term for finishing a piece of furniture, it is not necessarily or exclusively

[2] See pp. 43–46 for further discussion of psychotherapeutic aims.

"clinical" in application. In the dictionary "treatment" is defined as "conducting oneself in a specified manner," "applying a special process to," and this appears to be a suitable over-all term for any consciously controlled process. The essential attribute of treatment is that whether one uses predominantly practical and environmental or predominantly psychological means, the aim is better psychosocial functioning or adaptation. Another characteristic feature is its interpersonal, multiple client focus. In medical and psychiatric settings [3] the relative was often "manipulated" in the interest of the chief patient although this emphasis is changing so as to include family treatment when relevant, but in family and child-guidance work the persons significantly involved in the problem will typically be treated in relation to each other as well as in their own interest. The point is that the treatment aim may be: (a) individual psychosocial, that is, toward an individual who because of disability or other problem requires social adjustment, such as a job, money, or attitude modification; (b) toward an individual, the solution of whose problem requires the treatment of the family in a peripheral, or major way, as in child guidance; (c) toward several members of the family who may become "patients" in their own behalf as well as with respect to each other. Each situation poses a different diagnostic problem and calls for a specific goal of treatment. It may be desirable to have more than one worker, whenever a "client" desires treatment for himself alone.

For simplification we shall discuss the main approaches under three classifications, namely, (a) administration of a practical service, (b) environmental manipulation, and (c) direct treatment. The first two may be utilized with a minimum of direct treatment (except that interviewing and the use of relationship are basic to all method), the practical resource or the modified situation or program or new opportunity being thus engaged as the principal means of change. In direct treatment, the weight falls on the use of relationship through the interview or, with children, the play interview. Supplementary practical services and the manipulation

[3] See pp. 273, 293.

of the environment will frequently, although not necessarily, be used as tools or components or phases in direct treatment. Often the psychosocial aim in direct treatment is achieved because of the fact of simultaneous interviewing of two or more interacting persons in the family, the improved relationship between such persons thus representing the primary adaptation or adjustment area. In general, because the client's functioning in society, as well as in respect to his own legitimate gratification, is involved, the caseworker is concerned not only to help him satisfy his immediate needs, but also to stimulate and release his capacity for constructive social living and his assumption of appropriate responsibilities in the community.

Administration of a Practical Service

This is one of the oldest and best known of the casework types of treatment. The first attempt to describe it was in Porter Lee's "executive and leadership" classification.[4] The current equivalent is "administration of a social service."[5] In the simplest version the worker assists the client to choose and to use a social resource afforded by the community. Casework relationship[6] is the medium, it is true, in so far as the interview is the means of discussion,

---

[4] Lee, *Social Work as Cause and Function*, p. 113: "the executive aspect of social treatment, because it involves chiefly the discovery of a particular resource and arranges for its use," and "the leadership aspect of treatment, because it involves primarily not the use of other resources but the influence of the personality of the worker,"—what today one would call the client's readiness and ability to change. It is well to remember the word *aspect*, since treatment is rarely all one thing or all the other.

[5] De Schweinitz, Elizabeth and Karl, "The Contribution of Social Work to the Administration of Public Assistance," *Social Work Journal*, July, 1948, and October, 1948, "That 'job' [financial assistance] is an *administered*, as contrasted with a clinical service. It centers in the requirements that go with the operation of a fund of nationwide visibility. In this service the public assistance worker finds many of the same problems which perplexed the pioneers of 1877, and other problems that are new. The dilemma of individual and social responsibility is as insistent as it ever was; the work of securing to the individual his rights as a member of the community and of keeping the doors of initiative open continues to be a major consideration; and the goal of security with freedom involves the maintenance of the most difficult of balances, that between the individual and the society of which he is a part."

[6] See pp. 28–33.

information, and explanation. A mature person may be scarcely conscious of the relationship, the resource itself being regarded as the important thing. If, however, the client is infirm or ill the relationship may be strongly supportive, and the worker may more actively bring the resource within reach of the client. If the client has little ability to deal with actual situations because of a weak "character" or "ego" structure, if he has a distorted sense of reality, if he must act out his impulse without regard to conditions, limits, or cultural mores, if he is too self-inhibiting to find satisfaction in and make his normal contribution to society, then an educational, manipulative, or therapeutic process may be instituted.

Some would say that only if a practical service is involved can the process be regarded as casework,[7] but this is not our view. The typical case formulation, as we have already indicated, is neither the purely social nor the intra-psychic conflict, but the psychosocial interaction. Services may be offered either through the operation of one's own agency or through the cooperation of two or more agencies. The proper use of a practical resource implies a diagnostic survey, appraisal of the client's own strengths and resources, and a movement toward intake or else preparation and careful referral to the appropriate agency or institution. Counseling may take place accompanied or unaccompanied by a social service.

Frequently the client knows what he wants, but does not know where or how to get the service or the resource; sometimes he knows what he wants only vaguely, and his need must be clarified by the worker; occasionally, he is too handicapped to act for himself, and then the worker must act on his behalf to procure the necessary aid. It is a professional obligation to serve the client in one's own

[7] Aptekar, Herbert, "The Use of Private Psychiatrists by a Social Agency," *Jewish Social Service Quarterly*, March, 1949, p. 387. "Casework in origin, by tradition, and by logic, should be regarded as a sphere of helping in which concrete services are always predominant . . . the caseworker must center his attention upon the service he is administering and its significance for the client. . . . Counselling as I see it is a form of helping which, like casework, is therapeutically oriented. Unlike casework, however, it does not derive from nor is it attached to the concrete service. What it is dependent upon, however, is an externalized problem. Casework attempts to meet externalized problems through the administration of social services with psychological understanding."

agency, if feasible, or to send him where he will be best served, either to a tax-supported or a voluntary agency. The worker, having a precise and thorough knowledge of community resources, uses them selectively and economically; otherwise, clients may be passed along from one worker to another and shuttled about, while no one takes the responsibility for preparation and referral. This service well performed is one of social work's most valuable contributions. A large part of all treatment is concerned with such practical services. The resource is the "treatment," but the casework method enables the person to use it constructively. Providing financial assistance, offering shelter, procuring legal aid or medical care, and arranging for camps or convalescent opportunities are examples of such tangible, practical activities. The understanding of cultural patterns, as well as of agency functions, is called for in determining the best sources of help. The worker is "trustee" not only of the particular resources his agency represents but also of all health and welfare resources of which it is his responsibility to have accurate knowledge.

Although the main objective of public assistance is the meeting of a need as defined by statute rather than as arrived at by diagnosis, and therefore the method may be thought of more as an "administrative" than as a "clinical" version of casework method, it is not always possible to make such sharp distinctions. How this is to be answered finally may depend on the evolving functions of public, family and child welfare services. In social work the line between the administration of a social service as an end in itself and its administration as part of an educational or therapeutic plan cannot be drawn hard and fast. Practical social services may enrich or reinforce other means of treatment. Reality testing which employs practical services may actually become an aspect of therapy.

What brings practical services within social-case method is the degree to which the worker in the relationship (a) individualizes the person, (b) has the diagnostic ability to understand the nature of the problem, and (c) motivates independence, self-help, self-awareness, and responsibility in the client so that he can continue to contribute something toward the solution of the problem or, if less competent, can be sustained in appropriate ways. Even in apparently simple situations a great deal of diagnostic skill is called for, not only because needs are unique, but because they are not always what they seem. People may displace emotional needs and conflicts on unemployment or an operation or a request for institutional care. There are many pitfalls, for if clients ask for a job and mean a job, they will not thank us for a deep exploration of their emotional needs. If, on the other hand, they ask for a job and we are not aware that this is only because they are too proud to ask for financial assistance, they will rightly think us obtuse. If they ask for a job, yet are really trying to tell us about their sense of discomfort and failure, unless we catch the overtones, we shall have given them a stone for bread. For example, when a man says, "I do not know whether to take out my small insurance in favor of my wife or my mother," he may want only a little practical advice; but he may be saying, "I am all mixed up in my feelings because of the pull between my mother and my wife. Please help me with them."

Environmental Manipulation

We do not use the term "manipulation," as it sometimes is used by laymen, to describe the undesirable attempt of the worker to force his concepts and plans on the client. We use the term in a more positive sense. After listening to and observing the client we may use our understanding of his personality structure, his patterns, his needs and conflicts, and his defenses in order to "manipulate" these configurations. We may make suggestions as to what steps may or may not help this individual to cope better with his problems; we may plan with him as to his emotional, professional, and recreational activities; we may give appropriate advice to members of his environment; we may modify his attitude and approach to his problems; or we may purposely activate relevant emotional attitudes in the client for the sake of adjustive change.[8]

[8] Bibring, Grete L. "Psychiatric Principles in Casework," *Principles and Techniques in Social Casework, Selected Articles* 1940–50. New York, 1950, p. 372.

All attempts to correct, or improve the situation in order to reduce strain and pressure, and all modifications of the living experience [9] to offer opportunities for growth or change may be regarded
as environmental manipulation, sometimes referred to as "indirect" treatment. "Manipulation" is not used in a coercive, any
more than "executive" is used in an authoritative, sense (above).
Relationship and interviewing are employed in the usual ways to
help to involve the client in the change, but the emphasis is upon
situational modification. One might prefer the term "social treatment," or "therapy," whenever social resources and arranged situations are the chief instrumentalities—homemaking services, camps,
and group experiences: substitute family care and educational, vocational, and other program adjustments. But on the whole, the
term "environmental manipulation" conveys a precise meaning
here. The approach may be predominantly toward a social or toward
an interpersonal adjustment—interacting roles.

The client may be placed in a more benign setting, such as a foster home, or encouraged to join a recreational or other group, so
that he will become able to function better in a kinder reality and
later, therefore, to deal with ordinary life situations.[10] The experience itself may neutralize certain attitudes or create new ones.
Progressive education emphasizes the living experience as the learning matrix for the individual. Growth and change may be stimulated
through any creative situation, as well as through interviewing.

Recreation may satisfy an inner need or craving; especially for
children and youth it discharges aggression in a healthy way and
supplies the need for action and the adequate expression of drives.
Environmental manipulation includes arranging programs to reduce strain, as for handicapped persons for whom competitive situations are to be avoided, for the overgraded school child, and to
promote growth, as in providing new stimuli and outlets through

[9] See Chapter IV and also pp. 105–14 for group experience.
[10] Austin, "Trends in Differential Treatment in Social Casework," *Journal of
Social Casework*, XXIX (June, 1948), 203–11.

social situations and experiences. Supplementing such attempts to arrange an experience, manipulation may also supply practical resources, but the administration of a social service would not be exactly comparable to the manipulation of the environment, especially since the modification of attitudes of others toward the chief client lies within this mode of treatment.[11] For such interpersonal adjustment, modification of the attitudes of significant persons, parent, teacher, spouse, may be a crucial objective. If a relative is peripherally involved in the patient's problem and counseling is limited to a specific situation, a superficial modification of attitude may be attempted. This effort is common in medical and psychiatric settings, when not only social programs but also negative attitudes toward the chief "patient" may be corrected. The appeal to school teachers on behalf of a disturbed child and to employers, friends, or relatives on behalf of the client, usually involves a single interview or at most a few contacts; a parent is less likely to be peripherally involved, although there are instances in which for practical purposes this is true. But we must remember that emotionally determined attitudes are not easily altered. Since casework frequently involves both spouses, parents, children, and various other members of the family constellation, treatment which makes considerable use of the interview in attempting to change attitudes may be regarded as "direct" treatment, that is, "counseling," guidance, or variants of psychotherapy discussed later in this chapter. When two workers [12] collaborate, the nature of the collaboration but not the details of the contact is known to parent and child and to each spouse in marital counseling. Confidentiality has to be explained, and its terms scrupulously observed so that what one partner reveals is not passed on to the other. On the other hand, collaboration among

[11] Florence Hollis, in *Women in Marital Conflict; a Casework Study*, uses the term "environmental support" to cover all steps taken to modify the client's environment, either by putting in a social service, or reducing external pressures by changing the attitude of someone in the client group through interpretation, or changing some physical aspect, as by finding an apartment or rearranging a school program.

[12] See pp. 48–50.

several members of a team may be necessary for a therapeutic result, and therefore should be assented to by the patient or patients, specifically or in general.

Interviewing either the client or the client group may include: helping with concrete plans; getting the permission of the client or his family for certain measures—releases for adoption and the like; the coordination of concurrent services and programs, explanation and suggestion, usually including a large component of emotional support. So far as possible the client is encouraged to make changes for himself, as he is encouraged to active participation in establishing eligibility and in the use of any practical service, but usually some intervention on the part of a social worker is required, because of his weak ego and his feelings of inadequacy and anxiety, to enable him to manage his own affairs. Sometimes the alleviation of environmental pressures proves to be enough, but often the quality of the worker-client relationship itself must also be "stepped up," either toward stronger support of the ego or inducing self-awareness which leads to better perception of reality. At this end of the range of methods the concept of direct treatment is applicable.

DIRECT TREATMENT

By "direct treatment" is meant a series of interviews carried on with the purpose of inducing or reinforcing attitudes favorable to maintenance of emotional equilibrium, to making constructive decisions, and to growth or change. The term also includes psychological support, always a large factor in casework methods of psychosocial adjustment. In all casework methods it is assumed that the client is helped to be more keenly aware of the situation and of himself in relation to the situation, but in the administration of a social service awareness is usually limited to understanding the problem, the conditions of eligibility, and the policy and procedures under which the service is available. In interviewing techniques not confined to the administration of a social service, the purpose is to help the client to be as aware as possible of the ways in which he is reacting to the reality factors in his situation and, perhaps, contributing to the problem. In the decade following the publication of *Social Diagnosis*, American casework was greatly influenced by psychoanalytic psychiatry, so that its basic method, especially in interviewing technique and the use of relationship, contains much that is adapted from psychoanalytic principles. The more one moves in the direction of psychotherapy, the more control there must be of the worker-client relationship and the more self-involvement, self-awareness, and some degree of emotional adjustment will be the goal. It is difficult and perhaps unnecessary to draw hard and fast lines among therapeutic casework, counseling, and forms of "limited" psychotherapy, but certain aims and emphases can be described. Just as all casework method is psychosocial, so at the therapeutic end of the scale psychotherapeutic aims retain their psychosocial characteristics.

Counseling

The most common expression of direct interviewing treatment is counseling, which is to some degree an educational process. Counseling is intended to help a person in a rational way to sort out the issues in his situation, to clarify his problem and his conflicts with reality, to discuss the feasibility of various courses of action, and to free the client realistically to assume the responsibility of making a choice. The term "counselor," which has become recently popular, is used indiscriminately; it is applied to those who teach arts and swimming in camp as well as to those who are engaged in a guidance process. We use the term only for individual counseling that calls for professional education, training, and experience in interviewing. Just as it requires knowledge and skill to help the client use practical services to ameliorate his situation, so it requires knowledge and skill to help a client so use the interview that he can make up or change his mind. The main technique is, perhaps, that of clarification of the problem and feelings and attitudes toward it. In general there is a specific social problem (what Mr. Herbert

Aptekar calls "an externalized problem" [13]—of which the client is already conscious) to be solved. Counseling though "educational" is not a purely intellectual exercise since all learning is emotionally motivated. Counseling may be said to differ from therapy chiefly in the goal, in the kind of awareness sought and therefore in the intensity of emotional impact between client and worker.

The focus of counseling is the immediate social situation which must be resolved—its aim is to enlist the cooperation of the conscious ego in dealing with social problems and making social adaptations. "Clarification," Dr. Edward Bibring [14] points out, "by making the patient aware of certain attitudes, feelings, or by clarifying reality versus the subjective concept of it, permits him to see himself and the environment in a more objective manner which permits better control." Counseling may include the giving of information, explaining a regime and analyzing its issues, and analyzing the steps involved in a course of action. It is invoked in discussing a request with regard to the realities of the situation and to determine how much of it is wish or phantasy. If the social problem involves another person—parent, child, spouse, or other intimate relation, in any but the most superficial way, counseling may turn in the direction of psychotherapy. In the early days of child guidance one might say that the child was treated "therapeutically" by a psychiatrist and the parent was "counseled" by a caseworker as to how to handle the child. Nowadays family and child guidance require understanding of the interfamilial problem and treatment based on diagnostic understanding. Termination of treatment [15] involves the questions of focus, aim, treatability, and timing. These again are determined by the desires and capacities of the client, the purpose and function of the agency, the equipment of the workers, and the needs of the

[13] Counseling requires "a full psychological understanding, a process which is therapeutic in essence, skill in the use of structural forms and above all the capacity to focus upon externalized problem while appreciating its inner significance." Aptekar, Herbert. "The Use of Private Psychiatrists by a Social Agency," *Jewish Social Service Quarterly*, March, 1949, p. 388.
[14] "Psychotherapy and Casework," *Journal of Social Casework*, XXX (June, 1949), 259.
[15] See also pp. 203, 236.

community. True, with immature parents a certain amount of counseling can be effective about simple matters of child care, but the psychodynamics must be grasped or the real meaning of the parent's problem may be entirely missed and both parent and child may suffer from superficial handling. In its simpler forms counseling aims at intellectual comprehension, although this cannot be achieved without a feeling response: in complicated interpersonal relationships clarification can hardly take place without "abreaction," or a reliving of emotions experienced elsewhere within the worker-client relationship itself. When change of attitude and behavior is the goal, counseling merges with therapeutic interviewing in the direction of what is commonly thought of as psychotherapy, and any client becomes, in a sense, the "patient."

Therapeutic Interviewing [16]

Therapeutic endeavor ("curative," "of the healing art"), implying the existence of a disease or disability, has traditionally been regarded as the province of the physician. In the hospital setting, nursing, physiotherapy, occupational therapy, and other therapies are adjunctive to the responsibility for healing exercised by the physician. But as the field of medicine has broadened to include psychological and social, as well as biological, components—as the approach to problems of maladaptation has altered so as to embrace the social sciences and allied professions for new knowledge and skills, as psychodynamic concepts have been assimilated, psychotherapy is less easily confined to one branch of knowledge. Its place must be reexamined by the medical psychiatrist, the psychoanalyst, the general practitioner, and also by the social worker, the psycholo-

[16] The problem is stated by E. Bibring and J. J. Michaels in the *Journal of Social Casework* of June, 1949, in "Psychotherapy and Casework," Symposium of the Boston Psychoanalytic Society and Institute, Inc.: "Inasmuch as there is an area of overlapping in the work of the psychiatrist doing psychotherapy and the caseworker doing treatment, there is some danger of each discipline (psychiatry and social work) either losing its identity or stressing it too much. Discussions have arisen and are still continuing as to the relationship between the two disciplines. Thus those who emphasize what they have in common tend to lose sight of the differences and vice versa."

gist, the educator, the priest, and others concerned with human behavior.

Differentiated Approaches

One may clearly distinguish certain areas: clinical psychiatry, dealing mainly with psychoses, psychosomatic diseases, and severe, usually symptom-producing neuroses; psychoanalysis, a self-contained method dealing with intra-psychic conflict as such, including a minimum of the social components; and, at the other extreme "sociological" programs, such as employment, social insurance, and kindred means of social security. But the area of "psychotherapy" is not easy to delimit nor to assign to a single profession. Actually its techniques have not yet been fully "spelled out."

Maladjustment or maladaptation in social functioning may be largely the product of a pathological environment for which welfare services and environmental manipulation may be the appropriate remedy, but when a person projects or displaces his intra-psychic conflicts upon the environment, when he acts out his neurotic tendencies or behavior disorders in marital or parent-child or other relationships, direct psychotherapy at some level is usually indicated. For casework, as we have already suggested, at some point on the scale the citizen-"client" becomes "the patient." Usually the client does not apply to a social agency for relief of symptoms, since probably he does not consider himself "ill" and therefore does not seek a medical therapist; he may or may not ever reach a mental hygiene clinic. He will be more likely to do the latter if he does have distressing symptoms; or parents with a child who is a "behavior problem" may project conflicts so as to ask that the child be treated instead of themselves. A large number of confused, unhappy, and disturbed persons turn to social agencies, asking that homes be mended, children placed, or counsel given in situations in which psychological components are dominant. Marriages of neurotics which cannot be permitted by the partners either to fail or to succeed may be brought to the attention of family and children's agencies under the guise of nonsupport, neglect of children, illegitimacy, and unmarried parenthood. Traumatic experiences and neurotic conflicts are as much involved etiologically in family disturbances as in neurosis and certain functional mental diseases.

One may make the following arbitrary classification: (a) classical psychoanalysis, which needs no definition here, and closely related schools of thought which are commonly termed "psychoanalysis"; (b) psychotherapy, which, using psychoanalytic principles, modifies certain techniques; and (c) psychoanalytically oriented casework, which attempts emotional adjustment through interviewing and the living experience to affect the relation of the individual to the external world. The last two overlap somewhat or at least to some extent use similar techniques.[17] All psychotherapy must rest on understanding psychodynamics.

The basic concepts to be understood in any psychological treatment concern the structure and functions of the personality, the phenomena of transference, including counter-transference, repression, and resistance. In psychoanalysis free association is the central method; in limited-goal psychotherapy interviewing is more channelized and directed. The psychoanalyst's goal is to change and reintegrate the patient's neurotic personality through insight derived from a thorough exploration and reliving of unconscious infantile conflicts; the psychotherapeutic aim is that of adaptation through emotional readjustment. Derivatives of the unconscious are the chief media for interpretation in limited psychotherapy.

As derived from psychoanalytic principles psychotherapy is usually defined as a process rooted in a two-person relationship which

[17] It is recognized, of course, that there is much psychiatry which has not incorporated psychoanalytical principles and that there are schools of thought, both in "psychotherapy" and in casework, in which Freudian psychoanalysis has little or no place, but the psychotherapeutic discussion here assumes a theory of personality which is Freudian based. Such concepts as the structure of the personality itself, the system of the unconscious, the role of the defenses, psycho-sexual aspects of growth and development, anxiety, resistance, and so forth, should be, therefore, understood in that context. In a first edition of this book, written in the late thirties, the writer, in common with the caseworkers of that period, assumed that psychotherapy was the equivalent of psychoanalysis. Today psychotherapy is conceded to embrace many variants. However, the continued interchanging of the terms psychoanalysis with psychotherapy makes for endless confusion as to what is meant.

has the purpose of modifying attitudes and behavior largely, though not exclusively, through psychological processes. It is essentially a reliving experience, though not always of the remote past. Clinical and dynamic diagnosis is at the center, and the whole course of treatment is therapeutically controlled and oriented through the transference relationship. It is assumed that all "brief psychotherapy" is "goal limited," [18] reorganization of the total personality not being the aim, the resulting change or growth being "adjustive" rather than radical, "appropriate" rather than fundamental. Usually there is a problem area or theme and related defenses are selected for treatment, rather than the whole defense structure. The psychiatrist who uses psychotherapy may add as adjuncts medical and social therapies; the caseworker will usually support his therapeutic efforts with social therapies, calling in medical consultants as necessary. To date the details of these adapted techniques have been far less studied and tested than has the classical psychoanalytic method. Much remains to be done to clarify and refine these processes. The solution of practical problems always involves psychological factors to a greater or a lesser extent. As in all casework, especially when its aim is therapeutic, the problem must be clearly defined, the client's responses and wish for self-involvement must be tested, the area for treatment must be determined, whether intra-psychic solely or psychosocial, and the desired goal decided upon. The first question is always "What is to be done?" the second, "Who is best fitted to do it?" Both therapeutically and professionally appropriate treatment can be given only by practitioners who are well equipped to offer it.

Some writers believe that caseworkers and psychotherapists, though using psychoanalytic principles, must look in different directions or at different aspects of psychosocial adaptation; others, that these techniques legitimately overlap in "goal-limited treatment." It may well be that although all psychotherapy is based upon the same psychoanalytic principles, psychiatrists, psychologists, social workers, and others will give it different accents and

[18] Felix Deutsch, *Applied Psychoanalysis.*

emphases, psychiatrists tending to relate the intra-psychic conflict largely to biological processes, although cultural factors are receiving increasing attention, psychoanalysts to deeper layers of intrapsychic material, and social workers to external reality, but this will certainly vary with the needs of each case and the special interests and tendencies of the therapists, as well as with the disciplines, philosophy, and preoccupations of the several practitioners.

The therapist in depth treatment (psychoanalysis) of the intrapsychic conflict obviously must have extensive and rigorous technical training for this task because of handling irrational elements within the transference neurosis, but any good therapy calls for considerable training beyond medical, psychiatric, or social work basic education, and also for special aptitudes. Many caseworkers today are well equipped to use the interview and the living experience dynamically for release, support, clarification, and ego-strengthening activities. There are still controversial elements concerning the managing of the transference and the use of interpretation for direct or derivative insight, which can be solved only through careful and patient study and experiment.

Everyone aspiring to be a therapist must have a sound grasp of psychological dynamics and their phenomena, no matter what the form of expression, in order to offer treatment, manage treatment, or refer the client to the appropriate place for treatment, in terms of his real needs and problems, not because of ignorance, panic, or barriers artificially erected among the professions. Consultation and collaboration among the professions is assumed as necessary for sound practice not only in psychotherapy but in the science and art of human relations.

Transference

The phenomenon of transference, which is to say irrational elements carried over from other relationships, particularly in the past, now displaced upon the therapist, reflects unconscious motivation which must be understood and controlled in various ways. Strong attachments, fears, and hostilities on a real basis should not be confused with positive and negative transference. It is unrealistic to assume that the subtler aspects of transference manifestation are easily grasped or readily managed by the worker without specialized training. Professional education and supervision are essential.

Much worker-client relationship is based on objective world realities, even though potential or actual transference elements exist. Transference, however, may be increased in certain treatment aims, since in order to change attitudes or behavior the emotional components are inevitably heightened. In casework, however, transference is developed in terms of psychosocial interaction to reveal specific relationships and situations rather than held within the worker-client focus, as such. Transference is designed to free the patient sufficiently so that he may think and feel more realistically about his behavior and relationships, to support him in greater feelings of adequacy and confidence, and to mobilize him to express his powers creatively in social situations (sublimation). The transference situation, which in goal-limited therapy remains basically positive, is utilized, but sparingly commented upon and never fully analyzed. The attitude of acceptance does not mean unconditional love or that the client can unload all his infantile needs and hostile and ambivalent cravings for love or aggression upon the worker. Ordinarily, in applications transference is controlled by getting essential information and by various forms of reality testing; in treatment it is controlled rather by clarification, which is also a form of reality testing, and by formulating with the client goals toward which he is willing to work. In limited goal therapy the feeling experience within the relationship is usually related to the current situation and is therefore channelized into real relationships—family and foster family, employer, natural groups, teachers, and friends, which may be discussed within the interview.

Transference, which permits abreaction, is a heightened experience in which there is some reliving of current and old affects. The person will not only express infantile and hostile and distorted feelings, but also will usually make conscious connections between his current and his past behavior and between his behavior with the interviewer and outside. These connections lead to important flashes of self-awareness and often to improved attitudes and functioning. Even without such connections there may be "transference cures" [19] through the relationship experience, the value of which are variously assessed. Supported by social therapy (environmental manipulation), and even unsupported these recoveries sometimes appear to have considerable stability when the neurosis is not too pervasive or deep-seated. In limited therapy transference is not fully analyzed, but is controlled by discussion of social material by generalization, spaced interviews, and other reality factors. Release and mobilization of feeling, support and clarification, are made effective only by the management of transference elements in the relationship, including counter-transference.

Mobilizing Affect and Clarification

In the case of a seventeen-year-old girl [20] in conflict with her mother, in a very pathological home environment, therapy is limited to giving her insight into her feelings, but not their unconscious motivation. Unconscious material is not provoked or elicited, but unconscious derivatives are handled in relation to reality. Specific defenses are commented upon from time to time. She has been in treatment for several months and is diagnosed as a character disorder with neurotic traits.

Audry was in for her appointment ten minutes early. She looked badly physically, held her stomach and her head—her stomach was upset and she had "one of my terrible headaches." I said I was sorry she felt miserably, wondered if it didn't reflect her feelings too. Audry went through several moments denying this, to establish a physical basis for her illness. She had been up late again working with her mother, etc. When I commented (handling denial) on the difference in her mood she acknowledged then that her feelings were involved. She became quite upset, doubted that she could ever live with her mother. She didn't mean to threaten to run away—she'd not do that again—but she was just waiting for the next eight months to pass, when she would be 18,

[19] See G. L. Bibring, "Psychiatric Principles in Casework," *Journal of Social Casework*, XXX (June, 1949), 235.
[20] Below are excerpts from several entries.

then she would say good-bye and never, never return. I asked Audry about yesterday, what had happened, and she described her fatigue the night before (relating feelings to specific reality). I let her cry for a moment, then commented on the difference between her feelings today toward her mother's wish for her to accompany her on errands and those expressed yesterday. I said that yesterday I had the impression that Audry felt fine, now she was resentful. Perhaps something had happened even earlier in the afternoon while Audry was with mother to make her feel so let-down, done-in, when she got home. Audry protested mildly at first, then acknowledged that it was so. She had gone happily on the errands, believing her mother when she said they were so important that Audry, instead of Ellen, must come along. She thought it meant that mother was "forgiving" her for the hurt Audry caused when she ran away. She had felt reinstated in mother's eyes and the happiest she had been for weeks. After she had cancelled her appointment with me, which, she acknowledged with a little help from me, was at her own rather than her mother's instigation, she was in an ecstatic mood, convinced everything would be all right, and they had gone out again. In the course of the afternoon Audry stopped to look at some beautiful handkerchiefs in a window and wanted her mother to admire them with her. Mother became snappy, impatient, said Audry was "good for nothing but wasting time." Audry felt this rebuff intensely, could make no allowances for why mother might have said this, began to feel completely rejected again. She became silent, sulky. As she spoke her mood with me became much the same as it must have been yesterday with mother. She withdrew, appeared angry. . . .

I tried to get her to speculate on what might have accounted for mother's reaction. I commented on Audry's angry reaction to me, and Audry acknowledged this saying when she felt hurt and angry at mother it extended to others, too. Again there was silence, complaints about her head, it was getting worse, etc. She blamed me then for making her remember what she wanted to forget. What good did talking do? I thought Audry had felt misunderstood by something I said, had taken out of it that I was on her mother's side, when my intention was rather to try to get her to see what it was which had made mother's comment seem so rejecting. (Transference is used to show girl how she is acting with mother, worker, and others, to identify the nature of the conscious feelings and to let her make connections.) I wondered if, perhaps, when Audry felt so rejected by mother she didn't become more sympathetic to father, since she left the home as he did, in a sense, and I wondered if Audry, too, thought there were any similarities here. Audry didn't know, guessed it was possible, but again differentiated herself from father, since *she* really wanted parents and a home, and *he* didn't. He wanted to be free of it, while she searched for it. I asked Audry about the latter, and she explained that it was always with the hope of finding a good home with gentle, understanding parents, who loved each other and their children, that she left her own house. I recognized this as her wish, her fantasy, but was it what she actually looked for? (The fantasy is brought into a real focus.)

I referred to the times she had left home, particularly this last time, when her associates came far from representing the fulfillment of her fantasy, in fact, were quite the opposite. Audry acknowledged this somberly, said it looked as though in her anger and disappointment there was "an all or nothing quality." She went from one extreme to the other when she could not have what she wanted in the way of acceptance and love from mother. The worst of it was, she added sadly, that she would never have it, so she might as well give up trying. Her mother wouldn't love her in the way Audry thought she should, nor would she let Audry go anywhere else. . . . I said I knew she was hurt and angry with mother now, was perhaps even setting the stage to leave home again (Audry denied latter, but admitted the former, and her wish to do, saying in an aggressive way, what she wanted when her conciliatory efforts with mother didn't bring the desired results). I wondered if in her anger she wasn't seeing things a little out of focus, just as she did when she was in her more ecstatic moments. Was it really mother who was objecting to the boarding plan (handling defenses) or didn't Audry herself have some questions about it? Audry immediately denied feeling one way or the other. I said I doubted this, and reminded Audry of how ready she was to put aside her appointment here when she thought she could be with mother as one of the most important of her children. It was as though she had, coming here, associated with her failure to get her mother's love, with a kind of defeat ("when I have it I don't need to come"), and so she must make this same association. In thinking about this Audry guessed maybe I was right to a certain extent; she could see it clearly in relation to the appointment, commented on how much better off she would have been had she come—"the said words would have remained unsaid and the world might have remained more real." I asked what she meant by the latter, and she said she guessed she lived most of the time in a kind of fantasy world where everyone is either very good or very bad, and she doesn't accept the in-between.

She then told with some irritation about a six-year-old child who had spent part of the holidays with the S family, and is from time to time kept at the S home while the mother works. The child is very annoying because she is so "spoiled," "tries to walk over adults," was spanked by Audry, who feels it harmful to "allow anyone to indulge impulses to such a degree as this youngster does." "As a result of the mother's neglect of the child, not feeding it properly, not giving it consistent guidance, the child doesn't know where its limits are and what it can safely do and not do. It doesn't know right from wrong." Audry really felt "sorry for the way the child would grow up with such a mother." Somebody ought to keep it from doing just anything it wants to, and therefore Audry viewed her spanking (displacement of the problem) of the child in terms of helping rather than punishing. When I asked Audry how this related to herself, she said with all the complaints she had about mother she did feel she had been given a sense of right and wrong that was pretty much a part of her. She didn't think she was really bad, because a bad person was one who knew what was wrong and went ahead and did it anyway.

Audry thought her mistakes were errors in judgment rather than "badness," since whatever she did seemed right to her when she started to do it. She might realize as she talked it over with me that she was viewing the situation wrongly, but this to her "is a mistake" rather than being "bad." Her mother, of course, in her anger calls it "badness," but Audry believes what she herself says makes more sense. The thing that troubles Audry is her "stupidity" when she is supposed to be so smart. How it is that she can repeat the same thing over and over again after recognizing it as a mistake could be classified only as "stupidity," such as leaving home. When I questioned as to whether or not Audry meant to put it in such intellectual terms, she thought for a moment, then shook her head, commenting that this made it too simple, didn't it? She did wish though that she could understand, because the effect of it was so stupid and hurtful to both herself and her mother. She sees each time we have discussed this the immediate causes and what started her thoughts going in such an extreme way, but what started it all anyway in the first place? This she doesn't really understand. She had noticed one thing and this was that she hadn't gone to church regularly, had kind of drifted away since last June—she was going to start back regularly now, had made a beginning. I said Audry's question about what had started it all was a good one, one we needed very much to understand. Perhaps it would help to go back to the first time and what had happened then. . . .

Hereupon she gave a long account of her previous religious practices, ending that she needed her "faith restored" now. She didn't really worry any more now about what happened last June. I said I had the impression that Audry's loss of faith in the church and deciding suddenly to leave home had specific causes, something which set what she had properly called "an impulse" going. I thought Audry knew more about this than she felt she could tell me right now, because she was afraid, might even be to herself thinking of me as nosey, like Lester B. Audry laughed a little, but acknowledged that what I said was true. I said she felt afraid and perhaps couldn't tell me until she felt safer. She nodded, said she knew it was important and that she couldn't really forget, maybe eventually she could tell me. In gay, lighter mood, Audry shifted again to tell me how "the devil" had been trying hard to get hold of her for the last few days, making her break dishes, spill things, etc. The kinds of things, she explained, that out of her anger at herself for stupidity, might well make her take it out on her sister and mother. (The worker had described her conscious feelings here, not the unconscious anxiety behind her wanting to forget. The transference feelings are handled in the same way.)

She complained of her head hurting by gestures rather than words, bit her lips and shook her head negatively when I encouraged her to let me know what was going through her mind that was so extremely upsetting. I sat with her silently for some time, finally saying I had the impression that in addition to the other unpleasant things she had referred to this morning by telephone, another point now getting in the way of her talking was perhaps her angry feelings towards me right now, her belief that I had somehow let her down. Audry responded to this by saying that she did feel this way, it was my fault that she hadn't been able to escape her home situation for a few hours with a friend, some one with whom she could just talk about movies, school, inconsequential things. . . .

She has no freedom, is constantly being asked to do things for her mother, no matter what part of the house she is in, never has any time to herself. She gave as an example mother's expectation that Ellen would curl mother's hair late yesterday evening. Audry had offered to do so earlier, the mother responded with the comment, "You only want your hands in my hair because it's clean now—you wouldn't touch it when it was dirty." Later, she wanted Audry to curl it, and Audry refused. She didn't feel sorry either. Mother is always saying that she can get along without the children, but they can't get along without her—well, let her see. That was one thing she also said to Ellen as well as to Audry, but mostly she sent Ellen out to "spy" on Audry. (The worker brings out the need she feels for her mother here.)

I said Audry was angry now but didn't she often, too, value the feeling of safety and protection that this feeling of belonging to mother gave her? Often she liked being asked to do things for mother, what makes the situation so different now? It was "just mood"—it changes—she can't explain it. She gets tired of mother's restrictions, tired of never having any privacy, of having letters and poetry in her dresser snooped into. I thought she had a right to some privacy and was old enough to be able to expect this. "It's not only that, but why can't mother see that I'm a lot safer being able to express what I'm feeling rather than keeping it dammed up inside, which is what she is trying to force by her attitude." "If I write about love, it's bad; she's stupid not to see that it's what I can't speak about that places me in danger." As soon as Audry had finished she caught herself up, then laughed easily, "that's what we've been talking about, isn't it, and I've done nothing but argue with you that getting things out in the open does no good—I really know better as you can see." I said I knew Audry knew this with her mind, but that her feelings were different, and I thought she still felt pretty torn about this; when her angry and hurt feelings get so strong she is afraid.

She didn't suppose worker really meant this literally—it was just a way of letting Audry know she knew her anger was strong. I agreed with Audry, asked her more about the mother. She had awakened with a feeling that she could not talk to me today, so perhaps something happened the previous evening which again made her feel unwanted and unloved by mother. Audry agreed that something had happened—it was a small incident, but "important." She had wanted to be near her mother, had gone to the couch where her mother was lying down to cuddle up for a few moments (at first she said it was only because it was cold, but then brought out her wish to be babied, loved by mother). Mother had shoved her away, but more than just physically; there was a look of real horror, repulsion on her face as she did it.

I asked Audry what she thought was going through mother's mind and what through her own. She began to have doubts as she talked that she had read mother's expression correctly; it was funny, wasn't it, that she wanted to be treated like a grown-up, but resented not being allowed to be like a baby. I said Audry's doubts about whether or not she had read mother's expression correctly and her inability to recall now her own thoughts suggested some guilty feeling. This comment clicked psychologically with Audry and for a moment, I thought, she was going to go on to recall her own thoughts. However, she blocked again, and said she couldn't remember, maybe some time she could. I said her thoughts were still pretty frightening to her, and that to defend herself "she forgot," still resented my seeming "to pry," much as she resented mother. Audry protested momentarily my connecting myself with her mother, but responded later with a more convinced "maybe you're right," when I said it was understandable and to be expected in the course of our work together.

Before Audry left we talked a little more about her initial feelings against me for having let her mother know she was not in my office when she called (after running away). Spontaneously Audry said she felt differently about this now, since she could see that had I lied to her mother her mother would inevitably have discovered it and would not have allowed Audry to return here. While Audry acknowledges at times even wishing this, most of the time she really knows that "my only hope" is to get things straightened out "inside me."

When we have to communicate with the families of minor children as we did in this case, it is important that each shall understand the nature of the communication. In general, if impulses are described, verbalized, and discussed, as here, there is less temptation to act out. In the above interviews one can see how certain defenses with respect to real external situations are handled; with the feeling mobilized about the specific incident, "What did you feel?" or "What did you do?" is discussed; the pattern of dependency and resentment is brought out, but not the deeper sources of anger and helplessness. This is not to say that this is the only method or that it should always stop at such a level, but it does illustrate one kind of typical handling for emotional relief, giving perspective on objective reality and inner feelings through a controlled transference relationship which allows the client to see herself in her situation with less distortion.

Interpretation Leading to Insight

In any form of casework explanation of the overt aspects of the problem, clarification of issues, of attitudes, of conscious and preconscious feelings, distinguishing between feelings and reality, pointing up patterns of behavior, are essential to self-awareness and may be regarded as forms of insight. One shares reality data with any client, but one uses caution in sharing data concerning psychological matters, inasmuch as the client may not be ready to face emotional motivation. In itself depth is not inevitably therapeutic. Insight, as defined by psychoanalysts, is the understanding of unconscious repressed material which repeated interpretation may induce. This insight is never quickly gained, nor is it easily assimilated, nor is intellectual insight an end in itself. Much of it cannot be achieved by interviewing techniques, but through free-association and the use of symbolic material and fantasies, as is done in psychoanalysis. Only the highly skilled therapist can pick up the feelings behind the distortions. Dr. Coleman [21] makes an interesting differentiation with regard to insight:

In psychotherapy, the appeal is again to the conscious ego, but as an aid in the process of dealing with painful intra-psychic conflicts. It is also a useful device in reducing tension levels in the therapeutic relationship. In short-term psychotherapy, insight into historical genesis or ego patterning is avoided as far as possible but it does find its place in cases of longer duration, although it may here lend itself to intellectual defense, and thus prolong treatment. The reality aspects of intellectualization may make the seeking of insight more useful in casework than in psychotherapy.

As therapist the caseworker makes cautious use of interpretation, of either social or personal factors and their interaction, usually employing techniques of clarification, and supporting the ego within the transference, with little penetration of defenses unless negative and unusually difficult phases of resistance and particularly negative transference, occur. No absolute lines can be drawn, since the patient permits himself varying degrees of insight in any therapy. The attempt to clarify induces degrees of self-awareness at any level, but can only achieve results when the client is ready for it. Premature attempts to penetrate defensive structures will be shrugged off or resented or will arouse anxiety states. Although changes in feelings and behavior, especially of young children, by releasing feelings and correcting the environment, are possible without conscious insight, usually some self-awareness is a concomitant of change. The timing of interpretation is important. Superficial layers have to be worked through again and again before assimilation takes place— even if nothing deeper is attempted.

21 Coleman, "Distinguishing between Psychotherapy and Casework," *Journal of Social Casework*, XXX (June, 1949), 250.

L. N. Austin uses the term "experiential treatment" for the combination of support and interpretation of behavior common in goal-limited therapy.[22] A new orientation in a living experience, especially if verbalized within the transference, may lead to a change in feelings. Although the problem may be located in the unconscious, many persons respond to treatment focused to the nonconflicted or healthy part of the personality. Self-awareness is obtained by exploring into conscious experiences, feelings, and dynamics which are derivative and therefore linked with the unconscious motivation. Nor is it possible to measure the effect upon the unconscious of this approach.

Defenses and Resistance

In psychotherapy the nature of the defenses must be understood, both in themselves and as used in resistance to treatment. In limited therapy one does not arouse tension (anxiety) more than is necessary for the goal, nor does one often go into the emotional roots of intra-psychic conflict if the defenses are working well. How much in any limited therapy the patient is to be made aware of dynamic energies depends upon highly skilled judgment and experience. Although helping the person to work through some destructive defenses, the caseworker is well advised to proceed cautiously in uncovering repressed unconscious material lying behind any defenses used, and in general the defensive structure has to remain intact. Certainly the caseworker typically concerns himself with releasing strength in cooperation with the conscious ego, and lays more stress on interpersonal factors than on the components of dependent and hostile impulses displaced upon the relationship itself.

Since for any therapeutic formulation the client must commit

[22] L. N. Austin, "Trends in Differential Treatment in Social Casework," *Journal of Social Casework*, XXIX (June, 1948), 207. "Change is brought about through the use of the transference as stimulating growth experiences in the social reality. In some cases, selected interpretations may be used. Treatment is primarily based on positive experience both in the transference and in life situations. Its objectives are mainly loosening restrictive ties to figures in the past, redirection of emotional energies, and promoting growth through increased satisfactions in living."

himself to the treatment objective, and he must participate every step of the way, the phenomenon of resistance must be understood. By "resistance" is meant using various defenses to resist treatment. There may be an early phase of normal resistance due to fears, unfamiliarity with procedures, unpleasant agency experiences which may be readily discussed, and this should be distinguished from the resistance aroused by anxiety when self-awareness or impulsivity threatens the personality. In all casework the client is helped to assume responsibility for himself, but in therapy the degree of self-involvement and assumption of responsibility for producing material against one's own resistance is stepped up.

Resistance to treatment must be discussed, and hostile aggressive elements in the transference may have to be verbalized. Sexual aims in children are verbalized, but with adult patients the necessity for doing this might often indicate that mistakes had been made in the treatment hitherto and that countertransference was operating. The more intellectual aspects of interpretation may free the healthy ego to look at his role more clearly and with greater detachment, but interpretation of unconscious repressed material can only lead, if assimilated, to greater involvement of the total personality. Transference reactions used as resistance are difficult to recognize and, if they are to be handled at all, call for great skill in the therapist. "Insight" given within the transference which enables the client to understand his conscious resistances and the defenses utilized in specific life situations may offer considerable help, even though insight into the deeply repressed is not attempted in limited therapy.

One technique, which is already a familiar adaptation within casework, seems typically useful, namely, to mobilize feeling around a specific experience, situation or relationship and help the client to become aware of his affect. Since the anxiety is related to its situational source the therapeutic result is that the client almost always recognizes the connection and may apperceive his own contribution to the difficulty to some extent.

Both caseworkers and group workers have a stake in the therapeutic treatment of deviant personalities, individuals, and families whose behavior results in failure or conflict with society. Casework in America has been deeply affected by psychiatric, particularly psychoanalytic, developments, and so it is predisposed to adapt psychoanalytic principles for its own professional purposes. Whether such adaptations should be called psychotherapy, or casework therapy, or simply casework, the fact is not altered that psycho-dynamics are increasingly used in the treatment of problems of human relationship. The caseworker approaches the problem of intra-psychic conflict as it is manifested in social adaptation, interpersonal relationships, and realistic aspects of the cultural milieu. He tends, therefore, to define the problem in these terms, and he constantly relates psychological treatment to the realities of the living experience. In psychotherapy with children the child's own reality, particularly the parental reality, is insistently present and constantly active. But except for medical psychiatry and psychoanalysis, we would assume that in the more specific versions of social breakdown any therapist tends to work either single-handed or with collaborators on both the psychological and social manifestations of unadjustment in a thematic, noninclusive sense. The basic questions are always whether and to what degree the personality organization can be changed and how much modification of attitude and behavior can be achieved by working with the relatively healthy part of the patient's ego with respect to his real external situation.

The caseworker in therapy addresses himself as far as possible to positive strengths in the personality and assets in the social situation, but therapy is also based on the worker's "ability to accept the unpleasant side of life," which leads, in favorable cases, to greater self-acceptance in the client. The therapeutic goal in casework is always twofold—to reduce pressures in the environment and to fortify the client to bear pressures. The minimum requirements for the caseworker in therapy are to understand the personality structure in terms of the life experience; in treatment, to keep dynamic diagnosis and dynamic evaluation of the person's functioning at the center of the picture and to understand relevant etiological factors.

There is a marked tendency in both the family and the child-placing fields, so-called, toward more direct work with children, which is certainly in the context of psychotherapy at some level. All newer concepts of work with children in casework and groupwork stress the importance of adapting treatment to age levels. One does not treat babies, children, and adolescents alike. One must know how the oedipal period is going to affect children placed at certain ages, and the unresolved oedipal conflict at any age. Children don't grow up uniformly in every respect, some are slower in emotional development than others, and most are uneven. One must understand the early developmental years to work with the phenomenon of regression, which usually takes place after family separation. One must also understand the child who, in growing up, has had too little time and opportunity for gratifications or proper restraints.

With adults, therapy may depend largely on verbal material in the interview; with children, therapy involves direct observation, knowing what the child is doing, and modification of the living experience. With delinquent children the situation must be structured to permit release of aggression. Near a camp for delinquent children there should be not a dangerous and prohibited, but a *safe* swimming hole. Children should not be asked to listen to rules about going on a hike in a fascinating hay barn full of pitchforks and delightful temptations. There should be playrooms furnished with unbreakable toys and those that may be marred or destroyed. One must be as permissive as possible and must exercise few restraints and frustrations, but restraints, when necessary, must be "made to stick." One should not flinch or be inconsistent or easily seduced. In play interviews it is important to have on hand outlets for aggression—drums, darts, buckets for setting fires, and so forth —so that the aggression can be channelized, but with older children the aggression should be, for the most part, verbalized. If the child is neurotic but also acts out in therapy, one has to adjust oneself to whatever is coming out.

To recapitulate: the interview is designed to stimulate and elicit feelings, to which end the worker-client relationship, essential to the casework process, is deepened by transference elements which must be carefully controlled interview by interview. The treatment situation is used to release feeling, to support the ego, and to increase the person's self-awareness by bringing to his attention his attitudes and patterns of behavior both in the life experience and in the interviewing treatment situation (although usually more of the former), the caseworker tending to use the transference to redirect the psychological energies into reality channels. The client's use of defenses must be understood, but in general, constructive defenses and adequate, even if neurotically balanced, family relationships are left undisturbed, unless the effect on children is marked. If more radical therapy is indicated the client would be prepared for and referred to psychoanalysis. In fact, preparation for referral to therapeutic procedures elsewhere has been highly developed within casework practice, and calls for as much skill in therapeutic management as in other areas. As we have repeatedly indicated, evidence of disease processes always suggests medical responsibility and collaboration.

CHAPTER X

PRIMARY AND SECONDARY SETTINGS

THE FACT that the trend of modern community life is in the direction of institution and agency rather than individual practice means that the social worker must achieve a philosophy and discipline with regard to the effect of setting and function on practice.[1]

Functional differentiation can be soundly developed only upon a broad generic base of practice such as we have tried to describe in preceding chapters, otherwise fragmentation and particularization will result. It is now generally accepted that all the major services in health, education, and welfare, including the functions of maintenance, protection of children, and treatment of the ill and the handicapped, must find expression in a unified structure of public services to all eligible persons. The prevention of social ills and the promotion of positive welfare will increasingly be the objective in public programs. The voluntary counterpart will, in general, be supported by fee and group memberships, contributions, dues, and so will meet the needs of special groups. Experimental and demonstration projects, pilot studies, "action," and other research will be carried on through the efforts of enlightened and responsible citizens. The tradition of citizen participation on boards and committees of voluntary agencies will, it is hoped, be taken over into public welfare activities.

Casework methods should be introduced into public employment and other "marginal" welfare fields if they are to offer optimal benefit to clients. As the social casework idea became part of one "field" after another—court, hospital, school—professional knowledge and skill were deepened and broadened. Thus, when the possi-

[1] See Chapter V.

bility of judicial discretion to suspend sentence reached the court system, *circa* 1899, through the children's court and the probation officer, caseworkers began to take an interest in new meanings for the protective function. The notion that families must be "supervised" merely because they were receiving a family allowance has been supplanted by a democratic casework approach. This should not be taken to mean that eligibility should not be properly reviewed or social services made available, but that the recipients of public assistance are not thereby deprived of their normal status of self-direction.

From time to time a function administratively carried in one "field" may be shifted into another. Much of the work that is administered in one country by social workers attached to courts, in another may be performed under more flexible child welfare auspices. In this country the greater part of so-called "protective" work may slowly be shifted toward family welfare, child welfare, and the public schools, away from court and correctional emphases. Although it is possible to distinguish roughly objectives which suggest a functional division of labor, it is difficult to say precisely where the responsibilities of a public family agency giving assistance and those of a family court dealing with adult behavior problems begin and end, where family and children's work begins and ends, where the guidance clinic comes in, and so forth. The whole problem of economic dependency, when uncomplicated by parental or marital behavior, is being referred in general to the area of "maintenance," away from relief and "supervision." The problem of juvenile behavior is being moved, but more slowly, in the direction of child guidance and children's and family work. Many child delinquents are not "delinquent" in the psychiatric sense, and can be treated by case and groupwork methods. For the true delinquent, court authority in commitment, as well as full resources for psychiatric treatment of this difficult problem, is indispensable.

In presenting emphases from established "fields," it is well to note that artificial barriers, because of the accident of time of inception, of special bequests, or the interest of an individual leader, should now be dissolved as a basis for "specialization," and integration which reflects professional growth and development should take place. In the primary setting,[2] that is, the social work agency, the main consideration in regard to the optimal groupings seems that of family, children's and child-guidance types of service within the community; in the secondary setting the role of social work, adjunctive with regard to the primary aims of medicine, law, education, and so forth, must be defined for a multi-discipline effort. The areas chosen for brief discussion are those in which certain issues seem of long-range, as well as contemporary, significance.

THE PRIMARY SETTINGS

It is no longer tenable to consider family service and child-caring functions as separate "fields." Although some family problems do not involve children, such as the aged, the unadjusted single adult, and marital disharmony where there are no children, children's problems never fail to involve the family either physically or psychologically. Approach to the family must, therefore, include family counseling, child guidance,[3] "protective" services, and child placing. All modern casework is concerned with parent-child problems, not in the older sense of a "child-centered" case, but with the focus of parents and children in an intra-familial constellation. In any setting one individual may be the "patient," yet the very nature of casework process emphasizes the interrelationships rather than the isolation of this central figure, and, as indicated earlier, there will typically in social work be more than one "patient" under treatment.

FAMILY CARE AND FOSTER CARE [4]

An understanding of family group interaction is essential in learning to know children. Psychological and medical experts, meeting troubled youth and obdurate parents in the office, often see

[2] See pp. 115–16 for discussion of generic and specific.
[3] The term "child guidance," which originated in connection with mental hygiene clinics, is used here in its wider application. For further discussion of traditional family emphases, see pages 95–102.
[4] Hutchinson, *In Quest of Foster Parents.*

parents only as "background," and all too frequently as negative background, for the child. The caseworker who adopts this attitude will be ineffective in treating the family group. Little can be done until parents are aware that they have a part in the child's disturbed behavior and unless they are concerned to try to change their behavior. In coming to a diagnostic conclusion participant observation of home life may reveal strengths and liabilities in the family sometimes hidden in the office interview. Learning to see a child in a family, however, is difficult, since the group may obscure as well as precipitate individual reactions. In any family, just as in the classroom or the club, one or two individuals may dominate the scene. Often an invalid or the "good child" or the "black sheep" takes the center of the family stage. As in any other group, it is desirable to develop flexible leadership—give and take—in contrast to the unremitting control of one person. Originally the man of the family was interviewed only because he was a wage earner; the present trend to consider the man also as husband and father is wholesome. Fathers and foster fathers are increasingly involved in guidance and placement considerations.

As we said earlier, the family is threatened in two major ways, lack of resources for maintenance as a unit and disruption through the behavior of its members, especially the spouses or the parents. One may examine functional problems between, for example, the agency dealing with income as relief and the agency dealing with income on a nonsupportive basis. Public assistance agencies have a small, but by no means negligible, number of nonsupport cases. It is no longer tenable, however, to try to use relief as a threat or a club for the man who "refuses to work," the parent, spouse, or young person who refuses to support, the industrially displaced worker, the young couple living at home who want separate maintenance, or the antagonistic adolescent. Problems of this type may be handled within the public assistance structure or may be dealt with through domestic relations action or through some other agency, but they should be handled by trained and skillful caseworkers. Sometimes the "refusal to support" charge, originating in court, is a misnomer.

The refusal may not be voluntary, but the result of inability and should therefore be routed to public assistance for diagnosis and treatment. The converse also is true, in that problems of nonsupport and "refusal to work," in so far as they are not due to illness, personality difficulties, accidents, or unfair labor practices may better be referred to the authoritative agency set up to handle "delinquency."

Child Welfare

Originally the domestic relations court was concerned with nonsupport and desertion cases, and the juvenile courts [5] (with a few exceptions) with neglected, dependent, and delinquent children, but recently the trend has been toward an integrated domestic relations court with broader functions. On the other hand, there has been a trend toward removal from children's courts of the administration of assistance in health problems, such as the program of aid to handicapped children. Child welfare was begun in modern times, except for the ministrations of neighbors and relatives and institutional care, often under sectarian auspices. When children were taken out of the general almshouses and workhouses and placed in orphanages a corner was turned. With the innovation of removing crowds of vagabond children from the city streets of eastern cities and placing them on farms west of the Mississippi, another corner was turned. When the practice of indenture ceased and the placing of children in free instead of working wage homes was begun, a milestone was passed. When the movement to pay board for placed-out children became widespread, the treatment of children made startling advances. The range of assistance, insurance, wages-and-hours legislation, control of child labor, health, and recreation has meant that more and more often children may be kept at home under reasonable safeguards. Also, it has become clearer that when the disturbance is not economic, but lies in affectional relationships, programs for foster care must be available. The traditional feeling about division of labor in the welfare field persisted, however, in the notion that the maintenance of children

[5] See pp. 46–47.

at home was "family" work and the maintenance of children in foster homes "children's" work.

It is increasingly clear, because the pathological family tends to act out its conflict in part through the children, that treatment of the child cannot be successful unless the attitudes of the parents can be modified. While in instances of gross pathology and unmodifiable destructive behavior the child or the adolescent must be removed if there is to be any chance of therapy, misguided efforts to remove the child from "the corrupting parents" [6] may do more harm than good. Rather, we should do what we can to support whatever family strengths there are and to help the child gradually to face the realities of his home situation. This throws the weight upon diagnosis and differential treatment rather than arbitrary and artificial agency boundaries. Recognition of the significance of age groups should not lead to rigid categories for practice among children, youth, and the aged.

Care of the Aged

With the lengthening of life expectancy one may observe a tendency to regard the care of older persons as a separate "field." Since old age is not a matter of precise chronology and many of the efforts in health, welfare, and social activities are good for all human beings, there are disadvantages in a segmental approach and categorically isolated programs. Because full productive wage earning is not usually feasible for the aged, the security system must provide insurance, pensions, and various forms of assistance. Infirmaries for the mentally and physically disabled, institutions and boarding care for the ambulant, and small apartments in housing projects for those able to carry on their own housekeeping should assure appropriate shelter. However, to achieve better care for the aged it is important to recognize certain things about the group as a whole.[7]

The casework approach recognizes characteristics common to the group, yet knows that each individual is different. Workers in

[6] See Johnson, "A Contribution to Treatment of Superego Defect," *Social Casework*, April, 1950.
[7] Lawton, *New Goals for Old Age*.

family agencies, medical institutions, and other settings must understand such characteristics, because there are many more old people outside of special settings than in them. Although the staff of a home for the aged must indeed come to know geriatrics well if they are suited to their task, they will know old people best as individuals.

Assuming an adequate pension or insurance payment on the basis of age and income level, this can be supplemented by natural resources when they exist; when they do not exist the recipient may apply to a public assistance agency, which, on a budget basis, may supplement the income and arrange boarding care or other social services as needed. It is possible to compute the income level on which grants for old people or free medical services for otherwise self-supporting persons may be offered. In fact, as the coverage for unemployment compensation, old age and health care broadens, income rating for eligibility should be easy. This should in no wise deter the concurrent development of casework services addressed to individual needs or the skills of the professional approach made available for recipients of various forms of benefit under social security and enlightened labor management facilities.

The diseases and disabilities of middle age and old age are likely to call for amelioration rather than absolute cure. Impairment of hearing, eyesight, and other faculties require hearing aids, glasses, and dentures to maintain health and comfort. There are special nutritional problems to be considered. Emotionally, old people are beset by characteristic feelings of inadequacy, not being needed or wanted, of being a burden, especially in cultures where the rewards have been to the aggressive and competitive personality, the physically able-bodied worker for heavy or mass-production labor, rather than to sagacity, sober judgment, and wisdom. Old people have a tendency to live in the past, the more so if the present affords no sense of status and little opportunity or challenge for creative contribution. When opportunity for such a contribution is offered, when talents and assets of the mature personality are accredited, regression may be negligible. Rigidity of personality is not peculiar to old age, and many of the old enviably preserve greater degrees of tolerance and flexibility than younger persons have.

Exponents of a separate children's "field" have expressed apprehension that because care at home is cheaper, foster care may be minimized in favor of assistance programs. Social workers everywhere are united in the stand that not only must assistance for persons in family care be adequate but that the special services for members away from home must be continuously provided for. Boarding care is costly, but is less expensive than crippled bodies and minds. The first lines of defense in any country are economic security and family stability and, therewith, closely associated differentiated programs to meet the special needs of individuals. Although still inadequate in most states, the Aid to Dependent Children and Survivors Insurance grants, to say nothing of the benefits for veterans, and the less adequate but slowly improving general assistance and other security programs make it possible for the majority of children to live at home. Longer life expectancy, the drop in maternal mortality and in industrial accident rates, and better control of disease have meant fewer orphans and half-orphans to be placed and point toward a new emphasis both for the traditional family and children's fields or parent-child relationships and family and child guidance functions.[8] Home care programs, however, are greatly needed.

Chronic invalids, old persons, and children may be boarded out because in this way they can be made more comfortable and contented than if placed in institutions, or they may be boarded because of pathological relationships in the family group (as in instances of a schizophrenic or an aged person) when the attitudes of the own family cannot be modified toward a congenial and emotionally supportive atmosphere. The cultural taboos should be eliminated from such placements, thus reducing the feeling of guilt ordinarily experienced by those who use them for their relatives. There should be as little stigma on institutions and foster homes as on boarding

[8] Richman, "New Needs and New Approaches in Foster Care," *Jewish Social Service Quarterly* (March, 1949).

schools. It is the fashion to blame parents too much, to criticize them for using institutions or foster care. Grown-up children may feel too guilty about their own unconscious hostility to permit elderly relatives, especially parents, to use institutional facilities. Cultural disapproval and the inadequacy of resources have reinforced natural, as well as neurotic, reluctance to use boarding care. Giving one's child away for adoption [9] is also stigmatized, but this has been worked through more successfully with the unmarried mother than with the married parents who want to be rid of a child. Current needs in adult placing as well as in child placing include more specialization in the types of institutional care offered and more adequate payment of foster and temporary boarding home makers.

IMPROPER GUARDIANSHIP AND JUVENILE DELINQUENCY

The phases of "delinquency" to which we shall give attention are those involving programs for the youthful delinquent and the pathological family from whom the child must be protected. We shall not consider the protection of society against crime, which is beyond the scope of this book.

One historical approach to the question of division of labor is from the angle of guardianship. Thus, if both parents or the mother were dead or disabled, or anti-social, the children must be maintained outside the home as a quasi-parental or fully legal responsibility. The commissioner of welfare, or the court, or both, would be charged with duties and responsibilities to dependent and neglected children, because of the common-law doctrine that the state, through its agents, is the ultimate parent of all minors who require care or protection.[10] The natural right of parental control can be superseded by the common guardianship of the community if the child's welfare requires. The trend to intervene and to take custody of the child has been modified, however, by the forces set in motion to ameliorate the lot of the child at home, whenever there is a

[9] See pp. 99–102.
[10] See Lou, *Juvenile Courts in the United States*, pp. 3 *et seq.*

home. With the aid of day nurseries and visiting housekeepers and relatives, as well as supplemental income, many homes, even when the mother is disabled, can be kept together. Since provisions for security for dependent children have been broadened, more kinds of broken homes can be shored up, and homes, temporary foster homes, and institutions can be used interchangeably.

At one time a child sent to an institution was likely to stay there long after custodial care was needed, or the reverse. Although it is still true that children tend to remain too long in institutions, it is because of the administrative cost of transfers, the pressures of public subsidies, or the lack of facilities, not because it is believed to be for the good of the child to keep the institutional population stable and the beds full. Complete surrender of the child by the parent is less common, and the whole process is far more flexible than it was at the beginning of the century. As one reviews the movement to consider the whole child in a whole situation—parental, substitute parental, institutional, and community—the question of guardianship, while no less important in an ultimate legal sense, has a clinical or diagnostic component which should affect the disposition of the case. The use of probation or protective supervision at home for behavior problem children has made removal because of "improper guardianship" less exigent. The relation between problem child and problem parent is too well known to make the "neglect" category anything but restrictive among family, child welfare, and guidance objectives.

In some courts today the "offense" is classified as "neglect," "dependency," or "delinquency" to match any available institution of the type which currently has a vacancy. Obviously, treatment of the "offender" rather than punishment of the offense is the remedy to be sought. Prevention of family breakdown through direct treatment and environmental safeguards—community planning in positive programs of health, recreation and, education—are the objectives in welfare. The aim must be to *help*, not condemn parents and children. Many problems of "neglect" and "delinquency" respond to family services; others need court disposition. Authority and restraint, which are necessary functions of society, should be distinguished from punishment, which rarely has useful effects.

Treatment for delinquency may be said to require money, housing, cultural and recreational opportunities, as well as family, group, and individual treatment, including psychotherapy. About half of any police load today consists of trivial offenders or those who are not offenders at all, but victims of cultural discrimination, inadequate schools and leisure-time facilities. The schools have an important function in early identifying behavior problems and pathology, but intensive treatment within the schools should be directed mainly toward problems which have specific educational significance, such as retardation, reading and speech disabilities and other handicaps, truancy, classroom behavior problems, vocational adjustments, rather than behavior deviancy expressed outside the school. School difficulties which have their origin primarily in family relationships should be referred to or shared with the appropriate community agencies by means of competent screening and referral.

Continued absence from school may be a symptom either of emotional disturbance or inadequate school programs. It is essential to have all agencies adopt treatment attitudes towards problem children and plan together as much as possible. One cannot overestimate the importance of long-range environmental modification and wholesome social and educational activities. Money to spend on the prevention of delinquency and research is still greatly needed.

The Separation Experience

Historically, children's work was segmental, intake occurring in court, family agency, or a special department, and placement being done in another agency. Often the child was referred only when a crisis arose; often the intake procedure was complicated by arbitrary sectarian and public-private boundary lines. This segmental administration tended to emphasize the placement at the time of separation and thereafter,[11] but not sufficiently in the home, since separation in many instances is the climax of a long series of trau-

[11] See also pp. 99–102.

matic relationships and events. Some workers would attempt a functional division of labor between the family field and children's field by emphasizing only the separation itself. Separation is a common problem in casework. Many families clearly belong and want to belong together; many families cannot, do not want, or are not competent to maintain themselves as units, because of death or other interruption, defect, or distortions in the child-caring and home-making capacities. When the break actually occurs, when separation is imminent because of incompetent parents or parents who do not want their children or because of extreme behavior problems or unusually severe handicaps, the placement process can be thought of as a clearly defined function. On the other hand, as caseworkers in all fields began to comprehend the needs of children, as work with parents progressed under child guidance and family casework, it was found that separation could often be anticipated diagnostically and could itself become a definite focus for treatment.

Taking a child out of his home is a peculiarly wrenching ordeal for parent and child alike, more rather than less so if hostilities are involved. It is frightening and dislocating to lose one's parents by death, by distance, and most of all by rejection. For the child whose conflicts with his environment have become internalized, placement, especially in a substitute home, may be impossible; the child may not be able to use the help of foster parents because of his affectional deprivations. However, if the child and the parent can accept placement, it often proves a successful form of treatment.

A large number of families are broken because of the death or permanent absence of the parents, and the psychological involvement is negligible in child placing; however, whenever parents stay in the picture one must recognize the problems created both for them and for the foster parents, and must develop new patterns of family guidance. Whenever parents remain intermittently or concurrently active in the child's life, the placement experience must be integrated so as to include own parents and foster parents.

The trend in child guidance, family casework, day nurseries, camps, and child placing agencies alike is to involve parents in the treatment and to recognize fully their role, rights, responsibilities, and feelings. Children can play a role in making decisions and meeting difficult reality experiences such as a temporary or a long-time separation. The old ruse of sending the child out of earshot on a meaningless errand has been abandoned in favor of including him in frank discussion and planning. Even little children can face adversity and take appropriate responsibility if they are allowed to. On the other hand, it is unfair to force upon children the anguish of trying to adapt to indecisive parents (or for that matter workers) who cannot make up their minds whether the child is to remain at home or be taken home on impulse, only to suffer the pangs of separation all over again. Planned visits on the basis of careful evaluation of the parental capacity should replace trial and error visits which may prove for the child a "cat and mouse" situation.

Preparation for Placement

Caseworkers have learned that the preparation of a child for placement is difficult, painful, and slow. In some cases the trend of the case toward separation can be seen in the first interview, but even in such instances a period of treatment to prepare parent and child for the experience is usually indicated. In the pioneer era, placement of children was characterized not only by rapid tempo, occasioned by the crisis method of child intake, but also by arbitrary prescription. Thus, at one time most dependent children and practically all behavior-problem children were sent to institutions; later, it was assumed that practically all such children, if money could be found, would be better off in foster homes. When the parental experience could be more accurately diagnosed, it was realized that institutions were suitable for some age groups and for some problem children, as well as for many exhibiting mental, physical, and psychoneurotic conditions. Just as the trend is to integrate the treatment of the foster family with that of the own family, so is it essential to integrate the process of institutional care with the foster home periods, since at different times the child may profitably be moved from one to the other.

This period of preparation has not the purpose, as it had earlier in social casework, of dissuading the parents from taking the step, but if they are resolved upon it to help them and the child to understand its implications. Some caseworkers contend that one cannot really prepare anyone for placement—that the separation must be experienced. In this approach treatment is focused wholly upon the placement experience itself and on the emotional problems created for child and parent in the use of the placement agency's program. True, treatment must be clarified and channelized in respect to the separation experience, as in family maintenance to the sustaining processes and services, but placement presents a less impossible burden when children have faced, with the help of the caseworker, some of their feelings toward their own home before being removed from it. Separation occurs *after* placement also. Separation is not a single event, but a long chain of intermingled actual and psychological family relationships, inconsistencies, threatened partings, and reconciliations. Actually it may never be accomplished from a psychological point of view.

Since the affectional family ties are primary in growth experience, it is easy to see why a loved and secure child may be easier to place than an insecure one. The rejected child clings psychologically, with an agonized longing, to the relationships which have failed him, and he must be prepared for placement. Often, too, the placed-out child needs a period of direct, as well as environmental, treatment. The rejecting parent, too, presents guilt problems with which he needs help, since parents and children have inner as well as outer reality—many phantasies—about the separation experience and the placement. Timing is important; time may be judiciously limited, but one must remember that both parents and children need time to adjust to painful realities. One cannot force the pace. It is important to distinguish between threatening the parents with possible failure and discussing the consequences of a course of action in advance and in impersonal terms. In order to be successfully placed every child must understand, and at least partially accept, the necessity for so painful a procedure. Only if this is done will it be possible for him to involve himself in using the foster home for his own growth and development.

The exploratory study period may be prolonged if subtle emotional factors and not gross pathology are threatening family life. Need for placement may be apparent long before parental attitudes will permit the actual separation. Replacements, so expensive from the point of view of child, agency, and community, may sometimes be avoided if conflicts between parent and child have been at least partially worked out before the threatening experience is effected. Preparation of both parent and child for placement, like preparation to use guidance or a psychiatrist, is an important casework process and deserves the time which it often takes. It is now known why it is easier to place loved children or, at the other extreme, wholly rejected children than to place the child of the ambivalent parent.

Most parents indicate at the outset, because of guilt feelings reinforced by cultural attitudes, that they expect to reclaim the placed child, but careful consideration of the request and the imagined outcome may clarify the ambivalence in the expressed intention. Since all parents are to some degree anxious, guilty, or ashamed about having a badly behaved child or about giving up their child, one must be prepared for active defenses of denial, displacement, reaction formation, rationalization, projection, repression, and the rest. Frequently all the blame is placed either on the child or on the social situation. If one is aware of these tendencies, the difficulties can be anticipated, some of the feelings worked through before separation, and the release of negative feelings about the foster parents or about the child allowed expression throughout the placement process. It is not enough to help the foster parents to understand negative parental attitudes. We must actively accept, sustain, and support the parents through a very trying experience. If the parents are very hostile and ambivalent, institutions rather than foster care may be preferable. Allowing parental feelings to be expressed and accepting them does not mean here any more than in any treatment that the worker should interpret their unconscious motivation. Repeated placements suggest not an incomplete evaluation of the foster home but incomplete diagnosis of the child's psychological problem in regard to unsolved parental relationships.

The worker must not act as if child placing or a child guidance expert will be able to cure the child in some magical way. Parents who have any affectional contribution are encouraged to participate in the treatment process as long as it lasts and to take the child home as soon as emotional and other factors permit a reasonable balance. Treatment must be directed not merely to adequate resources and arrangements but also to the emotional problems created for both parent and child by the placement itself. After spending unlimited time and patience in finding suitable homes children's workers have sometimes discovered that neither child nor parent could respond and use these good homes constructively.[12] The failures experienced have suggested that much more careful work be done with the child's own parents, not in terms of whether they should or should not be allowed to place their children, but in helping them to understand the conditions and the reality of the placement experience. Moreover, continuity of contact between the child and the agency, to say nothing of those parents who remain accessible from intake to discharge, is now held to be desirable; but since the family is the place where affections and rejections begin, study of the emotional problems of separation should begin there, partly in order to anticipate the child's use of the foster-parental experience, and partly in preparation for his return to his own home whenever feasible.

Child placement has gone through an interesting cycle with regard to group relationships. At one time the problem child was sent to group life in the institution, and the blue-eyed "good" child was placed in a foster home. This placing of the socially attractive child was partly a practical solution when foster homes were free or little board was paid. Later it was realized that the "normal" child

[12] For adoption see pp. 103–104.

could tolerate more easily group life pressures and that the problem child often needed the individualized support of a subsidized foster family which could be educated to treat these difficult children. Later still it was realized that for some deeply rejected problem children the use of foster parents was itself impossible, because the child cannot relinquish his own parents, no matter how unkind, and the more ideal the foster parents, the more conflicts may be aroused. For some such children, as well as for handicapped children, the use of an institution, with its diluted pressures on intimate relationships, whether parental or sibling, may be easier to tolerate. In short, a child's ability to use parental and family experience and his ability to use group experience can only be understood together, and his treatment in the home, in the foster home, and in the institutional group can effectively supplement one another.

SECONDARY SETTINGS

We cannot do justice, in limited space, to the many facets within the church, labor, industry, and other important areas of collaboration in which casework is adjunctive to another professional purpose. Casework is now established in the school system, where the theory and practice of operation are not dissimilar to that in other institutions. We have chosen here as illustrations only the legal and the medical professions, since the developments and principles of the multi-discipline approach found herein are, no doubt, susceptible of wider application. In child welfare, broadly speaking, many legal and quasi-legal functions are exercised for the protection and care of children, but as much of this has been already discussed in the preceding pages we shall confine ourselves to one or two of the formal aspects of the court setting.

Traditionally the community has assigned to the court the decisive role with regard to the safeguarding and withholding of domestic liberties and rights as expressed in protection of the person against himself or the community against the person. We shall discuss the role of legal authority in a few of its salient aspects.

Domestic Relations Court

It is not within the jurisdiction of the domestic relations court [13] to establish eligibility for assistance, but it is within its jurisdiction to establish responsibility for support. When public assistance agencies adopt comparable budget systems as a measure of need and flexibility in the approach to the responsibility of relatives, and when the court respects this approach, interaction between the two agencies will be more productive. The estimate of the standard of living on which support may be expected or relatives held liable remains a very difficult subject which is culturally determined. In modern domestic relations courts the basis is noncriminal and its objective is to interpret society's interest in the home through behavior affecting income, as forms of public assistance do through lack of financial resources. Generally speaking, the family court may compel relatives to contribute to the support of the family members for whom they are legally responsible, although its responsiveness to cultural standards makes it more ready to compel parents to support minor children, and husbands wives, than the reverse. In the case of liable grandparents the court is disposed to take a lenient view, and one might add that whenever the petitioners are parents of grown children or unemployed adult children any purely legalistic approach is futile. While today the judge frequently does dispose of the support petition without benefit of casework, the whole process is being slowly permeated with casework practices and concepts as to the meaning of behavior in economic areas.

Certainly compulsion to support may serve only to crystallize latent hostility in the family, while educational encouragement may lead to the assumption of normal adult responsibilities. Often the support problem is found to be a cloak for punitive attitudes exist-

[13] Complaints of marital abuse or other overt behavior may be heard in magistrates courts, police courts, or in rural counties by justices of the peace, where little casework service is usually available, so that when we speak of casework in the domestic relations area we must compare the function where either the family (or juvenile) court has developed a fully socialized administration. Family court is not often found as an independent agency, but usually as a domestic relations part of a city court.

ing between husband and wife, or parents and children. The complaint of nonsupport may cover a multitude of behavior problems—rejection of children, dislike of parents, protests against drinking. It is seen sometimes as a drive for dominance by the woman in the household, or as evasion of adult responsibility, or as deep dependency in some member. In court situations, as elsewhere, the client may project all his difficulties upon other persons or factors, without facing the possibilities of self-direction and inner change for himself. Cases reaching family courts are often in too advanced a stage for treatment by the casework method, and legal procedures must be invoked; in this respect we are beginning to grasp the "clinical" and dynamic principles in the use of authority.[14]

In the interest of society freedom may be curtailed and other sanctions imposed. Questions are raised today about casework in the authoritative agency much as they were once raised about casework in public assistance. The answer for the authoritative setting lies in the extension and adaptation, not curtailment, of professional knowledge and skill. The factor-by-factor analysis of home situations by caseworkers, which has contributed indispensable data to knowledge of the "anatomy" of home life, is now becoming part of the authoritative agency's approach.

The essential elements in the casework use of authority derive from: clinical understanding of the nature of super ego defects, (delinquency and character disorders); the definition, when necessary, of limits within which treatment must proceed; a relationship which is fundamentally a giving one on the part of the worker, who should have genuine liking for and confidence in the person's desire and capacity to improve, and fairness and scrupulous honesty with himself, as well as with the client. The worker should not connive with the delinquent any more than he should be pulled into the client's neurosis. As the client learns to trust such a relationship, a constructive identification may permit the strengthening of conscience within the client's personality.

In other respects, recognition of the child's part as a "symptom"

[14] See pp. 46–47.

of family disturbance, working with the parental attitudes, and so forth, follows the same paths as those discussed under improper guardianship earlier.[15] Most parents have no greater difficulty in deciding on legal commitment, either through hospital or court authority, than in coming to a decision about the voluntary placement of a child, and the procedure often involves the same dynamics. The decision should, whenever possible, be worked out step-by-step with the parents. Current experiments in having certain children, as well as the parents, go through the reality of the court hearing is worth further study to determine the effect of having the separation seen (by the child) as impersonal reality rather than as rejection by the parent. As the worker rarely exercises personal authority, so in those cases in which mental illness or unmanageable social conditions induce placement through commitment, the impersonal reality of authoritarian intervention may, if skillfully used, reduce the guilt of the parent and the bitterness of the child. Limits and frustrations should come from the situation, the "rules," not from the worker. Punishment is rarely constructive, but when it must be applied, the situation should suggest the rules, and the group may share in making and enforcing them. Infringement, then, brings a sort of impersonal punishment which is usually better assimilated. It is recognized that the motivation of the one who punishes must be mature for any favorable result, but actually the "therapeutic" use of punishment has not been adequately studied.

The neurotic character—adult "delinquent"—is not able through an effort of the will to give up anti-social behavior and conform to social standards and sanctions for which nothing in his life experience has prepared him. In the authoritarian setting the caseworker must begin with the meaning of the act to the offender, as the medical social worker the meaning of the illness. Defenses must be understood, and the relationship must be used dynamically as the new experience within which feelings can be expressed, fears reduced, and therefore less of the conflict discharged through hostile

[15] See pp. 95–99.

aggression. From such a generic casework base will the court worker proceed to help the client grasp the realities of his situation, in favorable cases help him see his behavior as contributing to or retarding his recovery, and through the support of the relationship itself channelize his efforts towards social opportunities for sublimation.

"Delinquency" falls into the general diagnostic category of behavior or character disorders of those who act out their conflicts against society.[16] These are persons with weak egos and poor conscience structures; those with limited ability to deal with their own impulses and life's demands. Behavior disorders have not had enough help and guidance in learning to cope with their instinctual wishes. As children always learn "from someone," the probation officer, court social worker, and others invested with protective functions, must fully understand the dynamics of behavior and know how to bring the wary, narcissistic and hostile child into a treatment relationship. As in all work with children, one must accept, understand, but not enter into or be tricked by delinquent actions. All children find it hard to bear frustration, are normally self-loving, and believe in magical omnipotence. Behavior disorders show this in an exaggerated way. Yet the facts of youth, fluidity of identifications, potentialities for growth, re-education, and reintegration along lines of modern treatment, instead of punishment, offer great hope.

A small proportion of persons are so resistive to guidance, where neglect and pathology are gross, that authoritative intervention by the community through court and social worker, or other officer, is indicated. Caseworkers occasionally have to resort to prosecution or forcible commitment as a form of control, but the application of coercive procedures is not within the ordinary scope of "casework," and often such duties are undertaken by special investigators, or workers with assigned protective or restitution or other quasi-police functions. But by far the greater number of pathological situations

[16] Eisler, *Searchlight on Delinquency*.

are improved by provision of an assured income, by educational counseling through a social agency, by farm agent or nutritionist, by attention to health problems and family counseling.

The chief difference between the "fields" of family casework and probation and parole [17] is that the client, whether a direct applicant or referred, may voluntarily accept or reject the proposed treatment. The "client" of a probation office has no such choice, but the fact of authority in the setting does not mean an authoritarian relationship. It is characteristic of social work that practice is substantially carried on in agencies and institutions, all of which have policies and limits within which one has to work. Authority is part of social reality which the probation officer must not only accept but also learn to use so as to help his client, in a positive instead of a negative way—much as other procedures may be incorporated in casework.

In case a child has been severely abused or neglected, when commitment of children without parental consent is used, or when abrogation of ordinary privileges or liberties is indicated, the court is the natural instrument of authority and of protection. Here, as in relief, the stigma is reduced as legal processes become socialized. Eligibility will, perhaps, be based on the need for "authority," much as eligibility for assistance is now based on the need for money. Cases not requiring authority will be referred to family and children's agencies, public or private, in the community. That is to say, "unofficial" cases or those that can be adjusted out of court may be sent elsewhere, and the court may reserve its function for instances where there is noncooperation, or noncompliance, or incompetence. While it is possible for courts to develop their own "adjustment" service, in most communities this should not be necessary if division

[17] See David Crystal, "Family Casework in Probation," *Federal Probation*, XIII (December, 1949), 47–53: "The probation officer can feel perfectly comfortable about accepting a social reality that has been determined both for him and his client, and for which he has no redress. This is a common bond uniting probation officer and probationer and within this bond and this area it is possible to utilize the basic concepts of casework, which involve a nonjudgmental attitude on the part of the worker, an understanding of the total personality of the client, mutual participation of client and worker in a common effort and, finally, the individual choice of the client who goes to a voluntary agency requesting help."

of labor in the welfare field is well worked out. In so-called "protective" work in many instances the problem suggests lack of family strength rather than anti-social patterns.[18]

Court adjudication is essential and there is an essential police function, but there is little ground for assigning the duty of intensive treatment to the police department. Children are rarely independent applicants for help, but are brought to an agency for help by parents, guardians, and other protective agencies. Aggressive and delinquent children must be exposed to and experience treatment before they can ask for it. Skilled persons must be engaged for treatment. The police function is constructively discharged through a well-trained personnel engaged in observing, patrolling, inspecting, gathering evidence of family or neighborhood pathology, gang and individual delinquency, and legal restrictions, interpreting the law and apprehending adults charged with offenses against children, and the like. The duty of the police to protect society is now being extended to the initial steps in the prevention of delinquency in a kind of first aid—getting hold of the offender without threat or punitive methods and making suitable referrals. Youths over sixteen out of school require special handling with attention to late hours, sex behavior, street fighting, truancy, and stealing.

Many sorts of official and unofficial agencies may be used, and they should more and more frequently work together. Competent screening and referral services prove far more effective than admonition or punishment. As do severe neurosis and psychosis, true delinquency, of either parents or youths, needs all the resources, medical and social, of science for study, treatment, and, most of all, prevention.

The Medical and Psychiatric Setting

The oldest and the most clearly articulated "secondary" setting for social work practice is that of hospitals and clinics. Since the significant feature is collaboration with physicians, goals and methods of treatment, this section will cover the medical and psychiatric

[18] See pp. 46–47.

purpose and its social work components in an all inclusive discussion.

Throughout this book the assumption has been in one aspect that psychiatry is a "permeating" subject [19]; it runs through all the healing and helping professions. Medicine itself is being gradually infiltrated by the psychiatric point of view so that not only psychopathology but also the understanding of normal personality and of emotional reactions is becoming part of the general practitioner's equipment.

The Person as a Patient

When casework is practiced under medical auspices certain emphases are to be expected, since the purpose of the institution, its staffing and concerns, are primarily for medical, not social, care. The well-equipped caseworker in or outside the medical institution has to comprehend the meaning of symptoms, to understand disease processes within the personality, the effect of disability on social functioning, and the typical expressions of anxiety and dependency in illness. The young doctor must balance his medical training by learning to see the "patient as a person"; the social worker, by learning to see the "person as a patient." In the strictly medical setting the accent on illness and disability means deepening one's understanding of the body-mind unity; recognition of the course and treatment of major pathological syndromes, mental and physical; evaluating the possibilities of maintaining or regaining health; providing for convalescence, special treatments, terminal care, communicability, and community aspects of illness and public health.

Since the inception of medical social work in this country, about 1905, it has continuously interpreted the meaning of illness in terms of social handicaps and disabilities. This contribution was reinforced by psychiatric social work, which, emerging about 1918 (although with earlier antecedents), became integrated with the

[19] H. M. Bartlett, and W. W. Beckman, "Teaching of Social and Environmental Factors in Medicine," *American Association of Medical Social Workers' Bulletin*, September, 1949.

newly established child guidance movement of the twenties, from thence spreading to all casework fields. The patient's anxiety about illness, how illness may be used to play into the needs of the personality, the role of the ego in resisting as well as in cooperating with disease, the use of illness to dominate family relationships, and the supporting or obstructionist roles which relatives may play in helping the patient and his group adjust to handicaps have been gradually translated into a core of knowledge and technique. The psychosocial case must be seen as the bio (physical and psychic)-social case.[20]

Of all medical specialities, psychiatry stands out as the discipline which can least be isolated from the total patient in consideration of a social cultural situation. Whereas in the medical school the teaching of the importance of social and cultural influence has been only recently and often inadequately introduced, psychiatrists, especially in child guidance, and many individual medical practitioners have been sensitive to interpersonal environments and to larger social and cultural influences. In progressive settings those working with behavior problems of children have begun to see the whole child in the whole situation. The psychosocial environment, particularly early home and parental environment, has come to be recognized as significantly determinant of behavior. Up to the introduction of mental hygiene, physical rather than emotional or ideational environment had been stressed, both inside and outside the hospital. Casework itself, more generally perhaps than medicine, was deeply influenced by the point of view of psychiatric, particularly of "dynamic" or psychoanalytic psychiatry, so that caseworkers from any accredited school of social work enter upon practice not only equipped with knowledge and skill in the manipulation of social environmental factors but also attuned to the emotional responses of patients to physical or mental illness. Nevertheless, there are a great many specifics to be learned about the care

[20] Cockerill, "Casework and the New Emphasis on an Old Concept in Medicine," *Proceedings of National Conference of Social Work*, 1948, p. 284. One wishes that a simpler term could be found for the "person-environment interaction."

and treatment of persons suffering from heart disease, tuberculosis, diabetes, cancer, or manic depressive, schizophrenia, and other psychoses. Only with such specific knowledge can casework treatment be properly adapted to the medical problem and aim.

Caseworkers must not only ally themselves with the healthy parts of the personality struggling with disease or neurosis but also make a new appraisal, as it were, of how the ego is weakened and dependency needs exacerbated by illness. They must be able to accept regressive behavior without being drawn, because of countertransference, into sympathetic identification or flight and evasion. One must learn over again from a new angle the traumatic effect of loss of status as a wage earner because of *disability*, as in public assistance because of unemployment; of body narcissism; of mutilation, both realities and fantasies; of anxiety resulting in overactivity or immobilization. The relationship itself has to be adapted to clinical considerations; for instance, the use of emotional support, always an important tool, in preparing the patient for acceptance of handicaps without too great frustration and in educating the patient to assume responsibility for the use of medical treatment and programs. The tenuous and infantile nature of transference in the schizophrenic and his need to test and test again, fearing rejection; the tendency of the paranoid to play one person against another, the brittle nature of his defenses, and other variants must be understood. How to attach the hurt ego to reality interests, how to socialize and to sublimate, to protect and safeguard, is not different in principle from similar efforts in other areas, yet the means have to be constantly adjusted to the goal of the medical treatment as such. Timing is also constantly affected by medical considerations, and in many instances it cannot be adjusted to the regular once-or-twice-a-week interviewing, but must depend upon the necessities of admission, discharge, and the severity of the illness itself.

Relatives of chronically or intermittently disabled patients may be helped to undertake the responsibilities of home care, often so desirable, if their feelings of irritation and being burdened by the patient are permitted release and frankly faced. Families feel particularly guilty about admitting such negative feelings about a sick person and tend to suppress them, with unfortunate results. Through explanation and interpretation relatives can often be persuaded to take a more realistic attitude about the performance of the patient, expecting neither too much nor too little either of the sick person or of themselves. The tendency to equate illness with badness may add additional burdens to the sense of rejection which the institutionalized child may feel. The guilt and failure felt by the parent of a child who is a behavior problem may be seen again in the care of the sick child, in overprotection or complaints against the treatment, or through other disguises. Heavy expenses leading to economic deprivation may foster a smouldering resentment against fate which may prove even more destructive to family life unless ventilated and faced. In approaching relatives the worker perceives in a different context how hard it is to cure a child against the unconscious opposition of the parent.[21]

The Clinical Team and the Social Work Role

Treatment cannot be departmentalized; whether the services of nurse, social worker, and technician be regarded as "adjunctive" or "collaborative" to those of the physician, the approach must be integrated for the care of the patient. Treating a case concurrently with the same focus and goal as that of the physician is, therefore, part of the uniqueness of the medical or psychiatric setting. The primary contribution of the social worker to the medical or psychiatric team stems from his professional competence. The writer suggests that one day the professional designation within educational, court, and medical institutions may be "social worker" rather than "probation officer" or the hyphenated awkwardness of "school," "psychiatric" or "medical" social worker. The worker enters the clinical field having already assimilated in his training the idea of agency and institutional teamwork [22] and is disposed to assume a well-defined focus and role for his distinctive contribution. In earlier times he was expert in environmental conditions, whereas

[21] See pp. 95–99.   [22] See pp. 129–31.

now the graduate of the progressive school may be expected to have had considerable exposure to physical and psychiatric factors in illness and rehabilitation. Nevertheless, the social worker's primary contribution in the medical team is to accent the psychosocial, interfamilial component in study and treatment. His approach to the "patient group" remains oriented to the needs and recovery of the ill person. There are exceptions in cases of communicable diseases, and problems of psychogenetic origin, where the total family unit may be involved, and at times a relative becomes a major assignment for treatment, but in general the care is focused upon the medical patient.

In hospital settings the worker is responsible for preparing the patient for anxiety charged experiences, such as complicated treatments and examinations, unfamiliar procedures, and frightening terminology. In many settings he not only is responsible for taking the medical or developmental history, as well as the social history, but also carries the chief responsibility for whatever exploration of family and social background may be necessary to formulate a dynamic picture of the significant facts and interrelationships for diagnosis, treatment, discharge, and follow-up. In psychiatric settings he is likely to take social histories, although not so routinely as in earlier days, and to carry a larger share of the intake or admitting process, evaluating the immediate social pressures upon the patient and interpreting the hospital or clinic role. Possibly he will steer the applicant to other appropriate medical or social facilities. Responsibility for the admitting process is rarer in the medical setting, except on referral from the physician or, perhaps, in special clinics and services to which the worker is assigned. The psychosomatic or psychiatric history focuses more particularly on symptoms, etiology, and onset, reactions to illness, and so forth, than do some other psychosocial outlines, but the important stress is not on the details required, but on the skilled use of the relationship to get the picture with as little distortion as possible. In all settings in which pertinent history is required in early contacts, skill in interviewing determines the timing, sequence, deferments as to certain data, and effect upon the client's relationship to worker and the agency.

For participation in the medical plan and the carrying on of treatment, the role varies with the nature of the problem. Usually the social worker is more deeply involved in instances of chronic disability, physical and emotional, than in acute illness or uncomplicated surgery, except as he may be active in emergency plans for the care of a household during the mother's hospitalization, convalescent arrangements, or the like. Traditionally he has carried the main responsibility within the patient group [23] for attempts to modify the attitudes of relatives toward the chief patient. Today, with the inception of home care programs and the clearer recognition of the constructive or destructive role of relatives, physicians and psychiatrists are participating more freely in such family relationships, through selected interviews, as conversely the social worker may take selected or recurrent interviews with the patient. The question as to which member of the team conducts a particular interview is of less consequence than the emphasis and aim. While the clinical and psychogenetic formulation of the medical diagnosis is basically the responsibility of the physician, modern dynamic diagnosis may require the contribution of the social worker, since from the beginning he is observing the social functioning of the personality and eliciting, supporting, and building ego strengths. In so far as community resources, employment, placement, financial assistance, and other services must be used in recovery, this is appropriately the social worker's concern, but above all the social worker must understand the anxiety, the dependency, and the de-

[23] Garrett, A. "Historical Survey of the Evolution of Casework," *Journal of Social Casework*, XXX (June, 1949), 223. "One early attempt to solve the pendulum-swing problem was to attempt a division of labor assigning all external factors to caseworkers, all internal ones to psychiatrists. Thus early work in child guidance clinics was inaugurated with the idea that all psychiatric work with the child would be left with the psychiatrist while the caseworker would handle the environmental factors. This broke down because one of the chief factors in the child's environment is the mother. It was early found that the mother could not be 'manipulated' as could other aspects of the environment such as housing and recreation."

fensive structures if he is to help patients adapt to disability and to the realities of the social situation.

Whether the social worker within or without the medical institution should engage in "psychotherapy" is still a matter of debate and often seems to become a question of semantics. Actually the worker does engage in forms of psychotherapy when qualified to do so.[24] Some groups would limit the practice of psychotherapy to purely medical endeavor directed toward the improvement of the emotional health of the individual, and based upon the understanding of the biological psychodynamics and of the needs of the individual under treatment. In this view, "psychotherapeutic endeavor may include adjunctive professional services under the supervision of the psychiatrist." Others would restrict psychotherapy to a "systematic exploration of the unconscious," which seems to equate it with psychoanalysis. Still others, including the writer, would assume that psychoanalytic principles may be adapted with other therapies for various psychotherapeutic goals. Since a basic transference is the primary dynamic in psychotherapy, this, of course, cannot be confined to the guiding physician; the patient is more likely to improve if all the professional personnel in the medical setting share the therapeutic attitude which invites this relationship of trust. Beyond this, the caseworker must participate in a treatment program which includes release, suggestion, support, environmental manipulation, clarification, and usually some level of awareness of the disability and its meaning.[25] In most limited-goal psychotherapy the worker meets the unconscious feelings of sexuality, hostile aggression, and dependency through psychological derivatives which are, or can become, conscious. Fears of death and of incapacity, like other fears which torment patients, can sometimes be reduced if they are expressed and related to the reality of programs, of situations, and of family interaction. On the other hand, as is true of psychotics, when the irrational impulses are near the surface and break through, the worker must know how to help the patient repress them and carry on in reality.

[24] See pp. 251–52.   [25] See pp. 253–56.

Psychotherapy, whether inside or outside the medical institution, should always be carried on in a responsible relation to psychiatry, but this does not preclude appropriate activities for the competently prepared caseworker. In social agencies having therapeutic functions a psychiatrist serves on the staff. Functional differentiation, however, takes on somewhat different aspects when psychotherapy is practiced in a medical setting or in a social agency, or indeed between one medical institution and another. In the medical setting "the team" is always headed by a physician, and although certain aspects of therapy may be delegated or shared among psychologist, nurse, technician, and social worker, the tendency under such circumstances is to sharpen the distinctive roles for collaborative purposes, that is, the social worker in the hospital is most valuable for his knowledge of social therapy. In a social agency in which all treatment is carried on by caseworkers the client often has applied initially for a social service, but if psychotherapy is indicated the worker may help the client perceive his displacement and share in formulating the therapeutic problem and goal which have now emerged. The client may then be referred to a medical institution or a psychoanalyst for treatment, or may be treated within the agency itself by qualified social workers. Cases which are in neurotic equilibrium, as in many disturbed families, those without acute symptom formation (except as the child is "the symptom"), and such neurotic characters as typically express their conflict through social problems (long the province of social work) for practical, if for no other, reasons must be continued by the social agency. In many places direct application for treatment for problems of family relationship are now as common in the family agency as in the child guidance clinic. Cases of mental disease, psychosomatic illnesses, and severe psychoneuroses must be screened out and, in general, referred to medical auspices. Psychiatric consultants on staff or on call are indispensable for diagnosis.

Even when the social worker's contacts with the chief patient are minimal, he must be able to participate on the therapeutic level if he is not to block medical and psychiatric treatment. In working with the patient's relatives, if indicated he continually uses certain therapeutic techniques to encourage growth, reduce anxiety and discouragement, change unfavorable attitudes toward the patient, and promote an atmosphere of mental health. Adjunctive therapeutic support to the patient may make it advisable for the worker to treat a relative on his own behalf. At this point the relative may be referred to a psychiatrist inside or outside the institution, or he may, in certain cases, be treated by the worker himself in conference with the chief patient's psychiatrist or physician. The role of collaboration when families are undergoing psychoanalysis and other treatment simultaneously has special problems to be worked out, but they do not appear to offer insuperable obstacles as goals, and adaptations of social and psychotherapeutic techniques becomes increasingly skilled and controlled. As Dr. Paul Federn [26] puts it: "Freud's work was a contribution to the common task of all scientific professions which deal with the human mind and the human personality; it is dedicated to the whole of mankind."

In any setting the caseworker is most concerned with cases in which the neurotic conflict is projected or displaced upon persons or conditions in his environment. The goal in any form of limited psychotherapy is not primarily to change the patient's neurotic personality, through insight, but to use the transference for clarification to strengthen the ego, to manipulate the external circumstances on behalf of, and with the fullest participation of the patient. The social worker in interviewing treatment deals with the patient's reactions to the environment as well as the realities of the environment itself. His knowledge is acquired by interviews on the ward, or in clinic, or by visits to the home, school, or place of employment, and consultations with other agencies, and this special knowledge and skill are brought into the diagnosis and formulation of the medical or psychiatric plan. Interpretation, whether the main tools are direct or social therapy, is related to meaningful experiences—events, attitudes, behavior, with the purpose of sustaining or strengthening the ego.

[26] Dedication in *Searchlights on Delinquency* (*op. cit.*) in honor of August Aichhorn.

QUALIFICATIONS AND ROLES

In the light of psychological developments in medicine and in social work, the limits and roles of each practitioner cannot be too inflexibly set, any more than one would wish the doctor to confine his efforts solely to the psycho-biological without appropriate inclusion of the social material whenever appropriate. The multidiscipline emphasis, however, should mean, not the dilution, but the clarification of respective contributions. Since it is recognized that to treat illness or to influence behavior therapeutically requires a pooling of the knowledge and skills of several professions and the physical and social sciences, many of the principles of effective collaboration in the medical setting are seen to be equally applicable to the court, the school, and other institutions.

It is obvious that in social agencies the collaboration of a psychiatrist is essential to aid in diagnosis, in formulating the therapeutic objective, and for other consultations, yet typically he does not "supervise" the workers. Workers practicing psychotherapy should have had intensive and extensive supervision as part of advanced training, and consultation should be continuously available. Students in professional schools of social work are supervised in field work in ways which prepare them for the assimilation of psychological material and learning how to use the self in the interview. Psychiatric consultation is of little value, nor are social workers of maximum service in hospitals, unless the training schools of each profession create added curricula which further understanding of the whole human event and develop the language and techniques for interprofessional communication. In nonmedical settings safeguards are provided by agency standards and policies, a high quality of practice and supervision, specialized equipment, and the use of psychiatrists regularly on the staff.

The question of private practice in social work is far too complicated for comment here. It would seem obvious, however, that in welfare, as in other professions, institutional, agency, and group forms of practice are steadily increasing. It might, therefore, be regressive for social work to abandon its characteristic agency practice to develop private practice in any large measure; rather, salaries and conditions of work should be such that social workers of high caliber can be attracted and held within the agency setting. It is equally obvious that if private practice in psychotherapy is to exist, training must be rigorous and extended, licensing qualifications must be strict, and controls established. Charging of moderate fees by voluntary agencies and group membership and insurance plans similar to those in health and industry are regarded as promising trends for the future.

The chief problem for professional education today is to integrate the characteristic processes of social work with the larger purpose of social welfare. This means finding an effective balance between the technical core disciplines such as casework, groupwork, community organization, administration, and research, and the substantive knowledge derived from the social sciences, including philosophy and history, and the closely related professions such as medicine, law, and education. There is today a trend to abandon the narrowing aspects of field specialization for a generic foundation in social work, broadly considered. Specialization even though pushed ahead into further study in school and in in-service programs of training is shaping itself toward administration, supervision, and advanced practice, of which the therapeutic emphasis is only one of several possibilities. Other forms of specialization may emerge as current gains are consolidated. At the doctoral level, professional education should, no doubt, become again more generic, with the accent upon perspective, values, and the contributions of research to methods and the common store of knowledge.

CONCLUSION

In the foregoing chapters we have attempted to show in what characteristic ways casework concerns itself with the individual's adaptation to an ever-changing environment. Whether or not science comes to agree on ultimate constitutional and economic or other determinism, it seems clear that, pragmatically speaking, the social process, with its infinite number of variable factors, is relatively undetermined. Flexibility, change, and movement are of the very nature of social interaction. It is no wonder that social workers give close attention to behavior, which is the pulse of the human organism's attempts at adaptation. Even while complete causal explanations, because of their hundred and one component parts, elude us, through behavior we may come to a real, if limited, understanding of the individual and his culture. As Professor May puts it, "Human problems cannot be usefully divided into aspects that match the traditional divisions of science, biological science tending to ignore culture and social sciences the individual." [27]

Caseworkers use knowledge of psychological determinants in personality structure to stimulate the client to more creative choices; to help him assume social responsibilities for himself, his family, his community; to bear strains and pressures with less wear and tear; to modify habits of self-blame and feelings of inadequacy; and because of understanding and support to use less aggression, anxiety, rigidity, and projection in his social relationships in a real, economic, and cultural environment. The future of casework research is nowhere more important than in testing out theories as to the effect of identifications with neurotic personalities on the capacity to use group and community experience, or of anxiety-hostility patterns in wage earning, home making, and other activities. The findings of experimental and psychoanalytical psychology and of statistical and case study social science can no longer run in parallel lines and through isolated disciplines, if the profession is to make its minimum contribution. Researches, based on intimate knowledge of the family and other primary units, may prove not unrelated to the understanding of group identifications in national and political movements.

Social work should not be evaluated, as is sometimes alleged, by a self-liquidating test. Its purposes, historically based, are still concerned with making love instead of hostility effective in human relationships. Social work can release creative energies only as its purposes are accepted, not denied. Political democracy cannot

[27] May, "Is There a Science of Human Relations?"

survive unless based on the welfare of its people, but this welfare can neither be handed out nor handed down; it must be progressively achieved through enlightened participation of the commonwealth. Social work is still engaged, it is true, in furnishing the "commodities" of welfare—assistance, board of children, institutional care, recreational and neighborhood activities, and the like—but this is not its sole purpose. It is deeply concerned with programs, social planning, and social change which will make for a better social order, but this is not its entire contribution. The participation of labor in industry, of staffs in their own administration, of groups in their own education, of communities in social planning, of informed and responsible forces in social action, are constructive only as they involve self-determined, cooperative and altruistic behavior. All these movements are interdependent and all rest ultimately on the possibility of socializing the individual personality within the family and the group, for the development of a truly good society.

BIBLIOGRAPHY

Abbott, Edith, Public Assistance—American Principles and Policies. Chicago, 1940.

Abbott, Grace, The Child and the State, Vols. I and II. Chicago, 1938.

Ackerman, Nathan W., "Constructive and Destructive Tendencies in Children," *American Journal of Orthopsychiatry*, VII (July, 1937), 301–19.

—— "Dynamic Patterns in Group Psychotherapy," *Psychiatry*, VII (November, 1944), 341–48.

—— "Psychotherapy and 'Giving Love,'" *Psychiatry*, VII (May, 1944), 129–38.

—— "Technique of Therapy; a Case Study," *American Journal of Orthopsychiatry*, X (October, 1940), 665–80.

—— "What Constitutes Intensive Psychotherapy in a Child Guidance Clinic?" *American Journal of Orthopsychiatry*, XV (October, 1945), 711–20.

Addiss, Luise, and Elizabeth Guilford, "Home Economics Service in Family Agencies," *The Family*, XVIII (March, 1937), 16–19.

Aichhorn, August, Wayward Youth. New York, 1935.

Alexander, Franz, and Thomas Morton French, Psychoanalytic Therapy. New York, 1946.

Alexander, Franz, and William Healy, Roots of Crime. New York, 1935.

Alexander, Franz, and Hugo Staub, The Criminal, the Judge, and the Public. New York, 1931.

Aptekar, Herbert, "The Use of Private Psychiatrists by a Social Agency," *Jewish Social Service Quarterly*, March, 1949, 381–94.

Austin, Lucille N., "Trends in Differential Treatment in Social Case-work," *Journal of Social Casework*, XXIX (June, 1948), 203–11.

Bartlett, Harriet, Some Aspects of Social Casework in a Medical Setting. Chicago, 1940.

Bartlett, H. M. and W. W. Beckman, "Teaching of Social and Environmental Factors in Medicine," *American Association of Medical Social Workers' Bulletin*, September, 1949.

Benedict, Ruth, Patterns of Culture. Boston, 1934.

Bergson, Henri Louis, Creative Evolution. New York, 1911.

Bernard, Viola W., "Psychodynamics of Unmarried Motherhood in

Early Adolescence," *The Nervous Child*, IV (October, 1944), 26–45.

Bettelheim, Bruno, and Emmy Sylvester, "Therapeutic Influence of the Group on the Individual," *American Journal of Orthopsychiatry*, XVII (October, 1947), 684–92.

Bibring, Edward, "Psychotherapy and Casework," *Journal of Social Casework*, XXX (June, 1949), 219–59.

Bibring, E. and J. J. Michaels, "Psychotherapy and Casework," Symposium of the Boston Psychoanalytic Society and Institute, Inc., *Journal of Social Casework*, XXX (June, 1949).

Bibring, Grete L., "Psychiatry and Social Work," *Journal of Social Casework*, XXVIII (June, 1947), 203–11.

—— "Psychiatric Principles in Casework," *Principles and Techniques in Social Casework*, Selected Articles 1940–50, New York, 1950, 370–79.

Bowers, Swithun, "The Nature and Definition of Social Casework," *Journal of Social Casework*, XXX (October, 1949), 311–17 (November, 1949), 369–75.

Brown, Esther L., Social Work as a Profession. New York, 1938.

Browning, Grace, "Public Administration and Human Welfare," *The Social Service Review*, XXII (March, 1948), 10–19.

Bruno, Frank P., Trends in Social Work. New York, 1948.

—— The Theory of Social Work. New York, 1936.

Buhler, Charlotte, "The Social Behavior of Children," in *Handbook of Child Psychology*, ed. by C. Murchison. Worcester, Mass., 1933.

—— From Birth to Maturity. London, 1935.

Burns, Eveline M., The American Social Security System. Boston, 1949.

Cabot, Richard C., Doctor and Social Worker. Boston, 1919.

Cockerill, Eleanor, "Casework and the New Emphasis on an Old Concept in Medicine," in Proceedings of National Conference of Social Work (Atlantic City, 1948), pp. 284–92.

Colcord, Joanna C., Your Community; Its Provisions for Health, Education, Safety and Welfare. New York, 1939.

Coleman, Jules V., "Psychiatric Consultation in Case Work Agencies," *American Journal of Orthopsychiatry*, XVII (July, 1947), 533–39.

—— "The Teaching of Basic Psychotherapy," *American Journal of Orthopsychiatry*, XVII (October, 1947), 622–27.

—— "Distinguishing between Psychotherapy and Casework," *Journal of Social Casework*, XXX (June, 1949), 244–51.

Coyle, Grace, Group Work with American Youth. New York, 1948.

Crystal, David, "Family Casework in Probation," *Federal Probation,* XIII (December, 1949), 47–53.

Dawley, Almena, "Professional Skills in Intake Service," in Proceedings of the National Conference of Social Work (Chicago, 1937), pp. 255–65.

Day, Florence R., "Social Case Work and Social Adjustment," *The Family,* XVII (October, 1936), 197–204.

—— "A Study of Case Work Practice," in Diagnostic and Treatment Processes in Family Social Work, Family Welfare Association of America (New York, 1935), pp. 14–25.

De Schweinitz, Elizabeth, and Karl de Schweinitz, "The Contribution of Social Work to the Administration of Public Assistance," *Social Work Journal,* XXIX (July, 1948), 108–13; (October, 1948), 153–62.

De Schweinitz, Karl, People and Process in Social Security. Washington, D.C., 1948.

Deutsch, Felix, Applied Psychoanalysis. New York, 1949.

Deutsch, Helene, Psychology of Women. 2 vols. New York, 1944.

Dewey, John, Liberalism and Social Action. New York, 1935.

—— Experience and Education. New York, 1938.

Dollard, John, Criteria for the Life History. New Haven, 1935.

Dunbar, Helen Flanders, Emotions and Bodily Changes. 2d ed. New York, 1938.

—— Psychosomatic Medicine. New York, 1943.

Eisler, K. R., Searchlights on Delinquency. New York, 1949.

English, O. S., and G. H. J. Pearson, Emotional Problems of Living. New York, 1945.

Family Service Association of America. Practice of Casework in Public Agencies. 1950.

—— Primary Behavior Disorder in Children—Two Case Studies, by Staff Members, Jewish Board of Guardians, 1945.

—— Personalized Care for the Aged Client, 1946.

—— Developing Insight in Initial Interviews, by Alice L. Voiland, Martha Lou Gundelach, and Mildred Croner, 1947.

—— Techniques of Helping Children, 1949.

—— Family Counseling—Practice and Teaching, by Frances Taussig, M. Robert Gomberg, Frances T. Levinson, 1949.

—— Diagnosis and Treatment of Marital Problems, 1950.

Family Service Association of America. A Comparison of Diagnostic and Functional Casework Concepts, 1950.

Fenichel, Otto. Psychoanalytic Theory of Neurosis. New York, 1945.

Finlayson, Alan D., "The Diagnostic Process in Continuing Treatment," *The Family*, XVIII (November, 1937), 228–33.

Fitch, John A., "Social Action," in Social Work Year Book, Russell Sage Foundation (New York, 1939), pp. 398–401.

Follett, Mary P., Creative Experience. New York, 1930.

French, Lois Meredith, Psychiatric Social Work. New York, 1940.

French, Thomas M. and Ralph Ormsby, Psychoanalytic Orientation in Casework. Family Service Association of America, 1944.

Freud, Anna, "Child Analysis," *The Survey Graphic*, LXVIII (September, 1932), 389–99, 414–15.

—— The Ego and the Mechanisms of Defense. London, 1937.

—— The Psychoanalytical Treatment of Children. London, 1946.

Freud, Sigmund, Basic Writings of Sigmund Freud; ed. by A. A. Brill. New York, 1938.

—— Collected Papers. 4 vols. London, 1924, 1946.

—— The Ego and the Id. London, 1927.

—— A General Introduction to Psychoanalysis. New York, 1935.

Futterman, Samuel, "Ego Strengths and Therapy," *Newsletter A.A.P.S.W.*, autumn, 1946.

Garrett, Annette, "Historical Survey of the Evolution of Casework," *Journal of Social Casework*, XXX (June, 1949), 219–29.

—— Interviewing, Its Principles and Methods, Family Welfare Association of America. New York, 1942.

Greenacre, Phyllis, "The Biological Economy of Birth," in *The Psychoanalytic Study of the Child* (New York, 1945), I, 31–52.

Hamilton, Gordon, "Basic Concepts in Social Case Work," *The Family*, XVIII (July, 1937), 147–56.

—— Case Work in Old Age Assistance, Case Work with the Aged, Family Welfare Association of America (New York, 1938), pp. 1–7.

—— "Contribution of Social Case Work to Modern Life," in Family Life Today (Boston, 1928), pp. 193–207.

—— "Helping People—the Growth of a Profession," Anniversary Papers of the New York School of Social Work and the Community Service Society of New York, 1949.

—— Psychotherapy in Child Guidance. New York, 1947.

—— Principles of Social Case Recording. New York, 1946.

Healey, William, and Augusta Bronner, New Light on Delinquency and Its Treatment. New Haven, 1936.

Heyman, Margaret M., "Some Methods in Direct Casework Treatment of the Schizophrenic," *Journal of Psychiatric Social Work*, Vol. XIX, summer, 1949.

Hollis, Florence, "Some Contributions of Therapy to Generalized Case Work Practice," *The Family*, XV (February, 1935), 328–34.

—— Women in Marital Conflict; a Casework Study. New York, 1949.

—— "Individualized Service to Families in the Private Agency," *The Family*, XIX (October, 1938), 181–87.

—— Social Case Work in Practice: Six Case Studies. New York, 1939.

—— "The Techniques of Casework," Principles and Techniques in Social Casework (New York, 1950), pp. 412–26.

Howard, Donald, "The Changing Role of Public Assistance," *Proceedings of National Conference of Social Work* (San Francisco, 1947), pp. 154–62.

Hunt, J. McV., "Measuring the Effects of Social Casework," Transactions of the New York Academy of Sciences, IX (1947), pp. 78–88.

—— "Measuring Movement in Casework," *Journal of Social Casework*, XXIX (November, 1948), pp. 343–51.

—— Margaret Blenkner, and Leonard S. Kogan, "A Field-Test of the Movement Scale," *Journal of Social Casework*, XXXI (July, 1950), pp. 267–77.

Hutchinson, Dorothy, In Quest of Foster Parents. New York, 1943.

Isaacs, Susan, Social Development in Young Children. New York, 1933.

Jewish Board of Guardians. Conditioned Environment in Case Work Treatment. 1944

—— The Case Worker in Psychotherapy. 1946.

Johnson, Adelaide, "A Contribution to Treatment of Superego Defect," *Social Casework*, XXI (April, 1950), 135–45.

Josselyn, Irene M., "The Caseworker as Therapist," *Journal of Social Casework*, XXIX (November, 1948), 351–55.

—— Psychosocial Development of Children, Family Service Association of America, 1948.

Kardiner, Abram, "Influence of Culture on Behavior," *Social Work Today*, IV (February, 1937), 11–14; (March, 1937), 13–16.

—— The Individual and His Society. New York, 1939.

—— "The Role of Economic Security in the Adaptation of the Individual," *The Family*, XVII (October, 1936), 187–97.

King, Edith Shatto, "Social Service Exchanges," in Social Work Year Book (New York, 1939), pp. 422–24.

Klein, Philip, "Social Welfare Planning," in Social Work Year Book (New York, 1939), pp. 424–30.

Klein, Philip, and others, A Social Study of Pittsburgh. New York, 1938.

Kluckholn, Clyde, and Henry A. Murray, Personality in Nature, Society, and Culture. New York, 1948.

Koehler, Wolfgang, Gestalt Psychology. New York, 1929.

Knoepfmacher, Lia, "Child Guidance Work Based on Psychoanalytic Concepts," The Nervous Child, V (April, 1946), 178–98.

Lawton, George, New Goals for Old Age. New York, 1943.

—— Aging Successfully. New York, 1946.

Lee, Porter R., Social Work as Cause and Function. New York, 1937.

Lee, Porter R., and M. E. Kenworthy, Mental Hygiene and Social Work. New York, 1929.

Levy, David M., "Attitude Therapy," The American Journal of Orthopsychiatry, VII (January, 1937), 103–13.

—— "Release Therapy," The American Journal of Orthopsychiatry, IX (October, 1939), 713–36.

Lewis, Nolan, and Bernard L. Pacella, eds., Modern Trends in Child Psychiatry. New York, 1945.

Lindeman, Eduard C. Social Education. New York, 1933.

—— Social Discovery. New York, 1936.

Lippman, Hyman S., "Child Analysis," American Journal of Orthopsychiatry, IX (October, 1939), 707–12.

—— "Treatment of Juvenile Delinquents," in Proceedings of National Conference of Social Work, 1945, pp. 314–23.

Little, Ruby, "Diagnostic Recording," Journal of Social Casework, XXX (January, 1949), 15–19.

Lou, Herbert H., Juvenile Courts in the United States. Chapel Hill, 1927.

Lowrey, Lawson G., Psychiatry for Social Workers, 2d ed. New York, 1950.

—— "Current Concepts in Social Case Work," Social Service Review, XII (September–December, 1938), 365–73; 571–97.

—— "Objectives in Social Case Work," The Family, XVIII (December, 1937), 263–68.

McLean, H. V., "Psychodynamic Factors in Race Relations," Annals American Academy of Political and Social Science, CCXLIV (March, 1946), 159–66.

Maeder, LeRoy M. A., "Diagnostic Criteria—the Concept of Normal and Abnormal," *The Family,* XXII (October, 1941), 171–79.

Marcus, Grace F., "Social Case Work and Mental Health," *The Family,* XIX (June, 1938), 99–105.

—— Some Aspects of Relief in Family Casework. New York, 1929.

May, Mark, "Is There a Science of Human Relations?" *The Family,* XVII (July, 1936), 139–44.

Menninger, Karl A., Man against Himself. New York, 1938.

—— The Human Mind. New York, 1945.

Millar, Margaret W., "Common and Specialized Services in Family and Children's Agencies," *The Family,* XX (November, 1939), 222–28.

Millspaugh, Arthur C., Public Welfare Organization. Washington, 1935.

Mowrer, O. H., and Clyde Kluckholn, "Dynamic Theory of Personality," in Personality and the Behavior Disorders, ed. by J. McV. Hunt. New York, 1944.

Neumann, Frederika, "The Use of Psychiatric Consultation by a Casework Agency," *The Family,* XXVI (October, 1945), 216–20.

Neustaedter, Eleanor, "The Integration of Economic and Psychological Factors in Family Case Work," in Proceedings of the National Conference of Social Work (Chicago, 1930), pp. 198–216.

Newstetter, W. I., "What Is Social Group Work?" in Proceedings of the National Conference of Social Work (Chicago, 1935), pp. 291–99.

New Trends in Group Work; ed. by Joshua Lieberman. New York, 1937.

Peabody, Frances W., The Care of the Patient. Cambridge, 1928.

Perlman, Helen Harris, "Generic Aspects of Specific Casework Settings," *Social Service Review,* XXIII (September, 1949), 293–301.

Plant, James S., Personality and Cultural Patterns. New York, 1937.

Pray, Kenneth L. M., "The Place of Social Casework in the Treatment of Delinquency," *The Social Service Review,* XIX (June, 1945), 235–48.

—— "New Emphases in Education for Public Social Work," in Method and Skill in Public Assistance (Philadelphia, 1938), pp. 88–100.

Principles and Techniques in Social Casework, Selected Articles, 1940–50, from Social Casework. New York, 1950.

Redl, Fritz, "Group Psychological Elements in Discipline Problems," *American Journal of Orthopsychiatry*, XIII (January, 1943), 77–81.
—— "Diagnostic Group Work," *American Journal of Orthopsychiatry*, XIV (January, 1944), 53–67.
—— "Resistance in Therapy Groups," *Human Relations*, I (1948), 307–20.
Rennie, Thomas A. C., Mental Health in Modern Society. New York, 1948.
Reynolds, Bertha C., "Between Client and Community," *Smith College Studies in Social Work*, V. No. 1 (1934), 128.
—— "Rethinking Social Case Work," Social Work Today, V (April, 1938), 5–8; (May, 1938), 5–7; (June, 1938), 5–8.
Richman, Leon, "New Needs and New Approaches in Foster Care," *Jewish Social Service Quarterly* (March, 1949), pp. 308–18.
Richmond, Mary E., Social Diagnosis. New York, 1917.
—— What Is Social Case Work? New York, 1922.
—— The Long View. New York, 1930.
Robinson, G. Canby, The Patient as a Person. New York, 1939.
Robinson, Virginia, A Changing Psychology in Social Case Work. Chapel Hill, 1930.
Ross, Helen, and Adelaide M. Johnson, "The Growing Science of Casework," *Journal of Social Casework*, XXVII (November, 1946), 273–78.

Schmidl, Fritz, "On Contact with the Second Partner in Marriage Counseling," *Journal of Social Casework*, XXX (January, 1949), 30–36.
Simcox, Beatrice, "The Social Service Exchange," Parts I–II, *Journal of Social Casework*, XXVIII, November and December, 1947, pp. 331–37, 388–95.
Slavson, S. R., "The Group in Development and in Therapy," in Proceedings of the National Conference of Social Work (Chicago, 1938), pp. 339–49.
—— Introduction to Group Therapy. New York, 1943.
—— Recreation and the Total Personality. New York, 1946.
Social Case Work, Generic and Specific; a Report of the Milford Conference, American Association of Social Workers, New York, 1928.
Social Security Administration Publications, Federal Security Agency, Washington, D.C. Circulars.
—— General Publications.
—— Research and Statistical Reports.

—— Social Security Bulletin and Yearbook.

—— State Letters.

—— Technical Training Materials.

Social Work as Human Relations. New York, 1949. Anniversary Papers of the New York School of Social Work and the Community Service Society of New York.

Social Work Year Book (biennial), New York, articles "Catholic Social Work," "Jewish Social Work," and "Protestant Social Work."

Southard, E. E., and M. Jarrett, The Kingdom of Evils. New York, 1922.

Stevenson, George S., "Problems of Growth in Family Case Work," *Social Service Review*, X (September, 1936), 424–36.

Stevenson, George S., and G. Smith, Child Guidance Clinics. New York, 1934.

Sytz, Florence, "Unit of Attention in the Casework Process," *Journal of Social Casework*, XVII (June, 1946), 135–39.

Taft, Jessie, "The Relation of Function to Process in Social Case Work," *Journal of Social Work Process*, III (1937), 1–18.

—— "Function and Process in Psychiatric Social Work," *Newsletter* (American Association of Psychiatric Social Workers), IX (June, 1939), 3–10.

Thornton, Janet, The Social Component in Medical Care. New York, 1937.

Towle, Charlotte, "Factors in Treatment," in Proceedings of the National Conference of Social Work (Chicago, 1936), pp. 179–91.

—— "The Underlying Skills of Casework Today," in Proceedings of National Conference of Social Work (Atlantic City, 1941), pp. 254–66.

—— Common Human Needs, Social Security Board, Bureau of Public Assistance, United States Government Printing Office, Washington, D.C., 1945.

—— "Social Casework in Modern Society," *Social Service Review*, XX (June, 1946), 165–79.

—— "Helping the Client to Use His Capacities and Resources," in Proceedings of National Conference of Social Work, 1948, pp. 259–70.

Thurston, Henry, The Dependent Child, New York, 1930.

United States Children's Bureau, Washington, D.C. Handbook for the Use of Boards of Directors, Superintendents, and Staffs of Institutions for Dependent Children. Publication No. 170, 1927.

United States Children's Bureau, The ABC of Foster Family Care for Children. Publication No. 216, 1933.

—— Public Social Services to Children, A Decade of Progress, 1935–45. Child Welfare Report No. 1, April, 1946.

—— Child Welfare Moves Forward. Child Welfare Report No. 2, February, 1947.

—— Children's Services in the Public Welfare Agency. Child Welfare Report No. 3, May, 1947.

Van Ophuijsen, J. H. W., "Therapeutic Criteria in Social Agencies," *American Journal of Orthopsychiatry*, IX (April, 1939), 410–20.

—— "Primary Conduct Disturbances; Their Diagnosis and Treatment," in Modern Trends in Child Psychiatry (New York, 1945), pp. 35–42.

Waelder, Robert, "Scientific Approach to Social Casework, *The Family*, XXII (October, 1941), 179–85.

Wajdyk, Beatrice, Edna Astley, and Ruth Davis, The Sustaining Type of Case Work. Family Welfare Association of America. New York, 1938.

Waller, Willard, "Social Problems and the Mores," *American Sociological Review*, I (December, 1936), 922–33.

Warner, A. G., Stuart A. Queen, and Ernest B. Harper, American Charities and Social Work. Rev. ed. New York, 1930.

Warner, W. Lloyd, and Paul S. Lunt, The Social Life of a Modern Community. New Haven, 1941.

Webb, Sidney, and Beatrice Webb, English Local Government. New York, 1929.

Weiss, Edward, and O. Spurgeon English, Psychosomatic Medicine. New York, 1943.

White House Conference on Child Health and Protection, United States Government Printing Office, 1930.

—— The Handicapped Child, Report of the Committee on Physically and Mentally Handicapped. Section IV, Committee B, 1933.

—— Delinquent Child. Report of the Committee on Socially Handicapped. Section IV, Committee C–2, 1932.

—— Children in a Democracy, 1939–40. General Report adopted by the Conference, January 19, 1940.

Wilson, Gertrude, and Gladys Ryland, Social Group Work Practice. New York, 1949.

Witmer, Helen L., Social Work. New York, 1942.

Young, Erle Fiske, The Case Workers' Desk Manual. Los Angeles, Calif., 1937.

Young, Leontine R., "Helping an Unmaried Mother to Make a Decision about Her Baby," *Journal of Social Casework*, XXVIII (January, 1947), 27–34.

—— "Placement from the Child's Point of View," *Journal of Social Casework*, XXXI (June, 1950), 250–55.

Zilboorg, Gregory, "Sociology and the Psychoanalytic Method," *American Journal of Sociology*, XLV (November, 1939), 341–55.

INDEX

Ability to work asset, *see* Work capacity

Acceptance, interviewing skill rests on, 52; accrediting and, 53-55; technique of, in worker-client relationship, 106

Activity group therapy; *see* Group Therapy

Adjustment, anthropology and psychiatry throw light on factors involved in, 5; concept, 237-40; objective of psychosocial, 239

Administration of a social service, 182, 243-46

Adoption, 103-5; examinations and tests for, 195; diagnosis and evaluation, 234; giving child for, 279

Aged, care of, 276-79

Age levels, *see* Diagnosis; Treatment

Agencies, tax-supported, 17, 123; relationship of worker and client with, 28; interpreting functions and limitations of other, 65; variation between, 118; types, 118 ff.; structure and function, 125-29; functional approach, 127-29; policy and procedure, 126-27; exchange of information, 193; casework in the authoritative agency, 289; voluntary, 17; flexibility in functions, 123; master file of cases, 132; fees, 304

Agency and inter-agency practice, 39, 66, 115-44; field and setting, 115-17; significance of function, 117-25; structure and function, 125-29; inter-agency cooperation, 129-33; case recording, 133-41; staff and interdiscipline collaboration, 141-44; allocation or referral, 179-80

Aid to Dependent Children and Survivors Insurance, 278

Aggression, released within group experience, 112; channelized and verbalized, 269

Aggressive reaction, 72, 154-56, 189-93

Anxiety, 67, 72, 155, 210; in relation to ego defenses, 235; related to its situational source, 267; *see also* Fears

Application and intake processes, 147-80; continuity of study, diagnosis, and treatment, 147-49; in public welfare, 164; right to assistance, 149-68; application interviews, 153-59, 164-65; resistance and defenses, 169-79; allocation or referral, 179-80

Application blanks, 200

Aptekar, Herbert, quoted, 244n, 251

Asocial conduct, 40; *see also* Delinquency, protective work

Assets, utilized, 200; liquidation of, 201; and liabilities, 221

Assistance, right to, 149-68, 187; attitudes toward seeking, 149-53; "a full and patient hearing," 153-59; focusing through the request, 159-62; essential social facts, 162-65; readiness to use help, 165-68

Assumptions, basic, and methods, 3-26

Attitudes, negative, 173; modification of, 184, 255

Austin, L. N., quoted, 266n

Authority, use of, 46-47; essential elements in use of, 289; *see also* Legal authority

Behavior, in economic and cultural security, 12; professional, 39-43; pointing out or pointing up patterns of, 73-76; interpretation at level of motivation, 77-79; unconscious determinants of, 78; in interview, 149-53, 183; motivation of, 184; lack of adaptation in, 185; purpose of therapy to modify, 255; juvenile, 272, *see also* Child guidance; dynamics of, 291; treatment

Study (*Continued*)
tory, 183-86; home study and observation, 186-93; special examinations and tests, 195-96; clue and pattern, 196-212
Summaries, 135 ff.
Supervision, 120; *see also* Qualifications and roles
Support, responsibility for, 194, 202, 288; eligibility for, 201, 202; refusal to, 274; *see also* Public assistance

Taft, Jessie, quoted, 128n
Team, psychiatric and medical settings, 48-50, 293 ff.; application of concept in multi-discipline approach, 142; social worker's contribution in medical, 298
Technical core disciplines, effective balance between, 304
Technical knowledge for diagnosis and evaluation, 215
Tension, 64, 155
Termination of treatment, 57, 79-82, 236
Tests, examinations and, 195-96; Rorshach, 196; aptitude, 231; projective, 231
Therapeutic attitude, 74
Therapeutic interviewing, 74, 252, 300; *see also* Therapy; Psychotherapy
Therapy, 120; group, 110 ff.; play, 189; responsibility in, 267; requirements for caseworker in, 268; *see also* Psychotherapy
Thinking, reflective, 217; *see also* Evaluation
Timing, in counseling, 73; in interpreting, 77, 203, 296; in separation experience, 284; *see also* Limits; Restraints
Tolerance, 21; and self-awareness, 39-43
Transference, 256-58; and object relationship, 29-31; insight given within, 210-16, 267

Treatability, and termination, 79-82; psychological readiness, 211
Treatment, 25; treatment relationship, 29, *see also* Relationship; beginning of, 45, 49; termination, 57, 79-82, 236; direct, or interviewing treatment, 79, 249-70; money as a tool in, 92-95; summaries, 135; based on diagnosis and evaluation, 214-18; psychosocial, 230; methods, 237-70; concept of adjustment, 237-40; objectives and focus, 239-40; classification of methods, 241-43; specific means, 241-49; main approaches, 242; administration of a practical service, 243-46; environmental, 246-49; counseling, 250-52; therapeutic interviewing, 252; differentiated approaches, 253-56; mobilizing affect and clarification, 258-64; interpretation leading to insight, 264-66; defenses and resistance, 266-70; adapting to age levels, 269

Unconscious, 73, 254, 256, 300 ff.; Preconscious, 73; derivatives of, 258, 266 ff.; *see also* Ego
Unit of attention, 96, 181
Urgency, 177-79

Value judgments, 40
Vincent de Paul, St., 23
Voluntary agencies, *see* Agencies, voluntary
Voluntary association, democratic participation, 19

Waller, Willard, quoted, 7n
Welfare progressively achieved, 306
White House Conference, 118
Winant, John, 21
Worker-client relationship, *see* Relationship; Social worker

Youth, 293; *see also* Child welfare; Treatment